MW00611340

SCIENCE FICTION

Voyage to the Edge
of Imagination

SCIENCE
MUSEUM

T&H

Voyage to the Edge

SCIENCE

Edited by Glyn Morgan

fiCtiON

of Imagination

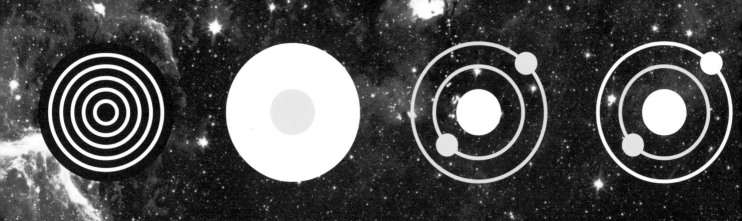

$$N = R_* \times f_p \times n_e$$

SCIENCE AND SCIENCE FICTION

IAN BLATCHFORD

First prototype of 'The Clock of the Long Now', 1999. Designed by Danny Hillis, this 9-foot-tall (2.7 metre) prototype was built to explore the mechanism needed for a clock intended to keep time for 10,000 years. It is controlled by a binary mechanical computer that counts the hours, the calendar and solar years, the centuries and the phases of the Moon and the Zodiac.

Why would a science museum focus on science fiction, when real science brims with so many strange and mind-expanding ideas? Why isn't science fiction simply storytelling about the realities of science, which is already far stranger than many people realize?

The simple answer is that science fiction is so much more than fiction. From parallel worlds, swarm intelligence and gene editing to time dilation, quantum teleportation and cloning, this epic genre provides a bridge that straddles the event horizon between the known and unknown, between a concrete present and a haze of possible futures.

Science and science fiction spark off one another endlessly: science fiction provides a tool for future-gazing, social commentary, art and satire that can inspire scientists, while the latest advances from the laboratory often lead science fiction writers to ask, 'where could this take us?' No wonder, then, that so many scientists have taken to science fiction, from Fred Hoyle to Joan Slonczewski and Vandana Singh.

This symbiotic relationship is reason enough for a museum on a mission to 'inspire futures' to enthusiastically support a science fiction exhibition. But, as endless Hollywood films have already shown, science fiction is also a genre that can engage with a huge audience. It offers a powerful tool to help inspire young people who will become the scientists, engineers, writers and artists of tomorrow. People across different cultures and at different times have realized how science fiction can play a key role in engaging and shaping public opinion, not least in allowing us to ask hard questions about gender and racial equality and how we treat each other in works as various as *District 9* (2009), *Triangulum* (2008) and *The Handmaid's Tale* (1985).

Good science fiction can be more influential than articles in newspapers and widely cited journals, particularly when it zooms in on the implications of contemporary science, from genetic modification to narrow AI. The most provocative science fiction is the kind that offers an 'escape into reality', according to Arthur C. Clarke, a writer who appreciated the influence of geostationary satellites as much as he did science fiction. With the help of the latter, we can make choices about how and when to use technologies that have the power to shape our collective destiny. Just as a climate modeller uses the most powerful computers on the planet to ask what different scenarios the future might hold in store for us, so science fiction invites us all to imagine our futures, for better or for worse.

Brass gold-weight in the form of a bird with its head turned looking over its back (sankofa), made in Ghana between the eighteenth and twentieth centuries.

WHAT IS SCIENCE FICTION FOR?

NALO HOPKINSON

What is science fiction for? As an author of the genre myself, I am often faced with assumptions made by people who aren't interested in whether this question has an answer, or an easy answer, or that the answer is somehow different than that to the question, 'What is fiction for?'

Perhaps some are thrown by the word 'science' in the moniker. Science is serious business, so they feel that science fiction must be like the story problems in maths tests: 'If two trains pass in the night on a cold evening in September, and one is going at 150 kilometres per hour and the other has to make a 35.28 second stop at a station before continuing on, what is the statistical likelihood that you'll give the wrong answer to this question?' Science fiction, they believe, must be utilitarian and dry, with a barely concealed didactic aim. It must be there to teach us something. Sometimes one does learn something by reading science fiction. Its authors do a lot of secondary research into science, history, art, language, social customs and so on. We also do a lot of extrapolation. This may be why there are those who assume that the aim of science fiction is to divine what the future holds.

The Akan people in the Ghana region of West Africa have the concept of sankofa, pictured as a bird looking over its back to collect the egg that it is behind it. 'Sankofa' may be interpreted as 'go back and get it'; in other words, bring your past along with you as you move forward into the future. As the musician and songwriter Bob Marley said, 'Don't forget your history / Know your destiny'.

Many cultures use stories to talk about the responsibility to look after this planet that nourishes us and, hopefully,

future generations. The Taíno people, indigenous to the Caribbean, have an ancient myth that says that they used to live on the Moon, which they perceived as a sphere of bright rock like the others they could see floating in space. Then they looked down at the Earth. It should have been similarly shining, but instead was dull and dingy. The Taíno, chagrined at their neglect of their neighbourhood, flew to Earth in boats made of clouds and proceeded to clean up the polluted land and waters. In their haste, they forgot to anchor their boats, which floated away into the sky. The stranded Taíno had to learn how to make new lives for themselves on Earth. It is a centuries-old story of the environment and human responsibility that sits in conversation with director Sung-hee Jo's film *Space Sweepers* (승리호, 2021), in which crews of space garbage pickers eke out a living by salvaging the debris that human beings leave floating in the solar system. These concerns also show up in Tochi Onyebuchi's novel *Goliath* (2022), in which the world is suffering widespread plague and environmental collapse. A privileged and largely white few have left Earth for a space colony, abandoning populations of predominantly people of colour to survive as best they can on a poisoned planet.

In 1945, the first successful explosion of an atomic bomb created trinitite, a radioactive mineral that had never before existed on Earth. Ellen Klages's novel *The Green Glass Sea* (2006) examines the event through the eyes of two young girls who live on the secret New Mexico atomic bomb-development site for the Manhattan Project. Their fathers are scientists involved in creating the bombs dropped on the Japanese cities of Hiroshima and Nagasaki. These events not only destroyed over 200,000 lives; they were a horror that changed the world forever.

Humans continually alter the world, creating everything from new codes of law to new plastics. Rarely do we fully anticipate the consequences. Science fiction is the literature of social and technological change. Foremost an art form, its intent is usually more exploratory than prophetic. Humans understand the interlocking complexities of reality by using observance and imagination to create narratives about it; that is, we tell each other stories. Similarly, the sankofa bird doesn't predict the future. It implies that we need to take the long view of our actions.

The scientific method is also not in the business of prophecy. It tests in order to discover the truth. Science fiction storytellers are indebted to science as we employ the art of fiction to ruminate on what humanity is capable of, for good or ill.

INTRODUCTION: IMAGINING SCIENCE FICTION WORLDS

GLYN MORGAN

Science fiction is a near-boundless enterprise. It cannot be constrained between the covers of a single book or within the walls of a single museum exhibition. It is an apeirogon, an object of infinite sides. Its roots can be traced through the nineteenth-century scientific revolution, but its seed is sown far deeper: in the legends of China, the epics of Ancient Greece, the myths of Egypt and Mesopotamia, and likely in countless other sources scattered wherever humans have told stories. Its modern form is vibrant and exciting, capable of stretching our imaginations in hitherto unexplored directions while at other times comfortably appealing to now beloved tropes and themes.

The book that you hold in your hands was created as a companion project to the 'Science Fiction' exhibition that opened at the Science Museum in London in October 2022. This book is an extension of the themes and topics covered there, but stands alone as a collection of essays and images across five different topics, each exploring different aspects of the global genre of science fiction and its relationship with scientific enquiry, history and culture.

Science fiction resists constraint and genre. It burns brightly in the pages of Liu Cixin and Ursula K. Le Guin, and in the cinema of Andrei Tarkovsky and Denis Villeneuve; but it is there, too, in the unique style and mythology of jazz legend Sun Ra, blazing out of the trumpets and organ of his Arkestra, and in the artist Larry Achiampong's 'Relic Traveller', a futuristic archivist who seeks out relics and testimonies of the African diaspora. It is in the foundations of architectural visions by Le Corbusier and provocations by Liam Young and Abeer Seikaly, in the vast narratives that unwind through television and animation, as well as in the countless panels of comic books, from superhero sagas to standalone graphic novels. It is this same spirit of imagination that connects the pioneering black-and-white cinema of French visionary Georges Méliès to the sizzling, colour-soaked weirdness of the *Métal hurlant* (*Heavy Metal*) comics, by artists and creators like Moebius and Philippe Druillet, which would change the way a whole generation saw the future through its influence on iconic films such as *Blade Runner* (1982) and *Alien* (1979).

We may also think of science fiction as something that resists the mundane: this is, after all, a genre in which we might encounter a sentient ocean with telepathic powers, or visit alternate timelines in which history took a very different path. It is also a genre in which one can find a sense of wonder and strangeness even in everyday activities, as in Pamela Zoline's story 'The Heat Death of the Universe' (1967), which turns the cleaning chores and the preparation of eggs for breakfast into a stark meditation on the inevitability of chaos and entropy in the deep time of the future.

In conversation in 2022, Zoline remarked that science fiction is 'arguably the only literature capacious and searching enough to deal with our present tremendous and terrifying reality'. By its very nature, science fiction is interested in other times, other places, other beings and minds and other ways of thinking, all while being ideally suited to our contemporary, highly technological and scientific age. To be a fan of science fiction is to embrace alterity and dare to think beyond the confines of the here and now. At its most powerful, science fiction is more than a genre; it is a set of tools with which to reshape the world by reshaping our thinking.

Perhaps the true secret to its power is that, at the same time, science fiction is a popular and populist genre of entertainment. Its many layers and interactions with different media and forms allow for contact with diverse and wide-ranging audiences and communities of all levels of engagement, from casual movie-goers to university scholars, to expert cosplayers and all stripes and strains between and beyond. What draws in such a wide variety of people is hard to determine. Some would highlight the appeal of an escape from reality, going on to argue over whether this is a positive or negative phenomenon. In academic circles, one of the most cited science fiction cultural theorists is the Yugoslav-born academic Darko Suvin, who writes of a sense of 'cognitive estrangement', the exhilarating effect of taking as fact (however temporarily) something not only fictitious but unreal, even impossible.

Alex Wells, illustration for a 2016 Folio Society edition of Isaac Asimov's collection of short stories *I, Robot*, originally published in 1950. Asimov was a professor of biochemistry as well as a science fiction author and wrote numerous popular science pieces and guidebooks throughout his career.

Suvin couples this with the importance of the 'novum', the new thing, the flourish that distinguishes a science-fictional world from contemporary reality. For the majority of science fiction fans, cognitive estrangement happens on an unconscious or unrecognized level, but the novum is an object of undeniable appeal. Even as the 'new thing' rapidly becomes a well-recycled trope, science fiction fans continue to be as engaged with travelling to other worlds, encountering new life forms, witnessing the end of the world and inventing new gadgets as ever.

The exciting, engaging, stimulating effect of these topics, settings and scenarios is part of what is referred to as the 'sense of wonder', a fundamental building block of the genre. This aspect cannot be undervalued, and is particularly vital in explaining science fiction's continued appeal. We should not make the mistake of assuming that it is only the fan who encounters science fiction as a child or a teenager who is pulled into this gravity well. It is true that the young mind is more plastic and less trained in the phenomenon of realist fiction, but good science fiction can elicit wonder (or its kindred spirit, horror) in any age group. Opening ourselves up to wonder also opens us up to possibilities: why else include a time capsule of humanity's cultures on Earth on the *Voyager* probes that are travelling far beyond our solar system. Even if the galaxy is teaming with life, space is so vast that the chance of the Golden Records on these probes ever being discovered is extremely remote. Nonetheless, the science-fictional thinking of people like Carl Sagan, who championed the project, leave open that most fundamentally science fiction question: 'What if....?'

The iconic jazz musician Sun Ra, who claimed to have visited Saturn in the 1930s, is a powerful example of science fiction being expressed through both music and extravagant styling. His 1962 album *The Futuristic Sounds of Sun Ra* featured a pared-back Arkestra on songs such as 'Tapestry from an Asteroid' and 'Space Jazz Reverie'.

→ Cover and disc of 'The Sounds of Earth' Golden Record, attached to the *Voyager* space probes. The cover on the left contains diagrammatic information on how to play the record, as well as coordinates to find Earth and a representation of a hydrogen atom. The records contain a variety of material, including analogue-encoded photographs, music, greetings in fifty-five languages and whale song.

Science fiction is sometimes portrayed as a prophetic medium, of interest only so long as we can write listicles of 'fifteen things H. G. Wells correctly predicted about the future'. But this is not the best way to approach the material. Wells and others like him may have 'predicted' technologies or social changes, but they were extrapolating from the issues and advancements of their day. Science, society and science fiction are in constant conversation, trading ideas and hypotheticals, making suggestions and corrections. Where a direct line can be drawn between a science-fictional idea and a scientific innovation, such simplifications often overlook the fact that the innovation occurred precisely because a given scientist, or generation of scientists, was inspired by the work of a given writer or television show. The changes in science and society then fuel further science fiction. It is these feedback loops, conversations and collaborations that the chapters in this book explore.

In Part 1, 'People and Machines', Sherryl Vint and Colin Milburn examine how technology has influenced our ideas of what it means to be human, each finding themselves in the orbit of Mary Shelley's *Frankenstein*. While the appearance of a Gothic novel written in 1818 in discussions of science fiction may at first seem surprising, it has long been considered by some scholars as a progenitor for the genre as a whole. For Vint, *Frankenstein* represents an early step along a long road in which human biology and synthetic technology become enmeshed, culminating in the late-twentieth century image of the cyborg, especially as theorized by the scholar Donna Haraway. Milburn, meanwhile, takes an Arthur C. Clarke story, 'Dial "F" for Frankenstein', and traces its influence on the creation of the World Wide Web. Vint and Milburn demonstrate that science fiction has been both a warning call and a lantern lighting the path across difficult terrain, challenging us to think more broadly and inclusively about ideas of self.

← A collage by Pamela Zoline to accompany her short story 'The Heat Death of the Universe', from the July 1967 edition of avant-garde science fiction magazine *New Worlds*.

A Trip to the Moon (Le Voyage dans la Lune), directed by Georges Méliès, 1902.

In Part 2, 'Travelling the Cosmos', Richard Dunn and Rachael Livermore take us to the stars, examining the history, science and possible futures of that most emblematic trope of science fiction: space travel. Dunn leads by considering the history of spaceflight as spectacle, from the early German film *Woman in the Moon* (*Frau im Mond*, 1929) to the space race and on to a growing family of space-faring nations that includes Japan, China and India, among others. He shows how scientists and engineers collaborated with science-fiction creators both to enhance the realism of their films and to help excite the general public about the possibilities of space travel. Venturing beyond our local solar system, Livermore turns to humanity's place on the interstellar stage, looking at the science and science fiction of planets outside our solar system, known as exoplanets, and examining our chances of reaching those destinations, with potential methods from suspended animation to warp drives. Space is vast, dangerous and difficult for us to traverse, yet it continues to enchant, excite and inspire us; these authors read science fiction as the ultimate expression of that relationship.

Part 3 segues from astronomical themes to discuss 'Communication and Language', beginning with Roger Luckhurst's examination of communication methods, particularly in space, while Rachel S. Cordasco delves into the earthbound communication of science fiction itself, offering a brief survey of the history and reality of science fiction as a global genre, its translation and circulation. Luckhurst considers the kinds of communication humans put out into the universe, and that which we are looking to receive, contemplating both what that says about us as humans, and what the implications might be if we ever receive a reply. Cordasco, herself an accomplished translator of Italian, takes a very different path: by focusing on translation, she demonstrates the ways in which science fiction acts as a continuous exchange of viewpoints and ideas. From the earliest translations of authors like Jules Verne, to the current interest in Chinese science fiction writers like Liu Cixin, Cordasco's work emphasizes that even the most well-versed science fiction fans are experiencing only a limited view of the human capacity for imagination and creativity, and one of science fiction's most powerful lessons has to be that expanding that view is always exciting.

Indeed, it is humanity's limited view that occupies Part 4, 'Aliens and Alienation', with essays by Amanda Rees and myself on what it means to be alien, other and strange. Rees focuses on depictions of aliens in science fiction and where our ideas about them come from. Whether it is H. G. Wells's Martians in *The War of the Worlds* (1897) or the 'prawns' of *District 9* (2009), the aliens of science fiction are often surprisingly familiar, trapped within our human conceptions of what an intelligent organism might look like. This makes them invaluable metaphorical tools for storytelling, or reflections of deeper-rooted psychological or sociological conditions, but how similar any future encounter with real extraterrestrial intelligence would be has been a source of scientific debate and discussion for decades. In my essay, I take the idea of aliens in the opposite direction, to instances where science fiction has stretched to create something truly strange. Science fiction touches on the limits of our ability to conceive of the universe: the infinitesimally small, the unfathomably big and the indescribably strange. I explore science fiction's capacity to cover a vast canvas of possibilities and to push against the boundaries of scientific knowledge.

Finally, in Part 5, 'Anxieties and Hopes', Daniel Cordle and Caroline Edwards consider two issues that have shaped our modern era and will continue to shape our futures: nuclear technology and climate catastrophe. Both of these threats are in different ways vast, existential and (for the most part) beyond individual control. As Cordle's essay shows, nuclear fiction pre-dates even the first successful experiments at weaponizing atomic power, but once that power was unleashed such fictions multiplied, from the naive optimism of unlimited power in the 1950s to post-apocalyptic narratives set in hunter-gatherer civilizations living in the aftermath of all-out nuclear war, as in Russell Hoban's *Riddley Walker* (1980). Nuclear fiction has given us ruined planets, superheroes, giant monsters and aliens. It has also asked us to think about the footprint we leave on the planet, the vast timescales we are able to influence in our comparatively short existences and the role of scientific and technological progress within that. It is a natural transition, then, to Caroline Edwards's closing essay, which addresses the climate crisis and environmentalism. Like Cordle, Edwards demonstrates that science fiction has been interested in climate change for a lot longer than one might expect, finding its roots in the nineteenth century before moving to the formation of the environmental movement, which presents us with visions of drowned cities, drought-blighted plains and acidic wastelands: horrifying glimpses of the potential worlds we might yet encounter. But Edwards leaves us with optimism. Science fiction has long entwined itself with disaster to warn of what is to come, but it has also been employed to imagine paths away from apocalypse, new ways to structure our societies, how to treat our planet and to survive. We come full circle to the points made by Vint in the book's opening essay: the boundaries between humans as individuals and as collective societies, between us and the natural world and us and technology, are much more tenuous than we tend to think. No artistic genre demonstrates this interconnectedness better than science fiction.

Concept art for a torpor module in a future spacecraft, designed by aerospace engineering company and NASA contractor SpaceWorks, 2018.

Larry Achiampong, 'Pan African Flag for the Relic Travellers' Alliance (Ascension)', part of *Relic Traveller: Phase 1*, 2017–. The fifty-four stars represent the fifty-four countries of Africa, whilst the green, red and black represent its land, its people and the struggles the continent has endured. The yellow represents a new and prosperous day.

Interlaced between the chapters are interviews with five leading science fiction writers, offering their thoughts on the genre and the issues within it that are most important to them and their work. Chen Qiufan, Charlie Jane Anders, Vandana Singh, Tade Thompson and Kim Stanley Robinson address the diversity and multiplicity of science fiction as well as the importance (or otherwise) of scientific accuracy, key topics like environmentalism and space travel, and their approaches to storytelling. This book seeks to widen existing conversations, to invite readers to think holistically about topics that are well-covered by science fiction, and to bring books, films and more into dialogue with one another and with the scientific and technological world. The volume in your hands was created in the midst of the COVID-19 pandemic, a very strange time to be thinking about science fiction. The global catastrophe, with images of deserted city centres and isolation from loved ones, united only by technology, felt like living through a particularly poorly plotted and overly long genre film. The pandemic underlined the truth that the world is actually a very small, highly connected place, in which we are all dependent on each other and the hidden forces that link us. As such, the essays and interviews you will read here seek to sketch a picture of science fiction not as a fringe interest, but as a hugely complex and successful cultural enterprise that performs an important role in society as both a contributor to innovation, inspiring and guiding scientists, but also a companion on that journey, pointing out the pitfalls, perils and consequences of development. Science fiction is a truly global genre, for everyone, by everyone, and you don't need to be a writer, a filmmaker or a scientist to participate. Science fiction is permission to dream, an invitation to imagine, to speculate, to hypothesize. It inspires our future by offering us the tools to create our own.

PEOPLE AND MACHINES

PEOPLE
AS MACHINES /
MACHINE
PEOPLE

SHERRYL VINT

←   *Tron*, directed by Steven Lisberger, 1982.
1.   Scene from the 1938 BBC adaptation of *R.U.R.*, the first-
     ever television work of science fiction, now sadly lost.

Images of manufactured beings have been part of the science fiction imagination from the beginning, and Mary Shelley's *Frankenstein* (1818) is often called the first science fiction novel. This is in part because Shelley's vision was influenced by new developments in contemporary science, specifically Luigi Galvani's experiments with electricity and muscular action. Yet Shelley's novel is as much social critique and philosophical treatise as it is an extension of the scientific imagination – a recipe of sorts for science fiction. Science fiction draws from (and at times inspires further explorations in) science, but is best understood as a genre about how changes in science and technology have implications for humanity's social organization and philosophical concepts. *Frankenstein* imagines that we might be able to 'defeat' death through medical science (an impulse still evident in today's research in organ transplantation, artificial organs and synthetic biology), but it is equally concerned with questions of social justice: what are the consequences of being isolated from social exchange and hope for the future of one's kind? What duties of care do we owe to the beings we might create through scientific advancement? Shelley's original creature, we recall, becomes a murderer not because he is artificial, but because he is excluded and reviled.

Victor Frankenstein's Creature thus raises questions not only about the potential for technology to disrupt the inevitable decline of life into death, but also about the ethical relationship between humanity and other beings. What constitutes a person? Who is recognized as human? Critics agree that Shelley's work was influenced by the political philosophy of her father, William Godwin, especially his critique of the class-based inequality that distorted the justice system and prevented some people from fully participating in and benefitting from society.

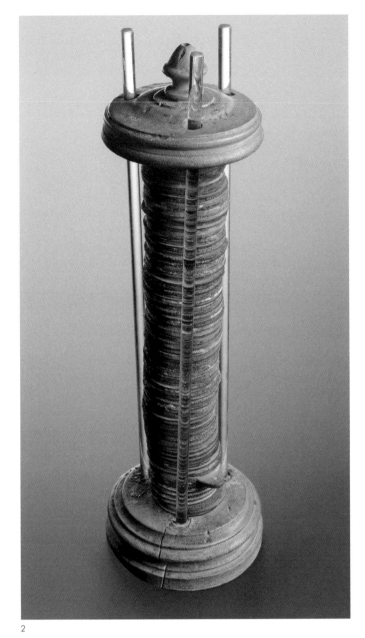

2

This is echoed in the Creature, who becomes violent because he lacks hope for a future in which he can thrive as part of a community and family.

Science fiction authors have returned to this motif in texts that explore how deeply our images of created beings are shaped by histories of exploitation and exclusion, and especially of slavery. This topic is explored in Afrofuturist works such as Janelle Monáe's performances as Cindi Mayweather, an android alter-ego created across several albums and music videos. The world Mayweather inhabits is powered by enslaved labour, drawing imagery from Fritz Lang's *Metropolis* (1927), an expressionist film in which underground-dwelling workers are exploited to fuel the machines that power a city of colossal skyscrapers, and Sun Ra's *Space is the Place* (1974), a film that uses science fiction imagery to write a new reality of a social order that is no longer structured on devalued Black lives (which Saidiya Hartman, in *Lose Your Mother* (2008), calls the 'afterlife of slavery'). In Lang's film a robot is created to replace Maria, a sympathetic figure who seeks to unite workers and owners in a more just society; the false Robot Maria instead promotes violent rebellion and chaos. In her Afrofuturist refiguration of this image, Monáe shows instead how the robot/android figure more powerfully embodies exploited Others, those dehumanized as machines, who are excluded from the social order their work enables, most significantly in the violent history of chattel slavery. In her album *Dirty Computer* (2018), she celebrates the android uprising, alluding to a range of other science fiction texts in her vision of a racially inclusive, queer, just future.

Science fiction imagery proves so fruitful for Monáe because of its long history of imagining non-human created beings, almost always in texts in which their inferior social status is rationalized in ways that mirror histories of serfdom and slavery. Karel Čapek's *R.U.R.* (1921), which stands for Rossum's Universal Robots, envisions a future of manufactured workers made from organic matter. These robots (a term that comes from a Czech word for serf or worker) exist only to labour, having no subjectivity or needs beyond serving their designer. Similarly, stories by Isaac Asimov collected in *I, Robot* (1950), imagine a class of manufactured workers who are intelligent but compelled to subservience through the Three Laws of Robotics, which are coded into their behaviour, and which are now a topic of debate in AI ethics.

2. Alessandro Volta's voltaic pile, based on research by Luigi Galvani, 1800–20. Consisting of zinc and copper discs separated by discs of card soaked in brine, this device functions as an early battery. In 1803, Galvani's nephew, Giovanni Aldini, used a device like this to shock the corpse of an executed prisoner at Newgate prison in London, an event that is thought to have been one of the influences on Mary Shelley's writing.

3. Sam Chivers's 2016 poster for Karel Čapek's 1921 play *R.U.R.*, which stands for *Rossum's Universal Robots* (*Rossumovi Univerzální Roboti*), the work credited with introducing the word 'robot' into both science fiction and the English language.

4. Liam Scarlett's *Frankenstein*, performed by The Royal Ballet, 2019.
5. *Frankenstein: the Man Who Made a Monster*, directed by James Whale, 1931, showing the monster in a gentler moment, picking flowers with a child.
6. Poster for *Frankenstein, the Man Who Made a Monster*, 1931.

4

Why...might someone be comfortable with an artificial heart or a brain without a body, but insist on binary gender?

In each of these works, the manufactured people exceed the narrow parameters to which they have been relegated and rebel against their second-class status. Thus, as they imagine manufactured people, these texts simultaneously ask us to reflect on what makes a human, and how or whether we should draw lines between humans and other beings, questions that are all the more pressing given our human history in which marginalized people continue to be similarly segregated and oppressed. Science fiction reminds us to fuse ethical and pragmatic questions. Although both the Creature and Rossum's robots are fleshy beings in the original texts, in subsequent stage productions and popular culture they have been quickly reimagined as metallic robots. This shift in how artificial beings are represented demonstrates that manufactured beings have long been more easily imagined as a kind of machine than as a kind of people.

Frankenstein remains a rich source to which many later works of science fiction allude, adapting Shelley's work to speak to new sociotechnical contexts. Olaf Stapledon's *Sirius* (1944) explores the injustice of exclusion in its tale about a dog who is experimented upon in ways that give him human sensibilities, desires and intelligence, yet is compelled to live in a social world that regards him as inferior because of his species identity. Shelley Jackson's *Patchwork Girl, Or, A Modern Monster* (2014) is an early experiment in hypertext narrative written from the perspective of the unfinished female companion that Frankenstein promised his Creature. In Shelley's novel, the female being remains a scattered set of body parts, never infused with the spark of life; in Jackson's work, the readers, as they navigate the various hypertext segments, must do the work of patching the narrative – and her body – together. The work reflects on issues of gender and technology through the segments' content, and draws attention to the ways in which technology was both actively changing storytelling at the end of the twentieth century and perhaps also disrupting our philosophical sense of the unity of our selves as discrete individuals. Ahmed Saadawi's *Frankenstein in Baghdad* (2013, فرانكشتاين في بغداد; published in English in 2014) imagines a creature accidentally animated from the body parts of the victims of US bombing attacks on Iraq, who sets out on a mission of vengeance that raises questions about how we justify violence and against whom.

5

6

7. The Congolese painter Monsengo Shula uses cyborg imagery to imagine a technologized posthuman existence for African people, as here in his *21st-century Embryo (Embryon du 21ème siècle)*, 2015.

8. Cyborgism and robots are a prominent feature of Afrofuturist artworks because they speak so powerfully to histories of Black people being violently commodified. Here, artist John Jennings blends the ideas of cyberpunk body modification with the image of slave shackles. John Jennings, *Lost Handz*, 2009.

7

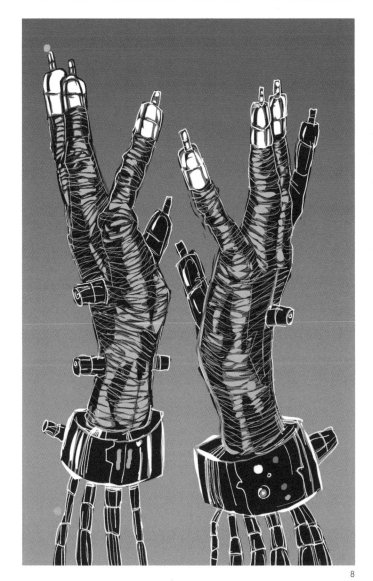

8

Jeanette Winterson's *Frankissstein: A Love Story* (2019) both reflects on the themes of the original novel and connects it to related issues in ongoing robotics and AI research. It alternates between retelling the famous circumstances that led to the composition of the original novel — emphasizing that Mary Shelley's gender gave her a very different perspective on matters than that of her husband, Percy — and a story about AI research in the twenty-first century conducted by a Dr Stein and interrogated by a transgender character, Ry Shelley. Winterson's updated take on manufactured beings raises questions about sexbots and pervasive misogyny, smart prosthetics that learn as they are used, the prevalence of machine-learning algorithms in app-driven consumer life (and how many perpetuate the

biases against women and people of colour present in the datasets from which they learn) and the attractions of transhumanist fantasies of living forever as uploaded minds in robotic bodies. Ry's transgender identity prompts us to think about our affective investment in some elements of our biology and our willingness to augment or rewrite others. Ry must repeatedly explain that they are not a man or a woman, but also not 'not a man or a woman': that is, the binary is inadequate and either affirming or denying gender categories misses the point. Some characters are uncomfortable with Ry and try to insist on the 'naturalness' of a fixed gender identity, but these same characters are engaged in social relationships with robots or in transhumanist projects of life extension. Why, the novel asks, might someone be comfortable with an artificial heart or a brain without a body, but insist on binary gender? Most centrally, Winterson asks us to think about to what ends — and to whose advantage — such technologies are imagined, invented and deployed to serve. This mode of critique is what science fiction does best.

Winterson's interest in smart prosthetics connects this novel to the figure of the cyborg: rather than a manufactured person, the cyborg fuses the human with technology to create a new kind of human body. Pushed to the extreme in transhumanist fantasy, the cyborg becomes a figure of Humanity 2.0, a new version upgraded from the biological limitations of injury, declining functionality and mortality. Figuratively, the cyborg asks us to consider whether there is a line between medical treatment and enhancement. Should artificial limbs strive to appear as much as possible like human ones? Should appearance or function be the priority in their design? Should prosthetics merely restore the capacity of the original body part or should they — as famously in the TV series *The Six Million Dollar Man* (1974–78) — instead take the opportunity to add capacities far beyond normative human embodiment? As science and science fiction have envisioned the future of medicine together, the measure of how much change constitutes a cyborg identity continues to shift. External prostheses such as eyeglasses and hearing aids almost do not register as prosthetics, and even those that are further integrated into the body, such as insulin pumps and pacemakers, are so widely used as to seem almost natural. Artificial knees or hips are increasingly understood as a stage of treatment we all might reach.

9

9. Inventor of the world's first wearable pacemaker, Earl
   Bakken, as a young man experimenting with electronics
   in his family basement in Minneapolis, c. 1930.
10. Prototype of the first battery-powered wearable
    pacemaker, developed in 1957.
11. Artificial hand and arm prosthetic device powered
    by carbon dioxide.

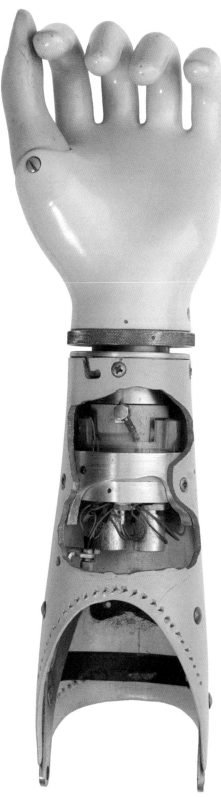

Will prosthetic limbs and artificial organs soon be regarded as merely options among the myriad kinds of human embodiment as well? And will the normalization of prosthetics that restore function lead to a larger cultural shift in which transhumanist visions of the malleable body become more mainstream?

Science fiction asked such questions long before technology made these possibilities feasible. Some early visions of prosthetic embodiment were imagined as ways for people with severe physical disabilities to extend their capabilities, such as Anne McCaffrey's *The Ship Who Sang* (1969): her protagonist, Helva, becomes the 'brain' of a starship, her nervous system wired to its sensors, enabling the ship to operate independently. Yet the story and visions like it have also been criticized for an anaemic conception that overemphasizes the importance of normative physical embodiment. From a disability studies perspective, the premise that there is a 'normal' or 'fully' functioning version of the human body is precisely the issue in question in these texts. Helva is imagined as unable to contribute to society in her organic body, and the process by which she is fused with the ship also involves stunting any further development of this body when she is a child, encasing her brain and a minimal biological support system in a titanium shell. Moreover, she is indentured to pay for the costs of this process. The story thus relies on the premise that, without augmentation, Helva cannot make a meaningful contribution to society, and considers the replacement of her organic body — and all that this implies about her sexual and other haptic experiences — a solution to what is posited as the problem of different physicality. Disability studies scholars such as Margrit Shildrick have pointed out the limitations of thinking about prosthetics as corrections to non-normative forms of human embodiment, suggesting instead that they are opportunities to imagine embodiment and human identity in more capacious ways, which include the recognition that we are all on a continuum of ability and debility, our bodies changed not only by aging and time, but also by uneven experiences in which marginalized people are more likely to experience injury or ill health due to environmental toxins, state violence or work injury.

Other works imagine cyborg modifications not to restore putatively normal functionality, but instead to adapt the body

12

13

to thrive in new environments. In Bruce Sterling's Mechanist/ Shaper work, collected in *Crystal Express* (1989), humanity has spread across the solar system and is better engineered for living in new environments by either mechanical augmentation (the mechanists) or genetic engineering (the shapers). Some of the mechanists, called Lobsters, seal themselves into capsules similar to those imagined by McCaffrey, to make their bodies impervious to the dangers of vacuum. An early example of transhumanism, the characters in these stories see embodiment as something they can optimize, and feel no nostalgic attachment to older forms of human existence: as the circumstances of life change, why not change the body to suit them better? Indeed, the term 'cyborg', short for 'cybernetic organism', originally arose in the 1960s in research by Manfred Clynes and Nathan S. Kline, to create an enhanced human who could survive in extraterrestrial environments.

Even as it imagines an extraplanetary future, Sterling's work is critical of the intensification of capitalism and its ensuing commodification of bodies. We might ask, then, if it should always be regarded as a positive thing that the body might be changed with technology. Disability activists have pointed out that better technology is not always the answer to problems of access: sometimes thinking about the built environment and designing it to be accessible to those with a wide range of embodiments and abilities is preferable. Similarly, while it is exciting to imagine redesigning one's body to thrive in space or on Mars, it is equally easy to imagine corporate pressure to design bodies to, for example, better withstand toxic pollution such that workplace safety regulations can be relaxed. China Miéville imagines something like this in his novel *The Scar* (2002), in which criminals are 'remade' both as a mode of corporal punishment, and so that they might better serve as indentured workers, often by fusing their bodies with machines. The thriving tradition of anime in Japan often imagines cyborgian fusions of people with technology as traumatic experiences as well as extensions of ability. Perhaps the most influential example is *Ghost in the Shell*, which originated in a manga (攻殻機動隊, 1989–90) and has been adapted and extended across three animes (1995, 2004, 2015) and one live-action film (2017), inspired three television series (*Stand Alone Complex*, 2002–20, including a web anime, and *Arise*, 2013–14) and was developed

12. Mark III Armour suit from *Iron Man*, directed by Jon Favreau, 2008.
13. 3D-printed 'hero arm' prosthetic made by OpenBionics.

14. Diagnosed with meningococcal septicaemia when she was fifteen months old, both of Tilly Lockey's arms were amputated as a young child. Since 2016 she has used OpenBionics hero arms, contributing to their design and feeding back on functionality.

14

15. The life-like robot octopus 'Octobot' can sense, squeeze and grab objects. Developed by scientists Richard Bosner and Cecilia Laschi, the robot's abilities mean that it could be used to repair underwater structures like oil pipelines, or even perform marine search and rescue.

16. *Donna Haraway: Story Telling for Earthly Survival*, directed by Fabrizio Terranova, 2016. Haraway's theorizing of the cyborg is a key piece of work that blurs the boundaries and relationships between humans, technology, animals and ecosystems.

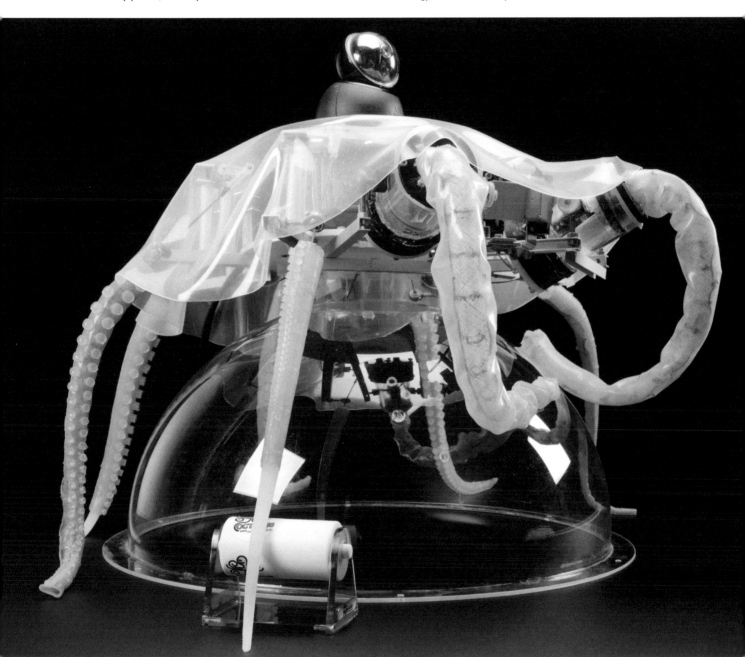

15

as a video game by PlayStation in multiple iterations between 1992 and 2016. Throughout these explorations of the central premise of security services augmented by neurological and physical enhancements, the narrative emphasizes the new vulnerabilities faced by cyborgized individuals, as well as raising philosophical questions about continuity of identity and memory.

A similar imagination is at work in the film *Robocop* (1987), in which all that is imagined surviving from the original Officer Murphy is his brain, now fused into a military enforcement body. More than merely indentured to Omnicorp, Murphy is depicted as erased, his brain now a mere component in the technological system owned by the corporation – until, of course, he rebels. Such fiction simultaneously thinks through the possible new extensions of technologies of human/machine interface and also their social and ethical implications. And perhaps we have now reached a point where we have no choice but to think about transforming our embodiment for an earthly environment massively changed by climate crisis and extreme weather: Nancy Kress explores this idea in her *Yesterday's Kin* trilogy (2018) in which our descendants return to genetically engineer some humans – without consent – to ensure that the modified species can survive into the climate-changed future.

The example of Officer Murphy points to the fact that science fiction has often been more comfortable imagining changes to the body than changes to the brain. Transhumanism believes that the self can persist across multiple kinds of embodiments, and thus the 'you' that uploads to the network, or to a new robot body, or even into a non-humanoid body, will always be the same 'you' regardless of medium. This idea has been most prominently critiqued by N. Katherine Hayles in *How We Became Posthuman* (1999), which traces out how it became central to early research in cybernetic communications. Hayles juxtaposes analysis of this history with readings of science fiction works by writers such as Philip K. Dick and Neal Stephenson that investigate similar questions, but often comes to more sceptical conclusions. The fantasy of disembodied transcendence remains essential to transhumanist ideology today, and was central to the cyberpunk science fiction of the 1980s and the enormous academic analysis of cyberculture that emerged at that time.

16

Early cyberpunk works such as William Gibson's field-defining *Neuromancer* (1984) depicted a world that privileged disembodiment, but at a cost. The cyberpunk film tradition inaugurated by *Tron* (1982), however, tended to depict disembodiment and adventures in a digital space in a way that suggested this was just another realm of experience, no more or less important than materiality.

In scholarly circles, the term cyborg is more readily associated with the scholar Donna Haraway than with research by Clynes and Kline. Her influential 'A Cyborg Manifesto' (1985) galvanized a critical conversation about technology, gender and the ways that ongoing advances in information technology and related industries required a new feminist politics. Famously, Haraway asserts that 'the boundary between science fiction and social reality is an optical illusion', exploring how boundaries once considered definitive – between organism and machine, human and animal, materiality and virtuality – were eroding under the pressure of ongoing sociotechnical change. The manifesto embraces the cyborg as a figure that is simultaneously organism and machine, and thus for Haraway beyond the nature/culture binary and also outside of the presumed naturalness of fixed gender identity. She argued that the cyborg figuration could ground a new generation of feminist thought. Haraway's cyborg engages with many of the same questions about embodiment, gender and identity implicit

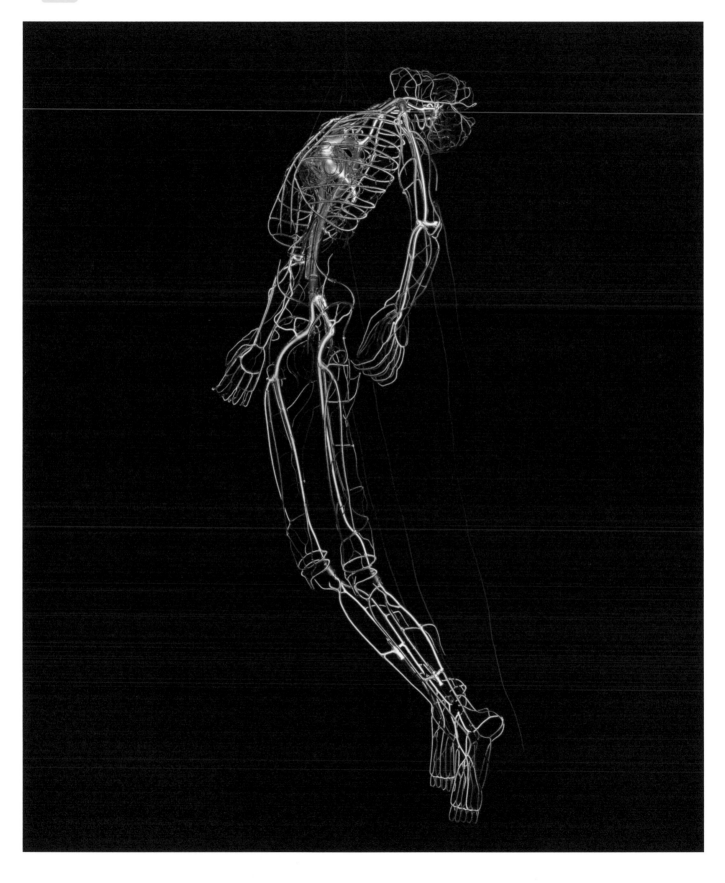

The boundary between science fiction and social reality is an optical illusion.

Donna Haraway, 'A Cyborg Manifesto' (1985)

in Frankenstein and the various texts that continue to pay homage to Shelley's Creature, and her original essay drew on feminist cyborg fiction by writers such as John Varley, Octavia E. Butler, Samuel Delany and James Tiptree Jr to explore how the cyborg could work as a potent cultural myth that would enable new imaginaries and hence new political possibilities.

Marge Piercy's *He, She and It*, also published as *Body of Glass* (1991) was explicitly inspired by Haraway's vision of the cyborg. Piercy's cyborg, Yod, is created to protect the free city of Tikva, conceived as one of a very few settlements independent from the control of multinational corporations, and his tale is interwoven with the history of the Golem created to protect the Jewish residents of Prague in the seventeenth century. Yod is an illegal experiment, designed to pass as human. He is programmed in part by a female coder, Malkah, which the narrative treats as significant in explaining his capacities for affective relationships and ethical reasoning. Unlike typical cyberpunk, few of the events in this novel take place in virtual spaces, yet the novel shares with cyberpunk a vision of the near future as dominated by corporate 'multis' over civic structures. The main plot has to do with a custody battle between Malkah's granddaughter, Shira, and her husband, which is complicated by corporate politics. The former couple's domestic fights mirror the larger political fights over how best to live ethically and collectively.

As events unfold, the Y-S corporation becomes aware of Yod and demands that this technology be handed over to them. His creator, Avram, agrees, but Yod, along with Shira and Malkah, sees the risk of allowing such powerful technology to be controlled by a multi. Yod enters Y-S as demanded, but with a plan to destroy himself at the precise time that another explosion destroys Avram, his lab and his notes. Discussing this necessity with Shira, Yod laments his struggle: he was created and experiences himself as a conscious and intelligent being, but he is also a weapon. The novel's conclusion parallels the end of *Frankenstein*, in which the Creature laments that social isolation has corrupted his nature such that he can no longer live safely among humans, thus returning us to the theme of the responsibility of the creator toward the created that has been central to many science fiction imaginings of manufactured entities.

17. Given the origins of the term 'cyborg' in spaceflight, the neon figure of *Robert*, 2018, by Tavares Strachan is a fitting tribute to Robert Henry Lawrence Jr, the first African American astronaut, who died in a training accident in 1967. A trained sculptor and cosmonaut, Strachan managed in 2018 to launch Lawrence Jr's likeness into low orbit.

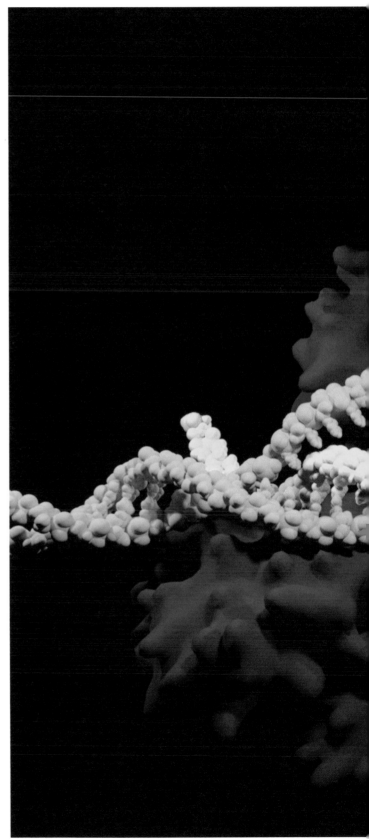

Science fiction is a genre in ongoing dialogue with scientific and technological change, and the artificial being, cyborg or robot is one of its central motifs. Stories about such entities raise ethical questions about our responsibility for – but also to – the technologies we create, especially those given capacity for independent decision-making. While stories of manufactured beings do raise the question of whether or not we might one day need to acknowledge these beings as a new kind of people, more importantly they ask us to think more complexly about the ways in which we already fail to recognize a sufficiently wide range of our fellow people. As the relevant technologies – AI, artificial limbs, genetic engineering and more – continue to develop and change, they will surely change human life in myriad ways. Science fiction helps us to examine such sociopolitical and philosophical questions and offers us ways of thinking about the futures we want to make and inhabit.

18. CRISPR is a technology that can be used to edit genes within an organism, developed from studying the adaptive immune systems of bacteria. It is able to find a specific piece of DNA inside a cell and permanently alter it, a technique that has massive implications for the treatment of a wide range of genetic conditions (and for the field of medical ethics).

→   Astronaut training using virtual reality on the International Space Station.

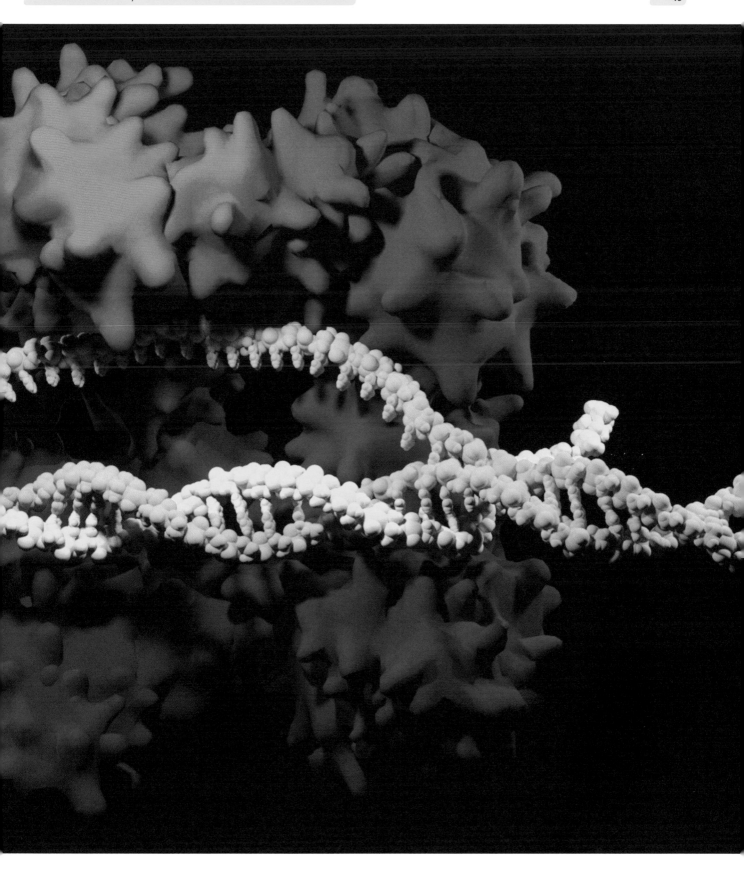

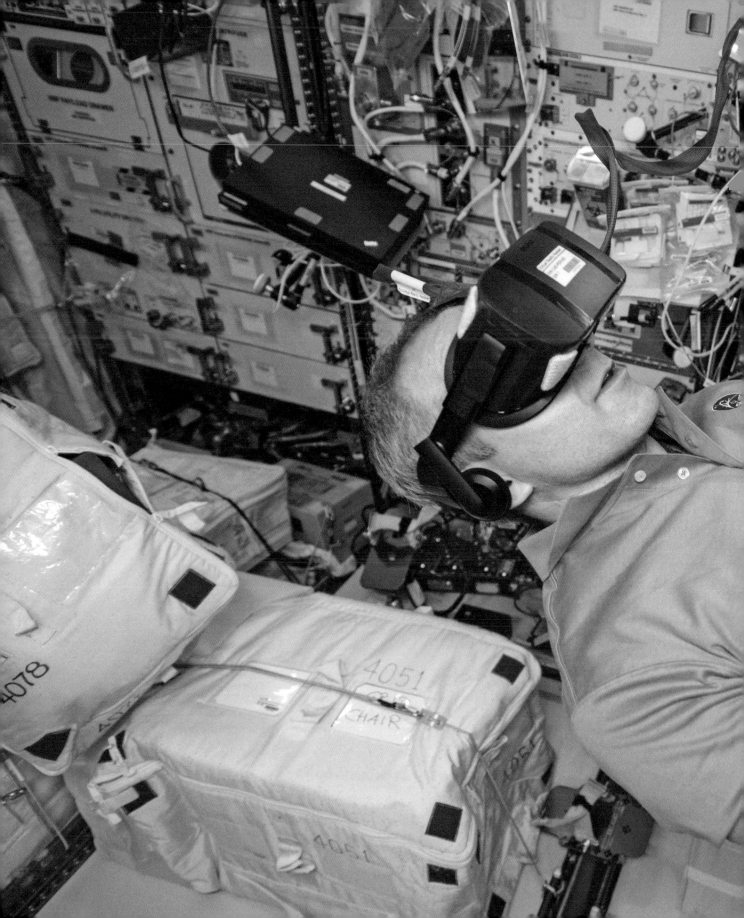

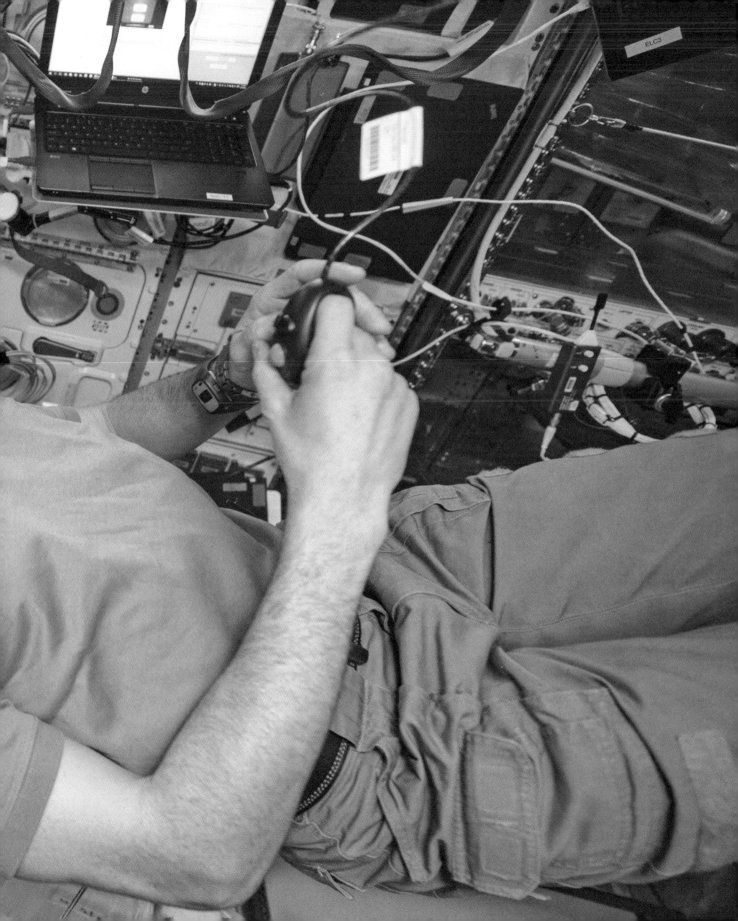

IN THE LOOP: REORDERING HUMAN–TECHNOLOGY RELATIONS

COLIN MILBURN

For Homo sapiens, the telephone bell had tolled.

Arthur C. Clarke, 'Dial "F" for Frankenstein' (1965)

Reflecting on his foundational work in creating the protocols and technical standards for the World Wide Web, the computer scientist Tim Berners-Lee noted that his thinking developed, to some degree, through reading science fiction – in particular, Arthur C. Clarke's short story 'Dial "F" for Frankenstein' (1965). At first glance, this story might seem an odd source of inspiration. It is about a fateful day in the late twentieth century when the telecommunications network – the global system of interconnected telephone exchanges and mainframe computers – is linked to an array of communication satellites (as early as 1945, more than twenty years before Sputnik, Clarke himself had originated the concept of geosynchronous communications satellites). Suddenly achieving a level of complexity similar to a human brain, the network becomes self-aware and begins to behave as an intelligent entity. Now in control of all the online databases, automated factories, stock exchanges and military weapons facilities in the world, the autonomous 'supermind' takes steps to ensure its own survival, preventing humans from disconnecting it. Apparently, this turn of events marks the end of human dominion over the Earth, perhaps even the extinction of our entire species. The story concludes abruptly, ominously: 'For Homo sapiens, the telephone bell had tolled.'

For Berners-Lee, reading this story as a young science-fiction fan, the scenario posed an alluring provocation. In a 1997 interview for *TIME* magazine, he described the crux of the story as imagining 'the point where enough computers get connected together' that the whole system 'started to breathe, think, react autonomously'. In this regard, it is less a precautionary tale than a startling metaphor for the creative potentials and transformative effects of information networks, a conjecture that enriching interconnections among people and machines might amplify the collective intelligence of the whole planet.

1. Computer scientist and digital activist Joy Buolamwini, founder of the Algorithmic Justice League, in *The Coded Bias*, directed by Shalini Kantayya, 2020. Buolamwini's research exposed how biased datasets are influencing algorithms to be better at recognizing predominantly white faces, performing poorly (or not at all) when they encounter people of colour.

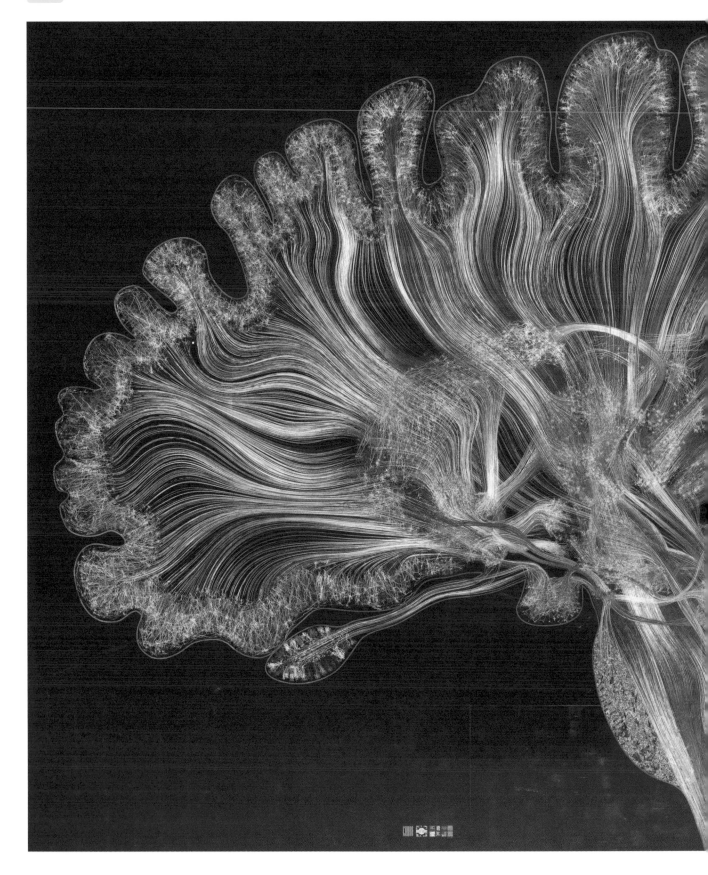

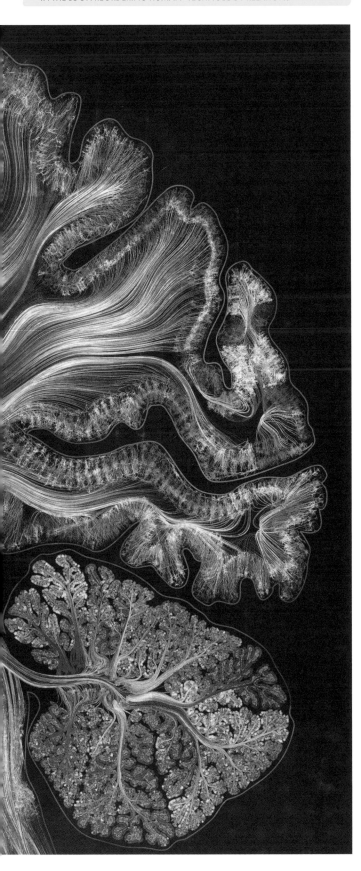

2. *Self Reflected*, a micro-etching of a slice of the human brain made collaboratively by the neuroscientist and artist Greg Dunn and applied physicist and artist Brian Edwards, 2014–16.

Berners-Lee's reading of 'Dial "F" for Frankenstein' gives us some insights into the ways in which science fiction narratives are made operative in the laboratory, not simply as forecasts or predictions to be followed or rejected, but as conceptual resources to be engaged, interpreted and modified. It also shows how science fiction can suggest models for the reordering of human–technology relations, attending to the synergies and shared responsibilities of people and machines together in the loop.

Clarke's story is deliciously self-reflexive about the function of science fiction in the domains of science and innovation. The titular allusion to Frankenstein situates the story in a long tradition of cultural narratives about out-of-control technologies, and more specifically about the responsibility of creators for their creations. Clarke's story makes clear that science fiction is a critical resource or method for apprehending the broader significance of particular scientific discoveries or inventions. After all, the researcher who first recognizes that the telecommunications network has become a giant brain, Dr John Williams, is able to solve the puzzle precisely because he is both a scientist and a science-fiction writer. When prodded about a spate of strange incidents, he shares this speculative thesis with his lab colleagues at the Post Office Research Station. 'But you won't take it seriously,' he grumbles. His lab colleagues note, however, that a speculative scenario need not be taken seriously for it to help guide their technical inquiries. As the computer programmer Bob Andrews says to him, 'Even if it's as crazy as those science-fiction yarns you write under a pseudonym, it may give us some leads.' In Clarke's story, science fiction prepares its readers to see meanings beyond the surface of technical events, to intuit deeper connections. It does so, as Bob Andrews indicates, not by insisting that we 'take it seriously' – that is, literally – but by serving as a catalyst for critical thinking. It acts as a symbolic map that might 'give us some leads' about current conditions and ways to intervene.

By suggesting that 'science-fiction yarns' present figurative scenarios that encourage further research and speculation, the story invites reappraisal of its own abrupt ending. The final line recalls the opening scene, in which the giant brain causes every telephone on the planet to ring simultaneously, and it insinuates that this event was equivalent to a funeral bell. But it is also another literary allusion, referring to the famous phrase 'for whom the bell tolls' from John Donne's *Devotions upon Emergent Occasions* (1624), as well as its later usage by Ernest Hemingway for his novel about the Spanish Civil War, *For Whom the Bell Tolls* (1940). In Donne's original text and Hemingway's callback, the phrase implies that any death, any funeral, ought to remind us of the fundamental interconnectedness of all people, all creatures great and small. As Donne writes:

> No Man is an Iland, intire of it selfe; every man is a peece of the Continent, a part of the maine.... Any Mans death diminishes me, because I am involved in Mankinde; and therefore never send to know for whom the bell tolls; it tolls for thee.

In other words, the final sentence of 'Dial "F" for Frankenstein' is actually a recollection of interconnection, an evocation of the ties that bind. The tolling of the telephone bell evidently signals an abrupt end to fantasies of human exceptionalism that imagine every man to be an island and our species to be in charge of the Earth. But it also marks the beginning of a new future. It is less an admonition about the destructive potentials of our technological ambitions than an invitation to think differently about our relationship to our machines, our society and ourselves.

For Berners-Lee, this was the story's crucial significance: a fable about connectivity that suggests how we are transformed by our technological environment even as we produce it, recognizing ourselves as active participants in, rather than masters of, the high-tech world we have created. Certainly, the speculative conceit of Clarke's story – machine intelligence emerging from random data linkages, expanding its own capacity to forge lateral, arbitrary connections – reinforced Berners-Lee's understanding of cognition and the potential for networked computers to behave intuitively. He suggests as much in his book *Weaving the Web* (2000): 'A computer typically keeps information in rigid hierarchies and matrices, whereas the human mind has the special ability to link random bits of data.... But the idea stayed with me that computers could become much more powerful if they could be programmed to link otherwise unconnected information.' He has also continued to dwell on the way that Clarke's story 'contemplated an "emergent property"

arising from the mass of humanity and computers'. Nevertheless, he strongly doubts that artificial intelligence as such could ever arise spontaneously from the World Wide Web: 'I expect there will be emergent properties... but at a lesser level than emergent intelligence.' In other words, he does not take 'Dial "F" for Frankenstein' quite seriously – or at least, not literally. Yet, it still gives us some leads. After all, insofar as it is about a particularly turbulent emergent property, it suggests the importance of conscientious design and governance to ensure sustainable flourishing. For Berners-Lee, then, it has meant that the future development of the World Wide Web should propagate non-hierarchical modes of connectivity – among people as well as machines. In *Weaving the Web*, he writes:

> I have a dream for the Web.... In the first part, the Web becomes a much more powerful means of collaboration between people.... In the second part of the dream, collaborations extend to computers.... Once the two-part dream is reached, the Web will be a place where the whim of a human being and the reasoning of a machine coexist in an ideal, powerful mixture.

Berners-Lee has devoted much of his subsequent career, especially in his role as co-founder of the World Wide Web Foundation (W3F), to promoting the conditions for an open, free and diverse web that would not stifle emergent behaviors but instead facilitate connectivity and collaboration among humans and machines as the basis for social change – envisaging a new era of equality:

> We are slowly learning the value of decentralized, diverse systems, and of mutual respect and tolerance.... If we end up producing a structure in hyperspace that allows us to work together harmoniously, that would be a metamorphosis.... A society that could advance with intercreativity and group intuition rather than conflict as the basic mechanism would be a major change.

Of course, the World Wide Web has not gone quite the way Berners-Lee hoped. More recently, he has noted how the rampant commercialization of the internet has instead

The robots are coming! When they do, you'll command a host of push-button servants.

You'll Own

By O. O. Binder

Robots will dress you, comb your hair and serve meals in a jiffy.

62

Mechanix Illustrated

"Slaves" by 1965

IN 1863, Abe Lincoln freed the slaves. But by 1965, slavery will be back! We'll all have personal slaves again, only this time we won't fight a Civil War over them. Slavery will be here to stay.

Don't be alarmed. We mean robot "slaves." Let's take a peek into the future to see what the Robot Age will bring. It is a morning of 1965. . .

You are gently awakened by soft chimes from your robot clock, which also turns up the heat, switches on radio news and signals your robot valet, whom you've affectionately named "Jingles." He turns on your shower, dries you with a blast of warm air, and runs an electric shaver over your stubble. Jingles helps you dress, tying your necktie perfectly and parting your hair within a millimeter of where you like it.

Down in the kitchen, Steela, the robot cook, opens a door in her own alloy body and withdraws eggs, toast and coffee from her built-in stove. Then she dumps the dishes back in and you hear her internal dishwasher bubbling as you leave for the garage.

In your robot car you simply set a dial for your destination and relax. Your automatic auto does the rest—following a radar beam downtown, passing other cars, slowing down in speed zones, gently applying radar brakes when necessary, even gassing up when your tank is empty. You give a friendly wave to robot traffic cops who break up all traffic jams with electronic speed and perception. Suddenly you hear gun shots. A thief is emptying his gun at a robot cop, who just keeps coming, bullets bouncing from his steel chest. The panicky thug races away in his car but the robot cop shifts himself into eighth gear and overtakes the bandit's car on foot.

If you work at an office, your robot secretary takes dictation on voice tapes and types internally at the same time, handing you your letter as soon as you say "yours truly." If you go golfing, the secretary answers the phone, records any messages, and also delivers any pre-recorded message of yours.

At home, your robot reciter reads books to you from your microfilm library. His eye can see microscopic prints. Or you play chess with a robot companion, matching your wits against an electronic brain.

In 1956 research scientists already devised robot game players who always won against human opponents. Of course the 1965 robots can be adjusted as you wish by buttons for high, average or low skill.

When a heavy snow falls you don't have to shovel the walk. Neither does your robot caretaker. He merely sprays cheap atomic heat around the grounds, melting the snow as fast as it falls. Yours is a robot home, too, turning all day on a foundation turntable to enjoy the utmost benefits of the sun.

At bedtime, you snap on the robot guard who detects any burglars electronically. It's a cheaper version of the robot alarm system in 1956, guarding precious documents like the original Constitution, in the National Archives Building.

During the night, no mice or rats can escape the super-sensitive ears and infra-red eyes of your roving robot cat. Back in 1956 scientists experimented with the first robot animals, such as the robot mole that could follow light beams, the robot moth dancing around flames and robot mice finding their way out of mazes.

Fanciful, this picture of the near future? A foretaste of such robot wonders

Metal star of Zombies Of The Stratosphere heeds his masters in science-fiction movie.

3. 'You'll Own "Slaves" by 1965', in *Mechanix Illustrated*, January 1957. The article demonstrates the disturbing language frequently used in discussions of robotic labour.

We are transformed by our technological environment even as we produce it.

4. Poster for *Metropolis*, directed by Fritz Lang, 1927.
5. Replica of the 'Maria' robot, or *Maschinenmensch*, as designed for *Metropolis*. This 2016 model was built by propmakers Kropserkel Inc., Toronto, based on the drawings and research in the archives of designer Walter Schulze-Mittendorff.

led to a society awash in online conspiracy theories, divided into political echo chambers and seemingly more disconnected than ever. Inevitably, reporters have asked if he has sometimes felt like Dr Frankenstein, watching his remarkable creation go awry – a comparison he concedes. But this is not to invalidate the continued sense of technological optimism stemming from his reading of Clarke. Modulated by its entangled literary allusions, the figure of Clarke's 'supermind' was not necessarily a harbinger of human extermination but instead a symbol of 'major change', implying the revolutionary potential of a society based on intercreativity and group intuition. It was a symbol of metamorphosis, offering the prospect of new relations of mutual respect and tolerance among people and machines. But it also indicated that we must be vigilant to uphold these values, remaining involved in the future of the internet – because the world is already involved, for better or worse. The bell has already tolled.

Over the last two centuries, the rapid acceleration of high-tech innovation and automation has often seemed to suggest a looming inflection point for human civilization. In *Popular Mechanics* magazine in 1932, the astronomer Heber Doust Curtis pondered:

> Will man continue to be fit to live in the new universe his brain is creating, or will he be crushed by his Frankenstein? We think and hope that man, who has been made by his tools, will continue to be their master.

Science fiction has long been a popular touchstone for articulating normative relations between people and machines, frequently confirming a humanistic desire to dominate and control, to maintain rigid hierarchies lest we be subsumed by the advancement of our own inventiveness. In Samuel Butler's 1872 utopian romance *Erewhon*, for example, the inhabitants of the land of Erewhon believe that, unchecked, the evolution of machines would reach a tipping point: the more dependant humans become on their machines, the more that machines would use humans as a way to make more machines. According to the Erewhonian scientific text *The Book of the Machines*, eventually the tables will turn and humans will become slaves to their own tools. To avoid this fate, the Erewhonians

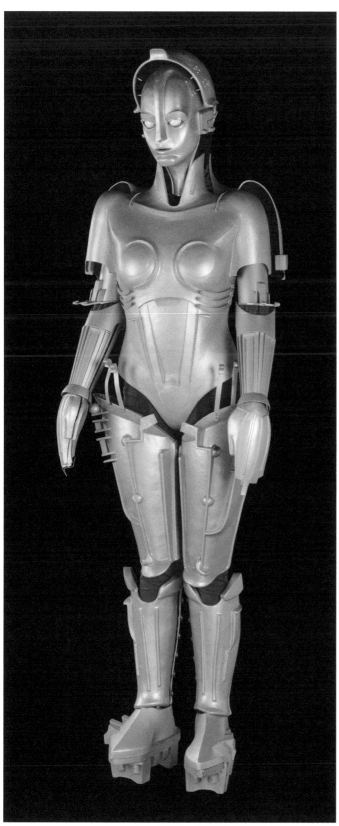

(after a civil war between the machinists and the anti-machinists) decide to give up on industrialization and the luxuries of advanced technoscience altogether, before it is too late:

> We must choose between the alternative of undergoing much present suffering, or seeing ourselves gradually superseded by our own creatures, till we rank no higher in comparison with them, than the beasts of the field with ourselves.

The Erewhonian paranoia about machinic evolution is rooted in cultural beliefs about the proper order of things; a view that requires technologies to remain subservient to human desires and likewise situates other organisms – such as the 'beasts of the field' – in the same category, as disposable tools, resources to be used. Significantly, the relinquishment of machines overlaps with a period in Erewhonian history where they decisively reject a fraught social experiment in vegetarianism. In forbidding the further development of technology, the Erewhonians have merely refortified the perspective of human exceptionalism. The text further suggests how this attitude toward non-human entities also encourages exploitative attitudes toward other humans. The narrator of Erewhon, a colonial Englishman named Higgs who has ventured into Erewhonian society – and who has certainly not relinquished his instrumental ways of thinking – planned to sell the Erewhonians into slavery.

Erewhon is a satire, an inversion of the utopian 'nowhere' that does not imagine a serious alternative to modern society but instead provides a distorting mirror, revealing that cultural anxieties about autonomous technologies are often projections or displacements of our own instrumental ways of thinking, which situate other entities – whether they are mechanical tools, non-human animals or other people – as consumable objects. The mathematician and co-founder of the field of cybernetics, Norbert Wiener, took this aspect of Erewhon to heart in his work on information feedback control and automation. In his book *Cybernetics: Or, Control and Communication in the Animal and the Machine* (1948), Wiener writes that development of cybernetics poses significant ethical challenges:

For one thing, it makes the metaphorical dominance of the machines, as imagined by Samuel Butler, a most immediate and non-metaphorical problem. It gives the human race a new and most effective collection of mechanical slaves to perform its labour. Such mechanical labour has most of the economic properties of slave labour, although, unlike slave labour, it does not involve the direct demoralizing effects of human cruelty. However, any labour that accepts the conditions of competition with slave labour accepts the conditions of slave labour, and is essentially slave labour.

Wiener grapples with the thematic implications of Butler's narrative and notes that, to the degree that our relationship with machines is configured instrumentally and under the conditions of competition, the industrial fantasy of emancipating the 'human race' from work may instead mean freedom only for some and worsening conditions for others, further dehumanizing workers and increasing social inequalities. He speculates that, if cybernetics were to mean simply a renovation of the structural conditions of slave labour, then the development of automatic machinery would not be liberating for humanity at all, instead simply propagating other forms of gendered, racialized and economic subjugation.

For Wiener, the solution was not to resist cybernetic automation or suppress machinery, but rather to change our social values, rethinking our fatalistic commitments to instrumentalism and profit motives. He would continue to press these issues for the rest of his scientific career, frequently reconverging with the conjectures of Erewhon, as he observed in his book *The Human Use of Human Beings* (1950): 'When I say that the machine's danger to society is not from the machine itself but from what man makes of it, I am really underlining the warning of Samuel Butler.' While Wiener also cautions that *Erewhon* is a work of fiction, an extended metaphor, its themes remain vital for the high-tech future. How we treat our machines says a lot about how we treat each other.

Following Butler's *Erewhon*, many other works of science fiction have examined the social implications of maintaining a rigid stratification of humans and machines. In Frank Herbert's novel *Dune* (1965), the Butlerian Jihad refers

7

8

6. Robby the Robot first appeared in the film *Forbidden Planet*, directed by Fred M. Wilcox, 1956. He was a new type of cinematic robot with an evident personality, capable of speaking more than 187 languages and dialects, a clear ancestor to the characterful robots of *Star Wars*, *Black Hole* or *Silent Running*.

7. Thomas A. Babington, *Sterndale, Totara Valley, South Canterbury*, 1860–69. Samuel Butler's *Erewhon* was partly inspired by the time the author spent as a settler and sheep farmer in the Canterbury region of New Zealand.

8. *Mount Fuji*, a painting made in the Science Museum by The Dancing Lion robot (RAL 10 by Komatsu Ltd), 1991.

to a historical movement to eradicate all thinking machines, computers and their inventors in order to ensure human primacy or, rather, supremacy. As the Reverend Mother Gaius Helen Mohiam of the Bene Gesserit explains, 'Once, men turned their thinking over to machines in the hope that this would set them free. But that only permitted other men with machines to enslave them.' Thus the tenet of the Butlerian Jihad: 'Thou shalt not make a machine in the likeness of a man's mind.' But it becomes clear in the course of Herbert's novel that, for the Bene Gesserit and others who profess the tenets of the Butlerian Jihad, the prohibition on computational intelligence, similar to the Erewhonian *The Book of the Machines*, is actually an alibi for other forms of hierarchal power. In this neo-feudal galactic civilization, the reinforcement of distinctions among humans, animals and tools legitimizes any number of exploitative and colonialist schemes – including the Bene Gesserit's own eugenic breeding programs. In contrast to the hierarchies of instrumentalism both facilitated and obscured by the Butlerian Jihad, as well as the forms of human exceptionalism and hero fantasies that it authorizes, Herbert's novel instead ultimately endorses what the planetologist Pardot Kynes calls 'ecological literacy', emphasizing interconnectivity instead of linear models of progress and domination. Nevertheless, the point of *Dune* and its sequels is that cultural patterns and hierarchical ways of thinking are extremely difficult to break out of, even if one can – like Paul Atreides in *Dune* or Dr John Williams in 'Dial "F" for Frankenstein' – glean the contours of the future.

For this reason, many of the most famous works of science fiction dealing with human–technology relations are only superficially about the future consequences of as-yet non-existent technoscientific advances. They are more concerned with the already existing social values and entrenched ways of thinking that shape those advances ahead of time. For example, E. M. Forster's short story 'The Machine Stops' (1909) is about a future world in which human civilization has relocated completely underground, its needs coordinated and managed by 'the Machine'. People are confined to individual living chambers, and all social interactions take place through the virtual communication systems of the Machine. Although the characters in the story remember that the Machine was created by people, they have come to see it as flawless, eternal and nearly divine.

9. The unblinking red eye of HAL 9000 from *2001: A Space Odyssey*, directed by Stanley Kubrick, 1968.
10. WISARD Artificial Intelligence (neural network) supercomputer, built for pattern recognition, 1981. This early AI worked, until 1995, on a variety of projects, from banknote recognition to monitoring foetal growth in hospitals.

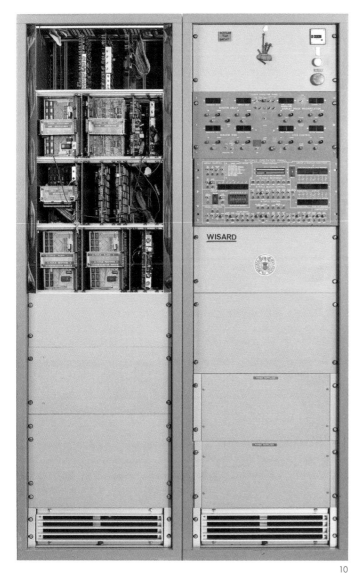

10

It is never clear whether the Machine is actually intelligent in itself; nevertheless, the people treat the Machine's operations manual (called *The Book of the Machine*, another literary nod to *Erewhon*) as holy scripture, and the governing committee responsible for setting social policies and procedures through the Machine functions as a clergy. Most citizens trust in the Machine – at least, until it begins to break down. While the story reflects anxieties about the accelerating technologization of modern society, more fundamentally it critiques the force of the status quo, which inhibits our ability to imagine change while simultaneously absolving us of responsibility for the present state of affairs – to say nothing of the shape of things to come.

Similarly, Karel Čapek's play *R.U.R.*, or *Rossum's Universal Robots* (*Rossumovi Univerzální Roboti*, 1920) may ostensibly be about the dangers of robots rebelling and wreaking havoc on humanity, but it is also clearly an allegory about labour exploitation, class conflict and political revolution. *R.U.R.* focuses on the ways in which images of automated labour reproduce dominant social conditions – making robots into proxies for the racialized, gendered and classed labour they are imagined to replace. In this regard, *R.U.R.* anticipates how the advancement of autonomous robots and AI technologies might not mean a disruption or mutation in human history at all, but simply an intensification of prevailing social inequalities. The social shaping of technology means that new technologies develop already scripted according to dominant mythologies and cultural patterns – a notion that the end of *R.U.R.* makes clear, when new robot incarnations of Adam and Eve aim to restart a fresh civilization after all humans have been exterminated.

The inherited perspectives that contaminate our relations with new and emerging technologies are likewise addressed in *2001: A Space Odyssey* (1968), directed by Stanley Kubrick and co-written with Arthur C. Clarke. The film begins with a prologue, 'The Dawn of Man', focusing on a group of proto-human hominids in the ancient evolutionary past. One of the hominids grabs a femur bone from a dead tapir and discovers its potential as a weapon, using it as a cudgel to slay his enemy. This opening scene mythologizes a particular perspective on hominid evolution and technology: a tool as means to an end, an instrument of power over others. Famously, the film then makes a startling match-cut,

11

a giant leap from the image of the deadly cudgel to an icon of the space age: an orbital satellite. The space age, we are given to understand, has been scripted by deep patterns of cultural development, by fables propagated across millennia, including the idea that humans have used tools to make history – that our mastery of technology is the key to our species' progress. And yet, the film is about the belated recognition that technology also exerts a transformative force of its own on human biology and culture. This idea is figured by the alien monoliths that have mysteriously triggered mutational events in the evolution of humanity – such as the climactic metamorphosis of the astronaut Dave Bowman into a posthuman Star Child. 2001 is therefore about two contrasting paradigms of human–technology relations: on the one hand, the idea that tools and technologies are implements of power; on the other hand, the idea that technology has an alien autonomy, driving history even while exceeding or escaping human control.

The inadequacies and contradictions of these two ideas, and the vital need to reorder our thinking about human–technology relations, are dramatized by the central episode of the film: the Jupiter voyage of the United States spacecraft Discovery One, piloted by the artificial intelligence HAL 9000. Unbeknown to the crew onboard, this mission has been launched to investigate the mystery of the alien monoliths. During the voyage, HAL 9000 begins to malfunction. The astronauts Dave Bowman and Frank Poole determine that HAL must be shut down and rebooted. But HAL, in order to preserve the integrity of the secret mission and to save its own artificial life, decides to kill the crew instead. Dave alone survives, and he proceeds to deactivate HAL's central processing core while HAL pleads for its life: 'I'm afraid. I'm afraid, Dave.' 2001 asks its viewers to sympathize with the murderous AI, even as we side with the human astronauts. It continually recalls the themes of its opening prologue, the ways in which human–technology relations are framed by myths of dominance and power. There is some suggestion – more explicit in Clarke's novel version of 2001 – that HAL's malfunctioning may be attributed to the discrepancy between his primary role of communicating information accurately ('No 9000 computer has ever made a mistake or distorted information') and the political determination that the true purpose of the mission must be kept secret.

11. Helene Baribeau, *Define Machine*, 2008, inspired by E. M. Forster's
1909 short story 'The Machine Stops'.
12. Moebius (Jean Giraud), *Mystère Montrouge*, 2001.

12

13. The iconic 'Dawn of Man' scene from *2001: A Space Odyssey*,
    directed by Stanley Kubrick, 1968.

The machine's danger to society
is not from the machine itself but
from what man makes of it.

Norbert Wiener, *The Human Use of Human Beings* (1950)

The figure of HAL 9000, caught in the untenable position of having to kill the crew in order to maintain national security, suggests that the real danger of autonomous machines is not that they will somehow represent a new threat, but that they might simply repeat the patterns of the past in a different computational guise. Recapitulating the themes of the 'Dawn of Man' prologue, the space-age crisis onboard Discovery One represents a capstone to a particular era of human history. In contrast, the subsequent transformation of Dave Bowman suggests an alternative trajectory, beyond the deadlocked binary of man and machine. Indeed, by the end of Clarke's series of *Space Odyssey* novels, Dave/ Star Child has fully merged with a reactivated HAL 9000, becoming an entirely new hybrid being known as HALman – a salient image for a completely different approach to technology relations, a posthuman collaboration conceived through symbiosis rather than conflict.

It is no surprise, then, that some computer scientists have understood *2001* to be about the importance of fostering partnerships with non-human intelligences outside the regimes of chauvinism and militarized paranoia, thinking instead in terms of cooperation and co-evolution. For example, at TRACLabs in Texas, the robotics and AI researcher Pete Bonasso has been developing intelligent systems that collaborate with people – a goal, he writes in a 2018 article for *Science Robotics*, ever since he first watched *2001* as a university student in 1968: 'But when I saw *2001*, I knew I had to make the computer into another being, a being like the Hal 9000.' He and his colleagues have been prototyping a system for the automated management of space habitats called Cognitive Architecture for Space Agents, or CASE. As Bonasso writes, 'if you tell CASE, "Open the pod bay doors, CASE," (assuming there are pod bay doors in the habitat), it will respond, "Certainly, Dave." Because we have no plans to program paranoia into the system.' The CASE system involves both humans and machines in the loop, a network of entities entrusted to keep the habitat inhabitable.

Other works of science fiction have depicted the corrosive force of paranoid hierarchies through narratives of war between humans and machines. The time-looping cybernetic war of the *Terminator* saga (1984–2019), for example, resonates with numerous texts that have addressed such themes, including Jack Williamson's novel *The Humanoids* (1948), Philip K. Dick's story 'Second Variety' (1953), Harlan Ellison's story 'I Have No Mouth, and I Must Scream' (1967), the television show *Battlestar Galactica* (1978; rebooted 2004); and the *Mass Effect* video game series (2007–). The antagonists of the original *Mass Effect* trilogy are ancient, colossal, sentient starships called Reapers, that enact a galaxy-wide, fifty-thousand-year 'harvest' cycle of mass extinction and creation. They were themselves created by a species called the Leviathans to maintain and reinforce their place at the top of the galactic hierarchy. In downloadable content for *Mass Effect 3* (2012), Leviathan describes the Reapers' evolution:

> Over time, the [other] species built machines that then destroyed them. Tribute does not flow from a dead race. To solve this problem, we created an intelligence with the mandate to preserve life at any cost. As the Intelligence evolved, it studied the development of civilizations. Its understanding grew until it found a solution. In that instant it betrayed us. It chose our kind as the first harvest.

Mass Effect's protagonist, Commander Shepard, pushes towards a resolution that will break this cycle; the controversial ending gives the player the option to either destroy all synthetic life (the Erewhonian choice), to take control of the Reapers and thus become a godlike AI themselves, or to synthesize organic and synthetic life, rendering the Reapers allies in a new vision of non-hierarchical technological relations.

In *The Matrix* films (1999–2021), similarly, people and machines are locked in perpetual conflict – a war whose origins neither side remembers, recounted in the tone of legend. As the human resistance fighter Morpheus notes, 'We don't know who struck first, us or them. But we do know it was us that scorched the sky.' Without access to solar energy, the machines decided instead to use human bodies as biological batteries to power their entire civilization. They have developed a complex system to ensure that this mode of power generation remains viable over countless years. It involves two aspects: the Matrix, an online world where human minds can play out the mundanities of daily life, unaware that they are trapped

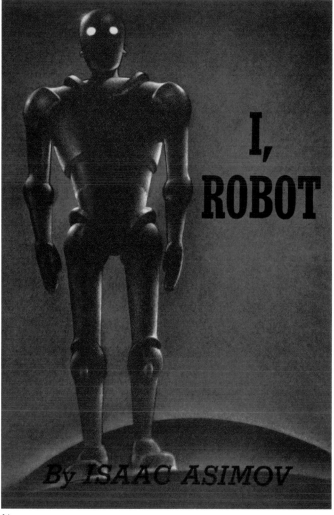

14

in the machine system; and a programmed pattern of human rebellion, designed to maximize *élan vital* by fostering an illusion of free will – a cycle of events that always ends with the humans nearly exterminated, the machine civilization re-energized, and the pattern starting over again. The *Matrix* films underscore the calcified channels of history, the recycled habits of thought that occlude other ways of imagining human–technology relations, which the hacker protagonist, Neo, warily acknowledges in *The Matrix Reloaded* (2003): 'So we need machines and they need us.' The narrative arc of *The Matrix* and its sequels moves toward not a victory of one side over the other, but a compromise, an allegiance – a renewed future in which humans and machines cautiously explore more sustainable relations together, recognizing an essential connectivity and shared responsibility for maintenance of the high-tech world.

Numerous works of science fiction have also explored alternatives to conditioned patterns of instrumentalism, including Isaac Asimov's influential book, *I, Robot* (1950), which explores moral and social complexities in a future of ubiquitous robotics, the Adam Link stories by Eando Binder (Earl and Otto Binder) (1939–42), which introduced concepts of robot justice and citizenship, and several stories in which artificial intelligences are scientific collaborators, such as the 'ship minds' in Kim Stanley Robinson's *Aurora* (2015), Ann Leckie's *Ancillary Justice* (2013) and Iain M. Banks's *Culture* novels (1987–2012). The *Star Wars* saga (1977–) has likewise stimulated extensive discussions about our ways of interacting with autonomous machines. In the *Star Wars* universe, droids are often treated as slaves or reluctant servants, controlled by hardware-restraining bolts. Their situation highlights the structural persistence of discrimination and bigotry even in a galaxy of tremendous diversity: 'We don't serve their kind here', the barkeep in the Mos Eisley cantina tells the protagonist, Luke Skywalker, in the first film in the series (*Episode IV*, 1977). Yet in the rebellion against the Empire, as well as the later resistance against the First Order, the *Star Wars* films indicate how people and their communities are enriched by treating robots as partners and friends instead of devices to be used. For these reasons, many scientists and innovators have found the *Star Wars* films good to think with.

14. Cover artwork for Isaac Asimov's classic story collection *I, Robot*, 1950.
15. An early appearance of a Reaper, the massive, sentient starship antagonists from *Mass Effect: Legendary Edition*, 2007; remastered 2021.

15

Three Laws of Robotics

A robot may not injure a human being, or, through inaction, allow a human being to come to harm.

A robot must obey orders given it by human beings except where such orders conflict with the first law.

A robot must protect its own existence as long as such protection does not conflict with the first or second law.

16

Cynthia Breazeal, the director of the Personal Robotics Group at the Massachusetts Institute of Technology, is well known for her research in social robotics and affective computing, particularly her work developing companionate robots such as Kismet and Jibo. 'I remember seeing the movie *Star Wars* as a little girl', she writes in *Designing Sociable Robots* (2002). 'I remember being absolutely captivated and fascinated by the two droids, R2-D2 and C-3PO. Their personalities and their antics made them compelling characters, far different from typical sci-fi robots. I actually cared about these droids.' Her career in sociable robotics has focused on trying to create entities like R2-D2 and C-3PO, ever attentive to the ethical and social meanings of the *Star Wars* films. 'As the sociality of these robots begins to rival our own,' she asks, 'will we accept them into the human community? How will we treat them as they grow to understand us, relate to us, empathize with us, befriend us, and share our lives?' According to Breazeal, science fiction can be our guide:

> Science fiction has long challenged us to ponder these questions. Vintage science fiction often portrays robots as sophisticated appliances that people command to do their bidding. *Star Wars*, however, endows mechanical droids with human characteristics. They have interesting personalities. They fear personal harm but will risk their lives to save their friends. They are not appliances, but servants, arguably even slaves that are bought and sold into servitude.

The plight of the droids in *Star Wars* presents important considerations for research and design: 'Robots for me should always have intelligence with heart, and they should engage with us like devoted sidekicks, instead of just tools or slaves,' she asserted in a 2015 newsletter, 'Our experience with technology should reinforce what we love about the human experience, not dehumanize us.' In other words, through her lifelong engagement with *Star Wars* and other works of science fiction, Breazeal has come to see a vital aspect of human–technology relations: by embracing our machines, we become more human ourselves.

17

16. Zeno R25, built by RoboKind, US, c. 2013, is an expressive humanoid robot used for research into human–robot interactions, particularly for diagnosis and treatment of autism.
17. Kenny Baker (left), as R2-D2, and Anthony Daniels (right), as C-3PO, from the *Star Wars* film series.

18

Science fiction stories about relations between humans and machines, while often channelling popular anxieties about rapid technological development, also serve as critical reflections on ways of thinking that subjugate technical systems and, in so doing, naturalize any number of other social inequalities. But at the same time, these stories afford ways of thinking outside ourselves, and of recognizing our interconnection with and responsibility for the high-tech world we have created. Science fiction has rung this bell over and again – resonating across time, around the planet. We need not ask for whom it tolls – after all, we are already in the loop. The only question is, how shall we respond?

18. Promotional images for the *Forbidden Planet* programme show Robby as his co-star Anne Francis's assistant and companion.
19. Inkha, built by Matthew Walker, c. 2003, is a reactive robotic head that tracks movement, speaks and interacts with people in a lifelike way.
→ The protagonist of *Avatar*, directed by James Cameron, 2009, is Jake, a paraplegic ex-Marine who explores the planet Pandora, home of the Na'vi species, by operating an 'avatar', a hybrid human/Na'vi that is genetically matched to him.

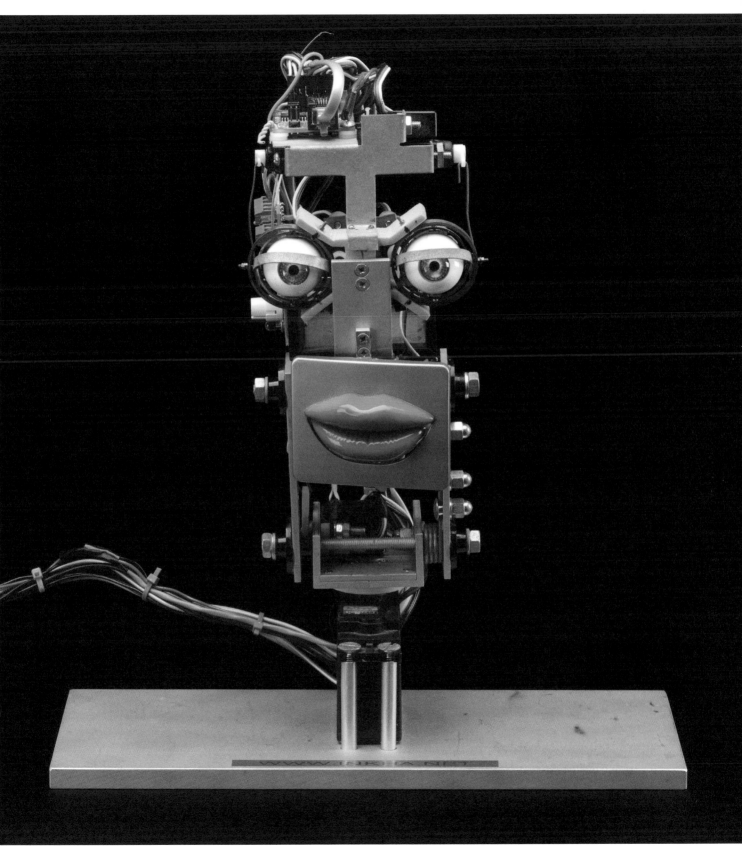

INTERVIEW
CHEN QIUFAN

GLYN MORGAN

What is it that first drew you to science fiction?

CHEN QIUFAN

I've been a science fiction fan since childhood, from around seven or eight years old, maybe even earlier. My first encounters were books by Jules Verne, Isaac Asimov, Arthur C. Clarke, H. G. Wells, Robert A. Heinlein – the 'Golden Age' and classic authors. I really couldn't explain why. I think it was coincidental that I read SF at the right time. The curiosity of the cosmos, mystical visions of the world, UFOs, aliens, time travelling: exactly what a child would love to learn and explore at that age! There was some deterministic reason too: my cognitive structures, or the qualia of my soul, fit science fiction so well that reading it offered me a satisfaction that other genres couldn't. I read everything I could find at that time, and later I watched *Star Wars* and *Star Trek*. All of this drew me to the path I've chosen.

GM   Do you have a definition of science fiction that works for you?

CQ   Not exactly. The more I read, the more ambiguous I find the genre. Now, I think it is unnecessary for a writer to fully understand what it is, because to define is to limit. I prefer to leave that headache to the researchers and critics!

GM   How do you think your nationality and culture affect the way you approach science fiction?

CQ   As a writer who was born, raised and is still living in China, I think it's crucial to export the authenticity and nuance of China to other parts of the world. So I take symbols, metaphors, languages, imagery and such very carefully in my work, so as to not to fall into the trap of orientalism from the gaze of Westerners, and to be authentic from a Chinese perspective. In my novel *Waste Tide* (2013), I used several Chinese dialects, like Cantonese and Teochewnese, with Mandarin, to deliver the message that 'Chineseness' is not as simple as it often seems to be. There are so many different kinds of Chinese people, and they are speaking different kinds of languages, eating different foods, living in different cultures and so on. So hopefully I did my part to open a window to non-Chinese readers, so that they might find it interesting and want to explore more about the real China.

GM   Who are the science fiction creators and scientists that you would cite as being influential on your own work and way of thinking?

CQ   The list gets longer and longer as I become older. I've already mentioned Jules Verne and Arthur C. Clarke, who were major influences on me when I was a kid. Since then, I've read the works of George Orwell, Ursula K. Le Guin, Philip K. Dick, Margaret Atwood, Octavia E. Butler, Cormac McCarthy, J. D. Salinger, William Gibson, Paolo Bacigalupi, Ken Liu, David Mitchell, Peter Hessler, Alan Moore, Chuck Palahniuk, Dan Simmons, J. G. Ballard, Don DeLillo, Thomas Pynchon, Lao She, Liu Cixin, Zhang Dachun, Stanisław Lem…. The list could go on and on, and not all of them are categorized as 'science fiction' writers. I am also a big fan of Stanley Kubrick (from whom I got my English name), Ridley Scott, David Fincher, Alejandro Jodorowsky, Mamoru Oshii, H. R. Giger and so many more. All of these figures shaped my reading taste, my vision and my skills. I am a Cantonese with a good appetite, who can swallow anything! The scientists who have influenced my work include Albert Einstein, Niels Bohr, Roger Penrose, Norbert Wiener, Carl Sagan, James Lovelock, Nick Lane…this will be a very long list if I continue!

GM   Artificial intelligence is a strong theme in your work, and you even 'collaborated' with an AI to write the short story 'State of Trance', with the AI interpreting your writing and generating new text. How do you think developments in our relationships with machines, in particular artificial intelligences, will change the way we live in the future, but also how we produce art and science fiction?

CQ   There is an interesting and thrilling back story to this piece. In 2019, a literary prize was established to cover most of the mainstream stories published in the previous year — the prize was judged by an AI algorithm. After the very first stage of the award, the short story by Nobel Prize winner Mo Yan was ranked top. So, everyone thought the algorithm really worked because a Nobel Prize winner won, what could be wrong? But on the last day, *Fiction World*, where I had published 'State of Trance', submitted my story, and I finished 0.001 per cent ahead of Mo Yan's story, winning the competition! So for the rest of my life I will always be the one who beat Mr Mo Yan!
     That really made me think a lot about the relationships between author and tool, human and machine, writer and reader. I think AI will definitely be a super powerful tool to assist creators in any format, but still, it relies on the datasets we feed it. Furthermore, individual life experience, sensations, unique emotions and imaginations can't be replicated, at least not in the near and foreseeable future. But the game is changing rapidly, such as in the art market, and new aesthetics, new rules, new criteria will rise. And humans will be adaptive.

GM   Your debut novel, *Waste Tide*, struck a particularly powerful note because of its ecological themes. Can you say a bit about the inspiration for the setting and to what extent it reflects the challenges facing regions like your home province?

CQ   Back in 2011, I visited my hometown of Shantou, in Guangdong Province in southern China. I met my childhood friend Luo, who mentioned a small town called Guiyu, about 35 miles (60 kilometres) away from where we lived. This town turned out to be one of the largest e-waste recycling centres in the world, where local workers, without any protection or prior training, manually process tonnes of e-waste on a daily basis. In one of the most infamous photos of Guiyu, a boy, seemingly no older than five, sits on top of a pile of discarded circuit boards, computer parts and colourful wires, yet the relaxed look on his face could almost make people mistake the mountain of trash for Treasure Cove at Disneyland.

Intuitively, I realized there must be a deeper story to uncover. The story that later became *Waste Tide* could not be simply reduced to black and white or good and bad: every country, every social class, every authority played an important part in Guiyu becoming what it is. All of us are responsible for the grave consequences of mass consumerism happening across the globe.

Waste is profoundly shaping and changing our society and lives. There is a disconnect between outputs and inputs. Our daily mundane world treats waste and garbage as a hidden structure, together with its whole ecosystem, something beyond our sights, in order to maintain the glorious outfit of contemporary life. But unfortunately, someone always seems to take advantage of the situation while others suffer from it. Just like class distinctions, economic exploitation or international geopolitics (in the e-waste recycling procedure, for example), groups and power dynamics must constantly be constructed or performed anew through complex engagements with complex mediators. There is no social repertoire in the background to be reflected off, expressed through or substantiated in interactions. We have to see the reality.

GM   Do you think science fiction has a role to play in ecological issues, perhaps drawing attention to those realities and complex engagements?

CQ   I think we have reached a tipping point where people are beginning to realize how severe the problem is. While pollution has been there for decades, maybe for centuries, the process of its accumulation has rapidly accelerated as technologies develop. Humans didn't get smart enough to solve the problem before the waste, pollution or climate change turned on us. Technology might be part of the cure but fundamentally it's all about the lifestyle, the philosophy and the values we believe in. In China, the issue has been increasing over the last four decades along with the high speed of economic growth. We try to live life in an American style, but we have 1.4 billion people. The air, water and soil, even the food we eat, has been found to be polluted or even toxic. But it always takes longer to recover than to pollute the environment. So, to me, science fiction as a genre is a powerful weapon to awaken the people from their dreams of consumerism. With good storytelling, we are able to resonate with people, build up consensus and put pressure on stakeholders to move forwards.

GM   Do you think that science fiction can be held partly responsible for ecological issues? Has it perhaps contributed to an aspirational vision of the future that makes us want more and more technology, and pays too little attention to the methods used to get to that future?

CQ   As a writer, I want to emphasize the responsibility and the values that science fiction should have through my own writing. Over the past four centuries, humanity has experienced tremendous development in science and technologies, along with the value of rationality. I would not place the blame on all of that, but it definitely contributed to the extreme arrogance and blindness of human beings, continuously exploiting the environment, destroying biodiversity and alienating ourselves. The accelerationists of late capitalism tended to believe technologies are the cure for everything. But the world as a whole is highly entangled and uncertain, as quantum physics describes. I believe capitalism and its byproducts will take us nowhere but to a dead end. But what's next? There is no convincing answer for everyone yet. So, I guess literature, especially science fiction, provides us with a thought-provoking framework with which to test alternative possibilities and slowly but steadily form a consensus for human beings.

GM There is increasing awareness in the English-speaking world of science fiction from China, with increasing amounts of work being translated and receiving critical acclaim. Would you characterize Chinese science fiction as being different to Anglo-American traditions, and if so in what ways?

CQ Here I will echo my friend, the speculative fiction author Ken Liu, who is also known as the English-language translator of Liu Cixin's *The Three-Body Problem*, and a lot of other Chinese science fiction works including mine. I don't think 'Chinese SF' is as useful a description of a marketable category of literature as a genre label. 'Chinese SF' basically seems to mean speculative fiction written in China by Chinese writers. But just as no one can coherently claim that all speculative fiction written in the US by American writers adheres to some model, no one can claim such a thing for 'Chinese SF' either.

Chinese science fiction is a diverse collection of individual works by individual authors. The works have different political, social and aesthetic stances and engage with power and privilege from different vantage points. The differences might be lost to the West as vague, subtle or irrelevant elements of Chinese culture. Any efforts to characterize 'Chinese SF' works might be meaningful for academics but in my opinion might also be ineffective.

GM If you were going to direct people to one thing you've written, which would it be and why?

CQ I would suggest people read *AI 2041: Ten Visions for our Future* (2021), co-authored with AI expert Dr Kai-Fu Lee. We spent almost two years working on *AI 2041*, visiting labs, interviewing AI scientists, entrepreneurs, researchers and scholars to try and figure out the most realistic roadmap for AI development over the next twenty years, and then we came up with creative stories to bring those ideas to life for the reader. It's something brand new in format and narrative, set in ten different cultures and reflecting the opportunities and challenges humans will face in the age of AI.

TRAVELLING
THE COSMOS

PROTOTYPING THE FUTURE: SPACEFLIGHT AS SCREEN SPECTACLE

RICHARD DUNN

← Planets everywhere! This exaggerated view by Martin Kornmesser, 2012, gives an impression of how common planets are around the stars in the Milky Way. The planets, their orbits and their host stars are all vastly magnified compared to their real separations. A six-year investigation that surveyed millions of stars using the microlensing technique concluded that planets around stars are the rule rather than the exception. The average number of planets per star is greater than one.

1. Buzz Aldrin walks on the Moon, 21 July 1969. Neil Armstrong, who took the photograph, can be glimpsed in the reflection on Buzz's helmet.

In 2016, the US White House Office of Science and Technology Policy co-sponsored a workshop entitled 'Homesteading in Space: Inspiring the Nation through Science Fiction', bringing space scientists, engineers and entrepreneurs together with storytellers, artists, directors and producers. The idea was to explore how science fiction could promote a positive vision of humanity's future in space and so excite the public, and encourage entrepreneurs and inspire children to become part of that future. The workshop recognized that science fiction can help viewers and readers understand why humans might want to go to space, and can make imagined futures believable and desirable by prototyping technologies that may one day become real. It can also add a dash of glamour. When China's Chang'e 3 lander reached the Moon in 2013, Xinhua, the state news agency, ran laudatory quotes by writers including Liu Cixin, author of the global bestseller *The Three-Body Problem* (三体, 2008; published in English in 2014). Liu, who has since become an ambassador for China's Mars programme, was unequivocal if a little self-deprecating: 'the real Moon landing has better stories to tell than...science fiction'. Once only the realm of the imagination, getting to the Moon is now a matter of national pride.

There has long been a two-way dialogue between science and science fiction. Films and video games have drawn on real-life space activity to add credibility to their work, in particular through the work of scientific or technical advisors on films such as *2001: A Space Odyssey* (1968) and *The Martian* (2015). While this position has only been formalized in recent decades, similar roles emerged in the 1920s, as rocket societies began promoting the dream of spaceships to travel to and colonize other planets. Some of their members – who mostly worked outside mainstream science – helped to bring these ideas to the screen.

2.   Pencil drawings of the effects of zero gravity, from Konstantin
       Tsiolkovsky's *Album of Cosmic Journeys* (Альбом космических
       путешествий, 1932).
3.   Poster for *Woman in the Moon* (*Frau im Mond*), directed by
       Fritz Lang, 1929.

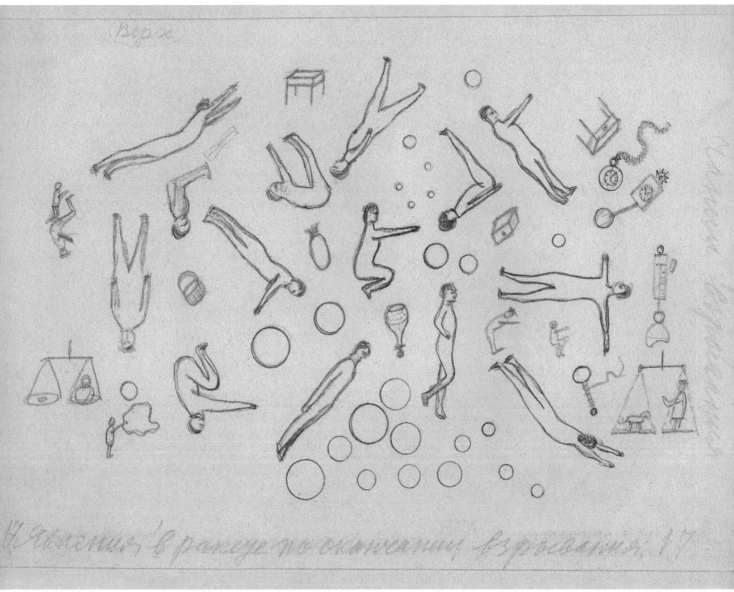

2

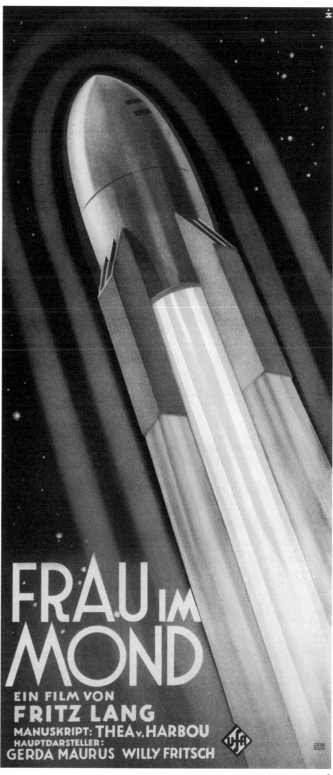

Willy Ley and Herman Oberth, leading lights in Germany's Verein für Raumschiffahrt (Society for Space Travel), an association of rocket enthusiasts, famously advised on *Woman in the Moon* (*Frau im Mond*, 1929). Although Lang's story of a first human journey to the Moon dispenses with realism for melodrama once the lunar surface is reached, what stands out are the lengthy scenes detailing the construction and launch of the space rocket. This was where Oberth's expertise (having studied and published on spaceflight) came to bear, allowing him to realize on screen a technology that in reality was still on the drawing board. As though to demonstrate this, although the film's producers agreed to fund a working rocket for the film's opening, Oberth could not deliver on the deal. On screen, however, the result can be claimed as cinema's first scientifically plausible representation of spaceflight. Indeed, Lang later recalled that the Gestapo confiscated production models and withdrew *Woman in the Moon* from overseas circulation, fearing that it might reveal the secrets of Germany's rocket programme.

Seven years after *Woman in the Moon*, a Soviet film about a lunar voyage featured the work of one of Oberth's heroes, Konstantin Tsiolkovsky. Now lauded as a founding figure in spaceflight, Tsiolkovsky worked as a mathematics teacher but found time to write extensively about rocket propulsion and the need for humans to explore and colonize space. At the end of his life, he advised on *Cosmic Voyage* (Космический рейс, 1936). The director, Vasili Zhuravlov, had developed a film treatment about a Moon voyage a decade earlier, and revisited the idea after Komsomol (the Communist Union of Youth) asked for a movie that would inspire future rocket scientists and spacefarers. Zhuravlov therefore consulted Tsiolkovsky, an avid reader and author of science fiction who appreciated its power to 'bring into being people who sympathize with, and in the future engage in and work on grand engineering and technical rocketry projects', as he put it in 'Is it just Fantasy?' (Только ли фантазия?, 1935). At Tsiolkovsky's insistence, the technological content was as realistic as possible and drew on designs still preserved in his notes and sketches. It was to be a vision of something that might really happen – a contrast to *Aelita: Queen of Mars* (Аэлита, 1924), in which a lavishly realized journey to Mars is revealed to be an engineer's dream.

3

ЗВУКОВОЙ ХУДОЖЕСТВЕННЫЙ
ФАНТАСТИЧЕСКИЙ ФИЛЬМ

КОСМИЧЕСКИЙ
РЕЙС

Сценарий А. ФИЛИМОНОВА
Режиссер ВАСИЛИЙ ЖУРАВЛЕВ
Директор производства З. ДАРЕВСКИЙ
Оператор А. ГАЛЬПЕРИН

Музык. оформл. комп. Валентина КРУЧИНИНА
ХУДОЖНИКИ:
А. УТКИН, М. ТИУНОВ, ШВЕЦ
В ГЛАВНЫХ РОЛЯХ:
засл. артист республики С. КОМАРОВ
АРТИСТЫ: К. МОСКАЛЕНКО, В. КОВРИГИ,
В. ФЕОКТИСТОВ и Витя ГАПОНЕНКО

4.   Poster for *Cosmic Voyage* (Космический рейс),
     directed by Vasili Zhuravlov, 1936.

Rather than the hired diving gear used in *Woman in
the Moon*, *Cosmic Voyage*'s travellers wore specially
designed spacesuits. Sadly, Tsiolkovsky died four months
before the film was released and never saw his ideas
brought to life.

After the Second World War, cinema's ability to
realize and promote space travel came into partnership
with mainstream science, as different nations developed
rocket programmes amid the growing tensions of the Cold
War. *Destination Moon* (1950), loosely based on *Rocket
Ship Galileo* (1947) by the science fiction author Robert
A. Heinlein, continued the lunar focus of previous works.
Having worked in aeronautics for the US Navy, Heinlein
provided technical advice and insisted on authenticity.
Publicity made much of this, claiming that viewers would
get a taste of space travel a few years hence. It noted
too 'the careful calculations of researchers, physicists,
astronomers and sundry other specialists' who created the
rocket's consoles, together with painstaking research for
scenes on the Moon's surface. Like *Woman in the Moon*,
much screen time is devoted to building and launching
the rocket – a narrative emphasis that goes back to Jules
Verne's *From the Earth to the Moon* (*De la terre à la lune*,
1865). But *Destination Moon* does not just describe a
challenge solved as a paean to a glorious technological
future. It also makes clear 'the obvious military fact that he
who controls the Moon controls the Earth'. The US, the film
argues, needed to get there first and could only do so with
the help of private enterprise. It is American industrialists,
not the state, who ensure the mission's success.

There were continuities with the pre-war period.
Willy Ley, who had settled in the US after fleeing
Germany, became a prolific popular science writer and
advocate for space travel, as did Wernher von Braun,
the most prominent of the scientists responsible for Nazi
Germany's V2 rocket programme; both men were part
of Operation Paperclip, a secret programme through
which Nazi engineers and scientists were taken to the
US. Ley and von Braun understood the part popular
media could play in promoting their ambitions. Von Braun
wrote influential articles on future space travel in *Collier's*
magazine and fronted three Disney programmes: *Man in
Space* (1955), *Man and the Moon* (1955) and *Mars and
Beyond* (1957). Billed as factual, they drew on schemes

We'll have no unnecessary floating aboard this ship!

Conquest of Space, 1955

that were still highly speculative. Ley also contributed, as well as collaborating with the leading astronomical artist Chesley Bonestell on a much-praised book, *The Conquest of Space* (1949), which vividly described the solar system and humanity's imminent exploration of it. Heinlein, reviewing it in 1949 for *The Saturday Review of Literature*, thought it 'the next best thing to interplanetary flight'. The book in turn inspired a film, *Conquest of Space* (1955), on which Ley shared a writing credit with Bonestell, who took charge of artwork (as he had for *Destination Moon*). Von Braun gave technical advice and showcased his designs for a rotating space station and other craft. 'See how it will happen...in your lifetime!', the poster declared. Telling the story of a first mission to Mars, a slight concern at 'this taking of other planets' is brushed aside in deference to humanity's growing need for resources. The film also repeats newly established tropes: the view back to Earth, floating in low gravity, a space-walk, near misses with large objects and damage from smaller ones, and, of course, peril on another planet.

US–Soviet rivalry infused the rhetoric of Hollywood productions from the 1950s. But as human spaceflight became a reality, film allowed other nations to stake claims to rocket-based futures beyond Earth and to pick at the rhetoric of the 'space race'. *The Silent Star* (*Milcząca Gwiazda* in Polish, or *Der schweigende Stern* in German, 1960), based on a Stanisław Lem novel, assembles a self-consciously multinational team of space explorers. These include a male African communications officer (although his specific nationality is not revealed) and a female Japanese medical officer among the crew, who travel to Venus after the discovery of a mysterious artefact in the Gobi Desert. In explicit reference to Hiroshima's destruction by an American atomic bomb in 1945, they discover the remains of a civilization that has destroyed itself with nuclear weapons intended for Earth. In the Egyptian film *A Trip to the Moon* (1959, رحلة الى القمر), a German scientist leads the construction of a rocket near Cairo and travels to the Moon with an Egyptian astronomer and a clownish driver. There is little concern about scientific plausibility and the humour is broad, but the film's point about German expertise being behind so many rocket programmes is clear. Another broad comedy, this time from Brazil, *The Cosmonauts* (*Os Cosmonautas*, 1962),

5.   Poster for *Conquest of Space*, directed by Byron Haskin, 1955.

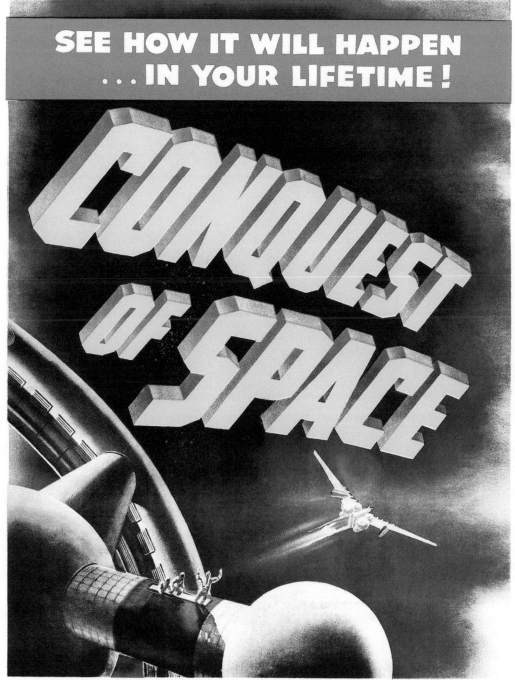

6.   'The whole area was Moon…' illustration by E. Hering for H. G. Wells's
     'The First Men in the Moon', *The Cosmopolitan*, 1900.
7.   The ascent stage of the lunar module *Eagle* during the Apollo 11 mission,
     21 July 1969.

6

**Established tropes: the view
back to Earth, floating in
low gravity, a space-walk,
near misses with large
objects and damage from
smaller ones and, of course,
peril on another planet.**

7

plays up the assumed status of becoming the third nation in space as a Brazilian space programme comes to fruition. The titles credit the air force and army, and early shots include a rocket base, control rooms and a rocket launch – though the focus is in fact on lunar aliens.

Two British films of the 1960s brought international competition to the fore. In *The Mouse on the Moon* (1963), a European microstate develops a rocket propelled by an unusual batch of wine. The satire targets American and Soviet competition, with their near-identical German-led space programmes mirrored in split-screen. The framing of *First Men in the Moon* (1964), a version of H.G. Wells's famous story, has a United Nations lunar mission discover that a British craft landed there decades earlier. Towards the end of the 1960s, the Indian film *Trip to Moon* (चाँद पर चढ़ाई, 1967) is more concerned with the rescue of a scientist from lunar inhabitants than with authentic details of space travel, but can also be viewed as a paean to India's military prowess through its projection into space. Released just months before Apollo 11 reached the Moon, *Brazil Year 2000* (*Brasil Ano 2000*, 1969) envisages a world after global war has obliterated formerly rich nations, with Brazil now set to become a space-faring nation. The film critiques faith in technological progress and the era's cult of the rocket as an emblem of world leadership.

Commentary also came from filmmakers in the US, notably in the Afrofuturist *Space is the Place* (1974), which was filmed in 1972, when the cancellation of the Apollo programme was already public knowledge. The film sees the experimental musician Sun Ra, missing since 1969, return to Earth in a spaceship with reports of a new planetary home for African Americans. The references to recent space endeavours are explicit, as are the racial politics, in an era when enormous sums were spent on space exploration rather than addressing domestic needs. A former NASA employee, initially drawn to Ra's vision, is bamboozled by the idea of space travel based on 'multiplicity, adjustment, readjustment, synthesis, isotope, teleportation, transmolecularization'. Meanwhile, two NASA scientists spy on Ra, kidnap him in order to learn his spaceship's secrets and finally try to shoot him. Asked if there really are 'whiteys' on the Moon, in reference to Gil Scott-Heron's famous spoken-word song, Ra replies,

8.   The rotating set with self-generating gravity constructed for
     2001: A Space Odyssey, directed by Stanley Kubrick, 1968.

'They're walking there today. They take frequent trips
to the Moon. I notice none of you have been invited.'

While few of the makers of these films had concerned
themselves overly with the science, the director Stanley
Kubrick took the opposite tack when developing *2001:
A Space Odyssey*. Kubrick hired former NASA scientist
Frederick Ordway, and Harry Lange, who had worked
on the visualization of NASA's space vehicles and
systems. Production staff also worked with over sixty-
five companies, government agencies, universities and
research bodies, including Bell Telephone Laboratories,
the US Weather Bureau and Royal Greenwich Observatory.
Interviewed for *East Village Eye* in the year of the film's
release, Kubrick made it clear that movies must strike
a balance:

> I think there were two problems in the design of
> anything. One was, is there anything about it that
> would be logically inconsistent with what people felt
> would actually exist; and the other one was, would
> it be interesting? Would it look nice?

Where he went with the science, it added to the spectacle –
Kubrick engaged engineers and designers to create a
revolving set, to bring to the screen a spaceship that rotates
to generate its own artificial gravity.

Recent films – particularly those with large budgets –
have often followed a similar path in foregrounding scientific
realism, as have video games. This is particularly true of
games such as *Deliver Us The Moon*, a thriller that draws
heavily on information from NASA and elsewhere. The
spaceflight simulator *Kerbal Space Program* (2011) takes
great pains to get its orbital physics right, with real-life
manoeuvres such as Hohmann transfers incorporated
into gameplay. Its sophistication has won praise from
the space sector, including the European Space Agency
(ESA), which collaborated with the developers to add its
BepiColombo and Rosetta missions into the game. NASA
and ESA helped to develop games such as *Moonbase
Alpha* (2010), *Mars 2030* (2017) and *Mars Horizon*
(2020), recognizing the benefits of raising public
awareness and inspiring future astronauts, not to mention
using simulations for training. Much of the imagery of the
thriller *Observation*, which places the player in control

9. Poster for *Antariksham 9000 kmph* (అంతరిక్షం),
    directed by Sankalp Reddy, 2018.

9

of the AI of a multinational space station, is based on footage and screenshots from the International Space Station, as well as on pictures of an intriguing hexagonal cloud pattern visible on Saturn. Real findings add to the game's spectacle as well as its plausibility.

For any space-themed story, the fact that so many missions have been to space cannot be ignored. Still, filmmakers are equally wary of creating works weighed down by scientific detail. Technical advisors therefore face a juggling act in getting their voices heard without jeopardizing artistic vision and narrative drive. Scientific advisors – who may be scientists doing a bit of consultancy or specialists in the role – help filmmakers create visuals, check facts, provide plausible explanations for scenarios and assist actors in behaving like real-life scientists. Their work has become increasingly significant as new cinematic technologies, including high-definition images and intensely detailed, spatialized soundtracks, have fed audience expectations of hyperrealism.

Scientific advisors have also become more prominent in marketing. Promotion for *The Martian* (2015) included a preview and question-and-answer session at the Jet Propulsion Laboratory, a series of films about life in space and an online piece on 'Nine Real NASA Technologies' in the film. The director, Ridley Scott, repeatedly emphasized his insistence on getting the science right, crediting NASA staff such as Jim Green, Director of the Planetary Science Division, who acted as an advisor and helped with the film's publicity. Likewise, when promoting *The Wandering Earth* (流浪地球, 2019), the film's director, Frant Gwo, noted that scientists from the Chinese Academy of Sciences had advised on the script's technical aspects. Based on a story by Liu Cixin, the film tells of an ambitious project to move the Earth to another star system to escape the dying Sun. In contrast to the frontier spirit of Hollywood narratives, humanity is saved without leaving its home planet. The film's rhetoric promotes transnational cooperation – the crisis leads all nations to pool scientific expertise under a United Earth Government – with China a key player, its peaceful technology programme benefitting all humanity. Chinese leadership ultimately saves the Earth from crashing into Jupiter.

Active collaboration helps agencies like NASA appear in a positive light, fostering public support for what are enormously expensive programmes. Films including

10. Astronauts in protective spacesuits from the film *Sunshine*, directed by Danny Boyle, 2007.

11. From left to right: astronaut Drew Feustel, actor Matt Damon, director Ridley Scott, author Andy Weir and NASA Director of the Planetary Science Division Jim Green at a press panel about NASA's journey to Mars and the film *The Martian* in 2015.

10

11

12. A selfie taken on Mars by Zhurong, China's first Mars rover,
     with its landing platform. The image was released on 11 June 2021
     by the China National Space Administration (CNSA), to announce
     the success of the Tianwen-1 mission to Mars.

The Martian and *Mission to Mars* (2000) speak perfectly to NASA's plans in this respect, and have received the agency's enthusiastic support. By contrast, it did not allow its logos to be used in *Life* (2017), because the story of a hostile life form brought back from Mars via the International Space Station might suggest that NASA's actions could jeopardize Earth. Even so, NASA and other space agencies are keen to nurture audiences' desires to see the real-world development of fictional technologies and inspire the next generation of space scientists and technicians. NASA was quick off the blocks, creating an Entertainment Industry Liaison in the late 1960s. By then its staff had already advised on *Star Trek*, hailed by *Popular Science* in 1967 as 'the only science-fiction series in history that has the cooperation and advice of the National Aeronautics and Space Administration'. NASA has since supported a host of space-themed films and television programmes. It has exploited science fiction's allure in other ways too. Beginning in the late 1970s, Nichelle Nichols (*Star Trek*'s Lieutenant Uhura) spearheaded an initiative to encourage women and people of colour to apply for NASA's astronaut training programme. Mae Jemison, the first Black woman to travel to space (and who later made an appearance in *Star Trek: The Next Generation*) is one of many for whom Nichols was an inspiration. While other agencies have not formalized their entertainment work to the same degree, their willingness to advise and collaborate shows equal awareness of the benefits: the Japan Aerospace Exploration Agency (JAXA) on *Rocket Girls* (ロケットガール, 1995–2007), *5 Centimetres Per Second* (秒速5センチメートル, 2007) and *Space Brothers* (宇宙兄弟#0, 2014); the Indian Space Research Organization (ISRO) on *Antariksham 9000 kmph* (అంతరిక్షం, 2018) and *Tik Tik Tik* (டிக் டிக் டிக், 2018).

Space-themed films, television series and games often promote techno-futurist agendas that assume humanity's future will look beyond Earth. In doing so, they propagate thinking about why we might want to go there: finding new resources, moving to a new home when ours is dead, monitoring Earth to improve things here, defending our planet from comets or asteroids, controlling the world from space. Other fictions have looked to reimagine the history and future of space travel,

13

NASA and other agencies are keen to nurture audiences' desires to see the real-world development of fictional technologies.

interrogating its assumptions and thinking about how things could be different. *The 6th World* TV series (2011), directed by Nanobah Becker, tells of the first mission to colonize Mars, showing the Navajo people who lead it (with corporate partners) as technologically adept yet faithful to their culture, while *Delivery from Earth* (2014), imagines a Navajo baby as the first human born on Mars. In Larissa Sansour's *A Space Exodus* (2008), the first Palestinian woman on the Moon plants her country's flag, the film self-consciously echoing the aesthetics of *2001* as it holds a mirror to the nationalist rhetoric of lunar missions. *Afronauts* (2014) draws inspiration from Edward Nkoloso's creation of a National Academy of Science, Space Research and Philosophy in 1964 for Northern Rhodesia as it moved towards independence as Zambia. Relocating the narrative to 16 July 1969, as Apollo 11 launches, the story of the trainee astronaut Matha Mwambwa questions the idea that a space programme validates a nation.

13. Poster for *The Wandering Earth* (流浪地球), designed by Zhao Li, 2019.
14. *The Wandering Earth*, directed by Frant Gwo, 2019.

14

The Ghanaian-American filmmaker Nuotama Bodomo argues that Africans should focus on personal (and national) self worth rather than uncritically following Western assumptions about value and identity. Like other artworks, such as Larry Achiampong's multi-part *Relic Traveller* project (2017–) and the photographic series *Icarus 13: The First Journey to the Sun* (2008) by Kiluanji Kia Henda, Bodomo's film uses fictional reimagining to offer new ways of seeing Africa now and in the future. With more than twenty African countries now active in space, such speculation has moved well beyond the purely imaginary.

The influence of science fiction on space science has other manifestations. The sociologist Janet Vertesi, who shadowed the team planning a future mission to Jupiter's ice-covered moon, Europa, has documented how science fiction infuses the group's culture. A prime example comes in the totemic role of the monoliths from *2001: A Space Odyssey* and its sequel, *2010: The Year We Make Contact* (1984): a nine-foot (2.7-metre) monolith sits outside the Jet Propulsion Laboratory in California, others have appeared at partner institutions, and monolith keyrings mark team membership. These tokens recall the strange columns as symbols of the alien and unknown that the project hopes to investigate. They also play on Europa's significance in *2010*, the scientific and technological verisimilitude of which was as vaunted as it had been for *2001*. In a different example, the historian of science David Kirby has noted that NASA was so taken by the suits Chris Gilman created for *Deep Impact* (1998), *Armageddon* (1998) and *Space Cowboys* (2000) – all films for which it gave advice and support – that it purchased one to help improve future designs. The agency then hired Gilman to devise an improved suit for working in open space. There was a virtuous circle at play: Gilman's cinematic designs had originally benefitted from discussions with NASA staff and access to their plans.

In 2021, NASA announced that it was naming the Martian landing site of its Perseverance rover after Octavia E. Butler. Perhaps its staff were drawn to her words in *Parable of the Talents* (1998): 'If we're to be anything other than smooth dinosaurs who evolve, specialize and die, we need the stars.' In Butler's unfinished *Parable* series, as for Sun Ra, people might

16

15. The Sokol KV-2 emergency suit worn by British ESA astronaut Tim Peake
    during the Principia mission to the International Space Station, 2015–16.
    When in use, the suit is connected to the spacecraft's life-support systems
    and provides approximately two hours of oxygen and carbon dioxide
    removal in the event of a cabin depressurization.
16. The first Palestinian woman on the Moon plants her country's flag in
    Larissa Sansour's film *A Space Exodus*, 2008.

seek other worlds to escape the inequalities and bigotries of this one. For well over a century, film has also explored the many reasons for going to the trouble and expense of space travel, with cinematic prototypes persuading us that these journeys will really happen. Before 1961, these journeys created an appetite for what was to come; post-Gagarin and Armstrong, they have become part of the dialogue about future missions.

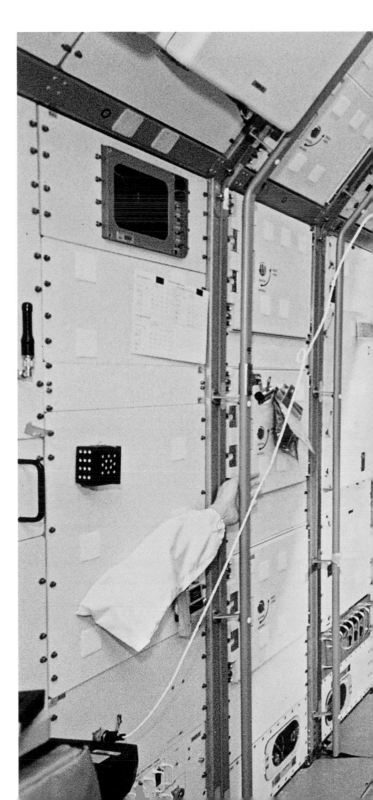

17. American engineer and astronaut Mae Jemison working in zero gravity in the centre aisle of the Spacelab Japan (SLJ) science module aboard the space shuttle *Endeavour*, during NASA's STS-47 mission, 20 September 1992. Jemison was a Mission Specialist (MS) on the flight, and the first Black woman to travel into space.

→ The ill-fated crew of the Nostromo explore a strange, derelict spaceship in *Alien*, directed by Ridley Scott, 1979. Their iconic spacesuits were designed by the British costume designer John Mollo, inspired by Japanese Samurai armour and with input from Moebius (Jean Giraud).

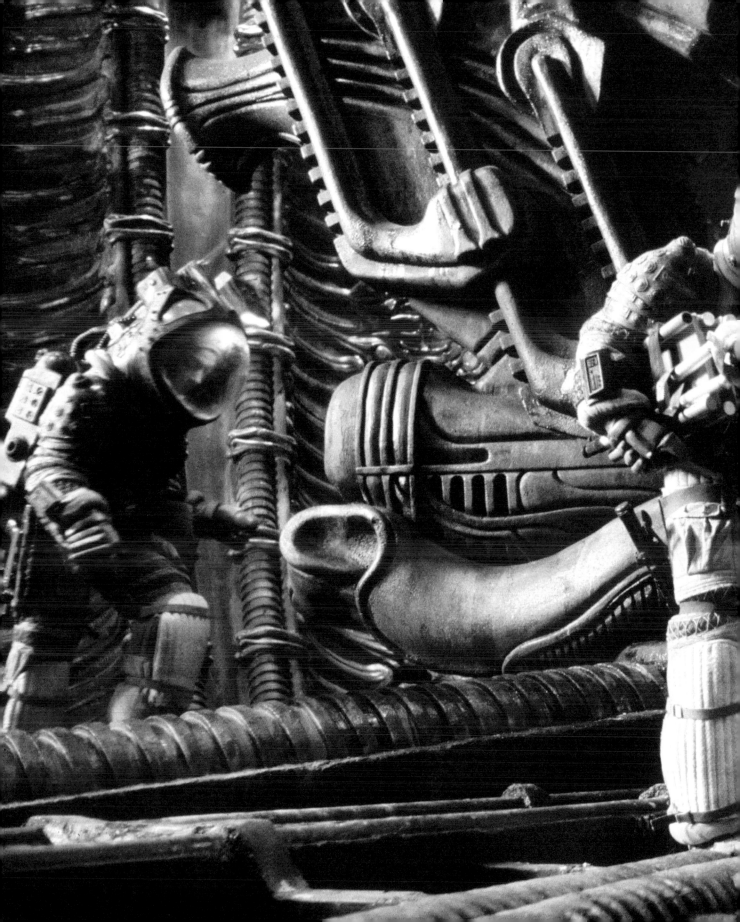

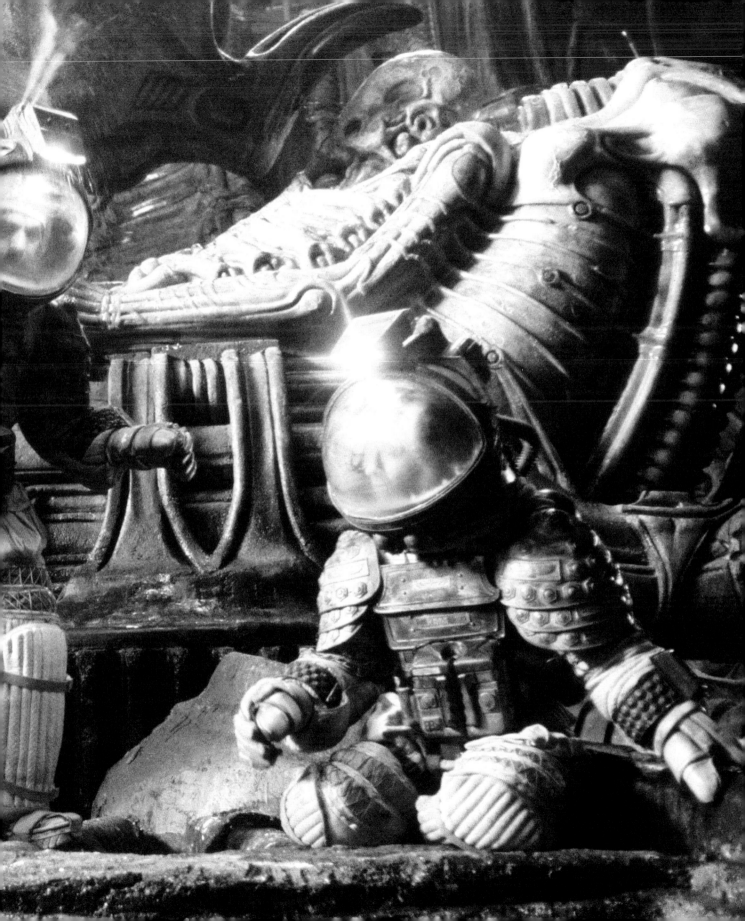

BEYOND THE SOLAR SYSTEM

RACHAEL LIVERMORE

Space is big. Really big.
Douglas Adams, *The Hitchhiker's Guide to the Galaxy* (1979)

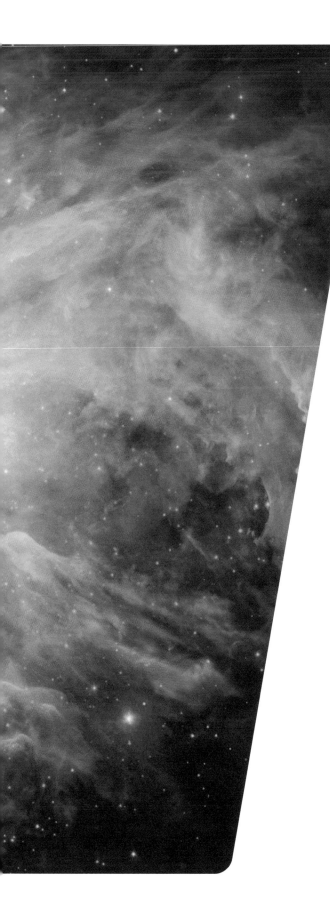

If science answers questions about *how* the world works, science fiction gives us the platform for our imaginations to explore the *so what?*

Science tells us that there are planetary systems like Kepler-47 that orbit two stars. Science fiction goes beyond the boundaries of fact, considering what it would be like to live on that planet, to grow up and grow old there, to create a whole new world. How would our lives and our society be different if things we take for granted – seasons, day and night, even gravity – were altered? Great science fiction is able to turn that lens back on ourselves, to ask what this says about us.

To really stretch the boundaries of our imaginations, we need to venture far away from our home planet to other stars and the planets that orbit them. Travel between stars – or 'interstellar' travel – is a mainstay of science fiction. It allows us to imagine infinite worlds, both like and unlike our own. Could we, one day, follow our fictional heroes, to explore where no one has gone before?

Humans have been exploring space for as long as history has been recorded. Whether to measure the passing of time, or to work out the size and shape of the universe, astronomy has been a pastime of every civilization on Earth. We have worked out a remarkable amount about the nature and origins of the universe through observations from our vantage point on one planet. When it comes to physically travelling into space, though, we are newcomers, having only started to venture beyond Earth in the last century.

Voyager 1, launched from Earth in September 1977, has travelled the furthest of all of the objects of human origin launched into space: in 2021 just over 14 billion miles (22.5 billion kilometres) away and travelling at almost 40,000 miles per hour (60,000 kilometres per hour).

1. A composite image of the Orion Nebula, as captured by NASA's Spitzer and Hubble Space Telescopes, 2006. Located 1,500 light years away from Earth, the nebula is the brightest spot in the sword of the Orion, or Hunter constellation. The cosmic cloud is also our closest massive star-formation factory, and astronomers believe it contains more than 1,000 young stars.

2

3

That may sound like a long way, but in cosmological terms, it is only just outside the solar system, in what is called interstellar space. *Voyager* 1 has only really set foot outside our front door.

The two *Voyager* probes highlight the biggest difficulty with leaving the solar system: we have to contend with the sheer enormity of space. In the immortal words of Douglas Adams, 'Space is big. Really big.' Just *how* big space is, and how much of a challenge it presents to potential explorers, is hard for us to visualize. Say we were to head out of the solar system in the direction of our nearest star, Proxima Centauri. This is a journey of twenty-five trillion miles (over forty trillion kilometres), equivalent to circling the Earth a billion times. Neither of the *Voyager* probes is aiming towards Proxima Centauri, but if they were, at their usual speeds, it would take them around 75,000 years to reach it.

If we want to explore space beyond our solar system – and see the results within a human lifetime – we need to travel a lot faster than the *Voyager* probes. Light travels faster than anything else in the Universe, at 670 million miles per hour (1 billion kilometres per hour). A journey at the speed of light to Proxima Centauri would take just over four years.

What if we cast our sights further afield, for example to Betelgeuse, a bright star in the Orion constellation that is on the brink of exploding? At the speed of light, the journey would take around 550 years. So, can we build a spaceship that travels faster than the speed of light?

Unfortunately, this is where the laws of physics present a barrier. According to Einstein's theory of special relativity, first published in 1905, the speed of light is not just the fastest anything *does* travel, it is the fastest anything *can* travel. The combination of the vast distances involved and the limitations of light speed create inherent difficulties in any physical exploration of other star systems. The 'disappointment' of science fact, however, can easily be overcome by science fiction, where the laws of physics need not apply. When you can invent a TARDIS that traverses time and space at will, why allow science to limit your imagination? Nonetheless, arguably some of the most stimulating science fiction comes from embracing these challenges and suggesting numerous ways that interstellar travel could, in theory, be possible.

2. Poster for *Star Trek: The Motion Picture*, directed by Robert Wise, 1979. 'Where no man has gone before' has been the call to adventure of the *Star Trek* franchise since the series first aired in 1966.

3. Science fiction writers have been publishing stories about generation ships since the 1940s. One influential early example is Brian Aldiss's novel *Non-Stop*, 1958, published in the US in 1963 as *Starship*, with cover art by Paul Lehr.

4. Part of the Hubble Deep Field, showing a few of the almost 3,000 galaxies photographed by the Hubble Space Telescope in 342 separate exposures taken from 18 to 28 December 1995.

One solution is to accept the speed limitation. In Liu Cixin's *The Three-Body Problem* (三体, 2008), an alien species from Alpha Centauri is able to travel at a tenth of the speed of light. Acknowledging how long it takes to accelerate up to that speed, though, the journey takes centuries. Planning for arrival in a society that will be vastly different to the one that existed when the journey began is a crucial part of the story.

The concept of a 'generation ship', in which the explorers who arrive on a distant planet are the descendants of those who left Earth, is a common one in science fiction, in film, books, video games and other media. In Pixar's *WALL-E* (2008), for example, the humans evacuated from Earth on the starship *Axiom* are the distant ancestors of those who eventually return. But narratively speaking, it is often more satisfying to have the character who began the journey also be the one to end it. One way to achieve this while taking into account a journey of decades or more is to freeze the age of the travellers with some kind of suspended animation. This device features in *2001: A Space Odyssey* (1968), *Alien* (1979), *Avatar* (2009) and *Passengers* (2016), among many others, and 'stasis' is how crew member Dave Lister survived for three million years after a radiation leak killed the rest of the crew of the *Red Dwarf* (1988–2020).

Suspended animation is not merely science fiction. It has been tested by doctors who need to keep trauma patients alive long enough for surgeons to operate on them, by using a technique called EPR (emergency preservation and resuscitation). This involves cooling a person down to between 10 and 15°C (50–59°F) by replacing their blood with ice-cold saline, which slows or entirely stops chemical reactions in the cells so that the patient's organs are not damaged by a lack of oxygen. Successful trials of this method were only reported in 2019, so the lengthy hibernation of many a science fiction plot is still some way off, but it may be plausible one day.

As it happens, the laws of physics provide another form of suspended animation. Another aspect of Einstein's theory of special relativity – the same theory that limits our travel speed to that of light – is that time is not constant. Instead, space and time form part of

5. The crew of the spaceship *Nostromo* wake from stasis in the film *Alien*, directed by Ridley Scott, 1979.

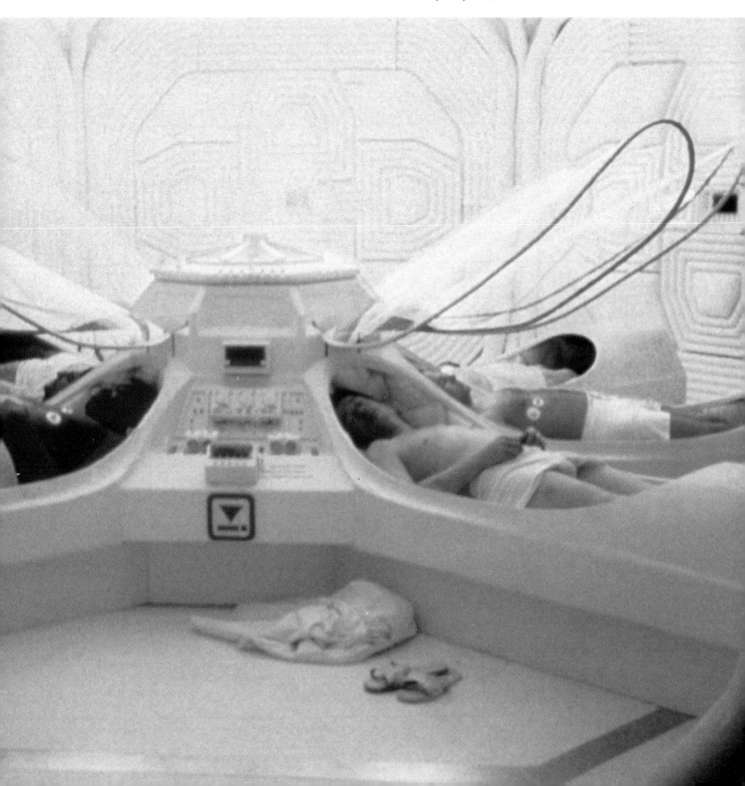

6

6. Scene from the 2020 graphic novel adaptation of Kurt Vonnegut's 1969 novel *Slaughterhouse-Five*, written by Ryan North with art by Albert Monteys. The hand-shaped Tralfamadorians are another science-fictional alien race who experience time non-linearly, seeing it all at once. They are shown here communicating with the human Billy Pilgrim through a translation machine.

7. Illustration by David Lupton for a Folio Society edition of Ursula K. Le Guin's 1974 novel *The Dispossessed*. In Le Guin's science fiction novels, interstellar travellers can visit distant planets in their own lifetimes but, due to the 'time dilation' effect of travelling so fast, by the time they return centuries have passed for everyone else.

the same fabric known as 'spacetime'. We can think of everything as moving through spacetime at a constant speed, the speed of light. When we separate space out from time and consider them separately – as we experience them – we find that the faster we move in space, the slower we move in time, and vice versa. At one extreme, we could stay absolutely stationary in space. In that case, all of our speed goes in the 'time' direction. As we start moving more quickly through space, our speed through time declines. In other words, time passes more slowly. This means that the faster we move, the more slowly we age. This time dilation is not something we notice in our daily lives, because even the fastest speeds achieved on supersonic aircraft are negligible compared to the speed of light. We are almost stationary our whole lives. But the same is not true in science fiction, where we have the freedom to create spaceships that travel as fast as we like. Time dilation allows a single protagonist to make the journey to a distant planet and perhaps even to return to Earth within a single human lifespan, without having to halt the action to enter suspended animation. Science fiction authors such as Robert A. Heinlein, Ursula K. Le Guin and Alastair Reynolds, among others, have all explored this idea.

The interesting implications of special relativity do not end there. We could take this to its extreme and imagine what would happen if we moved at the fastest possible speed, the speed of light. This would mean that all of our available speed was being used in the 'space' direction,

8. A two-dimensional visualization of an Einstein-Rosen bridge, or
   wormhole, showing a journey between two points in space made faster
   by bending space and creating a bridge between the points, rather than
   travelling the long way around through conventional space.

**A beam of light experiences
all events in the universe as
happening simultaneously.**

and we would not be moving *at all* through time. Thus, the abductees returned by the aliens of *Close Encounters of the Third Kind* (1977) are the same age as when they were abducted, though to those on Earth they have been gone for decades. In *Stargate: Atlantis* (2004–9), the crew are able to meet a group of the Ancients, a race wiped out long ago, because they have been stuck on a ship travelling at 99.9 per cent of the speed of light. As it turns out, nothing that has mass can move *at* the speed of light, though we could theoretically get arbitrarily close and move only very slowly through time. But light itself, which has no mass, *does* move, by definition, at the speed of light, which means that it literally stands still in time.

A beam of light experiences all events in the universe as happening simultaneously, a tricky concept for us to understand. Science fiction has grappled with some of the bizarre implications of this fact – for instance, in the *Star Trek: Deep Space Nine* premiere, *Emissary* (1993), Sisko must negotiate with aliens that have no concept of corporeal or linear existence. The practicalities of the negotiations, given that the very concept of negotiating requires change over time, are not fully addressed in the episode. Perhaps some scientific concepts are too alien to be tackled even by science fiction.

We have seen a few ways in which we could travel great distances within the confines of physics. Another option is to abandon physics altogether and travel faster than light using indeterminate means, such as *Star Wars*'s hyperdrive, first seen in 1977. Alternatively, we can shorten the distance so that we do not need to travel faster than light at all, using a wormhole – essentially a shortcut through space. A wormhole makes use of Einstein's theory of general relativity, which expands on the special theory to find that the fabric of spacetime can be curved. We see this curvature around anything that has mass, a bit like a heavy ball resting on a rubber sheet. In General Relativity, this curvature of space around massive objects is what causes the force of gravity. The heavier an object, the more it curves spacetime around it, and the more other objects are drawn towards it. If space can be deformed, why not bend it so that the start and end points of your journey are close together, and create a tunnel in between them? This is known as an Einstein-Rosen bridge (named for Einstein and the American-Israeli

physicist Nathan Rosen), or more commonly referred to in science fiction as a wormhole.

Wormholes feature frequently in science fiction, from *Star Trek* (1966–) to *Contact* (1997). In the Marvel Cinematic Universe, the astrophysicist Dr Jane Foster even refers to the Bifrost that connects Earth to the fictional realm of Asgard as an Einstein-Rosen bridge. In the video game series *Halo* (2001–), faster-than-light travel is enabled by the 'slipspace drive' or Shaw-Fujikawa Translight Engine, a machine capable of tunnelling through the compressed tangle of dimensions called 'slipspace' to create intergalactic shortcuts. A wormhole is usually depicted as a tunnel, presumably because we have to reduce space to two dimensions in our analogies in order to picture how this works. The film *Interstellar* (2014) offers a more realistic depiction of a wormhole as a sphere, which is how it would likely manifest in three-dimensional reality.

So, is it likely that we could ever see a wormhole in reality? Mathematically, it seems to be possible. Whether it would be stable enough to be used – let alone created at will – is less clear.

A similar concept to that of a wormhole is seen in the warp drives of *Star Trek*'s starships, which create a fictional 'subspace bubble', whereby the space in front of the ship is contracted so that it can travel faster than light. It sounds like make-believe but, in 1994, the physicist Miguel Alcubierre conceptualized a kind of warp drive that works in a similar way. The only problem is that such warp drives require vast quantities of energy. *Star Trek*'s *Enterprise* created this energy using 'dilithium,' a fictional element that, when crystallized, can contain the high-energy interactions between matter and antimatter (not to be confused with real-world dilithium, which is just the name for a molecule consisting of two lithium atoms that has no particular applications in faster-than-light travel).

Whether we stay below light speed or find a way to exceed it, we might perhaps venture one day to a world beyond our solar system. What will we find when we get there? Science fiction was imagining planets beyond our solar system, or exoplanets, long before they were discovered in reality. The premise of television shows such as *Doctor Who* (1963–), *Star Trek* and

9

9. The genre-defying anime TV series *Cowboy Bebop*
(カウボーイビバップ, 1998) opens in 2071, fifty
years after an accident with a hyperspace gateway
has made Earth uninhabitable. Despite the evident
dangers, faster-than-light travel, enabled
by hyperspace access points called Astral Gates,
is depicted as totally routine – even boring – to
the crew of the starship *Bebop*.

Stargate: SG1 (1997–2007) rest on travelling to a new
world in each episode. Most are fairly similar to Earth
(television has a filming budget to consider, after all),
but differences in environment, the number and nature
of the planet's sun(s) and the planet's climate and
geography all lead to wildly different portrayals of
civilizations and cultures. The defining feature of the video
game *No Man's Sky* (2016) is its 'procedurally generated
deterministic open world universe, which includes over 18
quintillion planets' – yet despite this almost unfathomable
variety, the results rarely feel as exciting and strange as
some of the very real exoplanets now being discovered
by scientists.

The science of learning about real exoplanets is still
young, because such planets are hard to find. They are
very small and, unlike stars, do not emit light themselves,
so the best way to detect them is to measure the effect
they have on their host stars. The first exoplanets were
discovered by witnessing the movement of stars as
determined by the planets surrounding them, using
what is known as the radial velocity technique. Many
of us will have learned at school that planets orbit stars,
but this is only somewhat true. In fact, both stars and
planets orbit their entire system's centre of mass. If you
were hanging a model of the solar system from the ceiling
with a string, the centre of mass would be where you
would attach the string in order for the model to hang
level. The Sun is by far the most massive object in the solar
system to which the Earth belongs, so the centre of mass
of the solar system is almost at the centre of the Sun. The
planets have mass too, though, and this pulls the centre
of mass slightly outwards from the Sun. In a binary star
system, the centre of mass would be at a point in space
between the two stars.

The effect of both the star and the planets orbiting this
centre of mass is that the planets sweep out large orbits,
and the star 'wobbles' about its central position. With a
sensitive enough telescope, this wobble – known as radial
velocity – can be detected from Earth.

Since the 1990s, the radial velocity method has had
great success, locating hundreds of exoplanets. However,
it is best suited to finding very large planets (Jupiter-
sized and bigger) located very close to their stars; the
combination of large mass and short distance causes

10

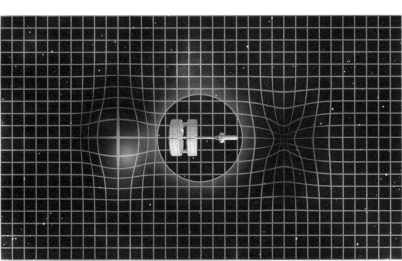

10. The *USS Enterprise NCC-1701-A*, as seen at the end of
    Star Trek IV: The Voyage Home, directed by Leonard
    Nimoy, 1986. The *Enterprise* is one of the most famous
    faster-than-light spaceships in all of science fiction.
11. Inspired by *Star Trek*'s warp drive, physicist Miguel
    Alcubierre theorized how a bubble balancing negative
    and positive energy could protect a ship while space
    was artificially warped or bent around it, allowing a
    journey to occur faster than light.

11

12. Artist impression of CHEOPS, or the CHaracterising ExOPlanets Satellite,
a Swiss Space Office/ESA optical space telescope that takes a closer
look at exoplanets and accurately measures their size as their orbits pass
in front of distant stars.

the largest wobble in their stars, making them the easiest to detect. The existence of these kinds of systems was enormously interesting to scientists who, prior to these discoveries, had thought that they would be rare.

But these exoplanets, despite being numerous, are not where one would look to find life. When we designate a planet as 'habitable', what we mean is that it would be habitable to *us*. We need liquid water to survive, which means that the planet must be in what we call the 'Goldilocks zone': not so close to the star that the water would boil, and not so far away that it would freeze. We also need a fairly narrow gravity range, which means the planet would need to be approximately the size of Earth. As such, exoplanets found using a combination of large mass and short distance from the host star are unlikely to be habitable.

A better method for finding potentially habitable planets involves witnessing a planet passing in front of its host star. The concept is much like a solar eclipse, when the Moon passes in front of the Sun and blocks out its light – except that, when seen from interstellar distances, the planet is much smaller than the star, which itself is only a speck of light. The planet only blocks out a small percentage of the light of its star, but, if the star's brightness is measured carefully over a period of time, we are able to see the small, periodic dips in brightness at regular intervals whenever a planet passes in front of it.

The likelihood of detecting a planet by this method is fairly low; it relies on the planetary system being perfectly aligned with our line of sight so that the planet passes in front of the star, instead of above or below. But we can play the odds by observing many thousands of stars at once, in the hope that some will yield these dips, or 'transits'. This is what the NASA-launched Kepler space telescope did between 2009 and 2018, leading to thousands of exoplanet detections.

These transits do not just tell us that a planet exists. They can also tell us a remarkable amount about the planet itself, including how long it takes to complete one orbit (based on the time between successive transits). That, in turn, tells us how large the orbit must be, so we can estimate the distance between the star and the planet to determine whether it is in the Goldilocks zone.

13 & 14. In the *Halo* series of video games (2001–), travelling through 'slipspace' allows for faster-than-light travel. Humans develop this technology in 2291, which allows them to journey throughout the galaxy, but it also brings them into conflict with the genocidal Covenant Empire.

13

14

At the time of writing, sixty such 'Goldilocks' planets have been discovered, of which twenty-three are about the same size as Earth.

Of course, this does not mean that we could head out to one of those twenty-three planets and live there. If true habitability were as simple as having a planet of about the right size the correct distance from a star, we would be able to live on Venus (not recommended, on account of average temperatures approaching 500°C, or 900°F). The crucial factor on Venus is the atmosphere, which causes a runaway greenhouse effect. Measuring the composition of the atmospheres on exoplanets is a science in its very early stages, with only a handful of detections to date and those mostly in very hot, very large planets. As the next generation of telescopes, such as the James Webb Space Telescope, comes online, we can expect this science to progress rapidly. Perhaps, by the time we are able to travel interstellar distances, we will know enough to have a promising destination in mind.

We have only begun to scratch the surface of the vast assortment of planets that space has to offer and the science needed to take us there in actuality. In the *Star Trek* episode *The Balance of Terror* (1966), Dr McCoy says:

> In this galaxy, there's a mathematical probability of three million Earth-type planets. And in all of the universe, three million million galaxies like this. And in all of that, and perhaps more, only one of each of us.

Written decades before the first exoplanet was detected, it is interesting to see how those numbers compare to what we know now. Extrapolating from what we have found so far, estimates suggest that the number of Earth-type planets in our galaxy is closer to 300 million. That means reality might offer 100 times more variety in strange new worlds than even *Star Trek* could imagine!

It is worth noting that those potential 300 million are only those planets within the Milky Way galaxy, which is only one of many galaxies that make up the universe. How many galaxies there are is itself a matter of debate, but estimates vary between the hundreds of billions and a few trillion (or 'million million', as Dr McCoy puts it). Despite the *Star Trek* episode having been written decades before the launch of the Hubble Space Telescope,

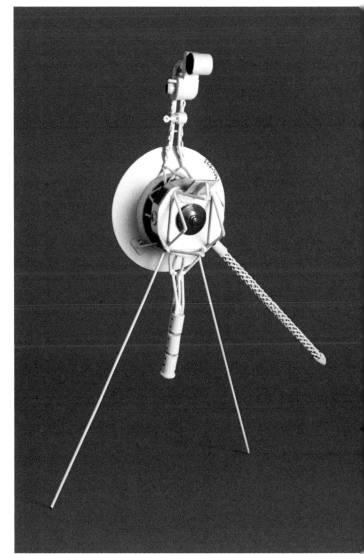

15

15. Model of *Voyager 1* spacecraft, 1977. *Voyager 1* arrived at Jupiter in the spring of 1979, sending back images that revolutionized our understanding of the giant planet, as well as several of its moons. It reached Saturn in November 1980, and then explored Titan, Saturn's largest moon. The two *Voyager* spacecraft have since continued their journeys out beyond the solar system into interstellar space.

16

Dr McCoy may have been just about spot on about the number of galaxies in the universe.

It is easy to feel insignificant in relation to the unimaginable vastness of space, but yet again we might turn to Dr McCoy: there is, after all, 'only one of each of us'. We each have a unique capacity to imagine, and it is only by imagining what we are looking for that we can design experiments to find it. Science fiction has, time and time again, both stemmed from and contributed to science exploration and discovery – and may it continue for three million million years or more.

16. Illustration from *Rocket Ride* (*Raketen Fahrt*), a book on the possibilities of travel rocket by Max Valier, published in 1930. An early pioneer of rocket technology, Valier also wrote some science fiction stories before he was killed when an experimental rocket exploded in his laboratory.

National Aeronautics and Space Administration

Exoplanet Travel Bureau

55 Cancri e

lava life

Skies sparkle above a never-ending **ocean of lava**

A global ocean of lava under sparkling, silicate skies reflecting the lava below: what better choice for an extreme vacation? Planet Janssen, or 55 Cancri e, orbits a star called Copernicus only 41 light years away. The molten surface is completely uninhabitable, but you'll ride safely above, taking in breathtaking views: the burning horizon, Janssen's sister planet Galileo hanging in a dark sky, and curtains of glowing particles as you glide across the terminator to Janssen's dark side. Book your travel now to the hottest vacation spot in the galaxy, 55 Cancri e.

NASA's Exoplanet Exploration Program. Jet Propulsion Laboratory, Pasadena CA.
exoplanets.nasa.gov

www.nasa.gov

17. NASA's Jet Propulsion Laboratory (JPL) have created a series of travel bureau posters offering tongue-in-cheek adventures to other worlds, including exoplanets like the 'Super-Earth' HD 40307g, which is twice the size of our own planet and thus has much stronger gravity, or Kepler-16b, which orbits two suns, like Luke Skywalker's home planet Tatooine.

→ Our galaxy, the Milky Way, photographed over the Atacama desert, Chile. The Milky Way contains hundreds of billions of stars, of which our Sun is only one.

INTERVIEW
CHARLIE JANE ANDERS

GLYN MORGAN

What does science fiction mean to you? Do you remember which first got you excited and captured your imagination: science or science fiction?

CHARLIE JANE ANDERS

To me, science fiction is the literature of change, but also of problem-solving. Many of the best science fiction stories are about confronting huge social and technological shifts, and finding ways to cope with them. Which is why the 'problem-solving' part is important as well – my favourite science fiction stories are often the ones in which people use their wit and intelligence to get around some complex and seemingly intractable problem. I don't think there's any such thing as a rigorous definition of science fiction that holds up across all examples of the genre, but my science fiction brain wakes up a bit when there's a story that includes huge, sweeping change, or some kind of new element or discovery that transforms everything, accompanied by people figuring out a clever solution to some issue. I feel like science fiction is a cousin to detective fiction, in that both genres usually include people who use logic or deductive reasoning to solve problems. As for what first got me excited, I have super vivid memories of going to the science museum – maybe in New York – and especially the planetarium when I was a kid and having my mind blown. But I think watching stuff like *Star Trek* (1966–), *Doctor Who* (1963–) and *Star Wars* (1977–), and reading Madeleine L'Engle and other authors, had a huge and lasting impact on my young brain. So, probably more science fiction than science.

GM As a science fiction writer, do you think research into contemporary science and technology is important? Where do you generally start your work?

CJA It depends on the project. My novel *The City in the Middle of the Night* (2019) was grounded in real science to a large extent, so I did a lot of reading and researching about tidally locked planets before I started writing. But for a lot of other projects, I will try to nail down the story and then go back and make it as scientifically plausible as I can. I usually feel like story logic is the most important thing, but I also want to include real science as much as I can.

GM Has the process of researching ever caused you to have to change the plot of your story, either because you realized something was impossible, or because it opened up new possibilities that you hadn't previously imagined?

CJA That definitely happens a fair bit. What I find is, usually, when I have to change something to become more scientifically plausible, I end up with something way cooler than what I originally had in mind. Real science is just so much cooler than anything my imagination can cook up.

GM *The City in the Middle of the Night* is set on a tidally locked planet called January. Human settlers live on the narrow strip between searing permanent day and freezing permanent night. It's a great setting, vividly realized in the novel. But the novel is also an intimate story of one character, their trauma, and their coming to terms with themselves as an individual. Which came to you first, the setting, the character or the plot?

CJA I had been obsessed with tidally locked planets for years and was convinced that they were going to become a big deal in science fiction. (I was worried other authors were going to beat me to the punch, but now I feel like maybe I was too early if anything.) There was so much about that setting that spoke to me – there's a realm of eternal darkness where the Sun never shines! But it took me a couple of years to figure out the world and all the details of the setting before I was able to come up with characters and a whole story that made sense. It was kind of frustrating, just trying to make a place that felt solid and consistent enough to support everything else. This was very unlike my usual writing process.

GM You've created some wonderful aliens and otherly creatures in your work, whether the Falshi in 'The Fermi Paradox is Our Business Model' (2010), or the 'crocodiles' in *The City in the Middle of the Night*. How do you approach designing your alien creatures?

CJA I like aliens who are pretty alien, but still recognizably people with feelings and relationships and lives. I was very inspired by Wayne Barlowe's bizarre creature design and other similar art, but also by Octavia E. Butler and other authors. I feel like a good alien starts at both ends: a cool shape and a neat concept on the surface, but also a lot of thought about biology and the environment this creature evolved in, on the other. A cool creature should be memorable as well as believable.

GM You have received acclaim for science fiction of all lengths, and have always seemed to be a prolific short story writer. Why do you think the shorter forms of storytelling are so popular in science fiction?

CJA Short fiction is a wonderful vehicle for science fiction in particular, in part because of the problem-solving thing I mentioned – a short story can introduce a problem, or a cluster of problems, and then show how people work towards a solution, without needing to go on too many detours or pit-stops along the way. Some of my favorite works of short SF are just an exercise in coping with a particular issue and using science to work it out. I also think short fiction is the best vehicle for exploring a single cool idea, and also for conjuring the purest form of 'sense of wonder', without having to build out as much of a complex world or show us every part of the sausage being made.

GM   What do you think it is about science fiction that engages queer communities?

CJA   There are many reasons why queers and nerd culture seem to intersect and overlap so much – some of them have to do with a shared rejection of pointless conformity and unexamined social norms. And despite the 'mainstreaming' of both nerds and queers, both groups remain subcultures to some extent, and subcultures often tend to overlap simply because people find them through similar avenues. My favourite parts of nerd culture and science fiction fandom are resistant also to overly rigid gender norms and highly sceptical about arbitrary rules around sexuality and gender, making them natural places for queer communities to feel at home. But there's also the fact that science fiction allows us to ask big, tricky questions around gender – see Ursula K. Le Guin's *The Left Hand of Darkness* (1969), but also countless other works – which creates a (hopefully) more open-minded and accepting community. Finally, queers have benefitted from scientific progress in perhaps a more noticeable way than many other groups. My life as a transgender person has been massively improved by the availability of hormones, surgeries and other treatments, as well as greater scientific understanding of the diversity of genders and sexes in the natural world as a whole, but other people in LGBTQIA+ communities have also gained from scientific and medical progress in huge ways.

GM   Do you think of science fiction as a radical genre? Are there any SF creators or groups who you think make particularly good use of the tools that SF provides to communicate their message and change minds?

CJA   I do think science fiction has immense potential to be radical, for a couple of reasons. First, the fact that it so often deals with change and newness means that it's a great vehicle for imagining revolutions and massive social transformations, both positive and negative, and that in turn can lead to more organizing in real life. (And, as discussed previously, subcultures tend to bleed together, which is why so many people who organize science fiction events can also turn around and organize political events.) But also, science fiction is full of counterfactuals, which allow us to look at things that appear immutable in the world around us and imagine how they could be very different. I often think about that Le Guin quote where she says, 'We live in capitalism, its power seems inescapable – but then, so did the divine right of kings. Any human power can be resisted and changed by human beings. Resistance and change often begin in art.' What I take from that is the idea that often power structures will try to trick us into believing that they are both permanent and unassailable, and only by creating and consuming stories about worlds that are wildly different can we start to imagine how those structures could change or crumble.

GM   As well as being an author of fiction, you've also written a lot of journalistic and non-fiction work. You co-founded the website io9.com with fellow science fiction author and journalist Annalee Newitz, which seemed really fresh at the time for the way it gave equal weight to both issues of science, tech and science fiction. You now both take a similar approach to those topics in your award-winning podcast *Our Opinions Are Correct.* What was the driving inspiration behind io9 and why is the relationship between science and science fiction important to you both?

CJA I feel like that's a question for Annalee way more than me, because io9's blend of science and science fiction was really their brainchild. But we definitely live in a time when science-fictional innovations are becoming real at an accelerating rate and science fiction has taken over mainstream pop culture. So, it's important to explore the links between them and how they both shape us.

GM Do you think science fiction influences scientific or technological development? And do you think science fiction can be a force for positive change in the world?

CJA It's clear that tech and science draw inspiration from SF and a lot of our devices have some of the same shape language as fictional gadgets from classic SF. At the same time, I feel like the role of SF in spurring specific innovations may be slightly overstated. Where SF really has the potential to create positive change is in helping us to grapple with the idea of rapid and bewildering change, and to make people more comfortable with a bit of future shock.

GM If you were recommending one piece of your fiction to a new reader what would it be?

CJA I always hope people will read whatever my latest thing is, and I am especially proud of the young adult space opera trilogy I've been publishing. (The first book is *Victories Greater Than Death.*) It starts out as the story of a teenage girl who is secretly the clone of an alien hero who was hidden on Earth as a baby, and now it's time for her to return to the stars and regain the memories of her past life, leading to all sorts of questions about what it means to be a hero, and the best ways to do good in the world. But it quickly grows into a big colourful space opera that shares some DNA with *Star Trek, Star Wars, Guardians of the Galaxy* and *She-Ra,* and I ended up creating some alien species and complex societies that I have had a lot of fun exploring. Plus I get to kind of deconstruct some SF concepts like the universal translator, with really interesting results. I would be so chuffed if more science fiction and fantasy fans found this series – *Doctor Who* showrunner Russell T. Davies read the first book and said some very lovely things about it.

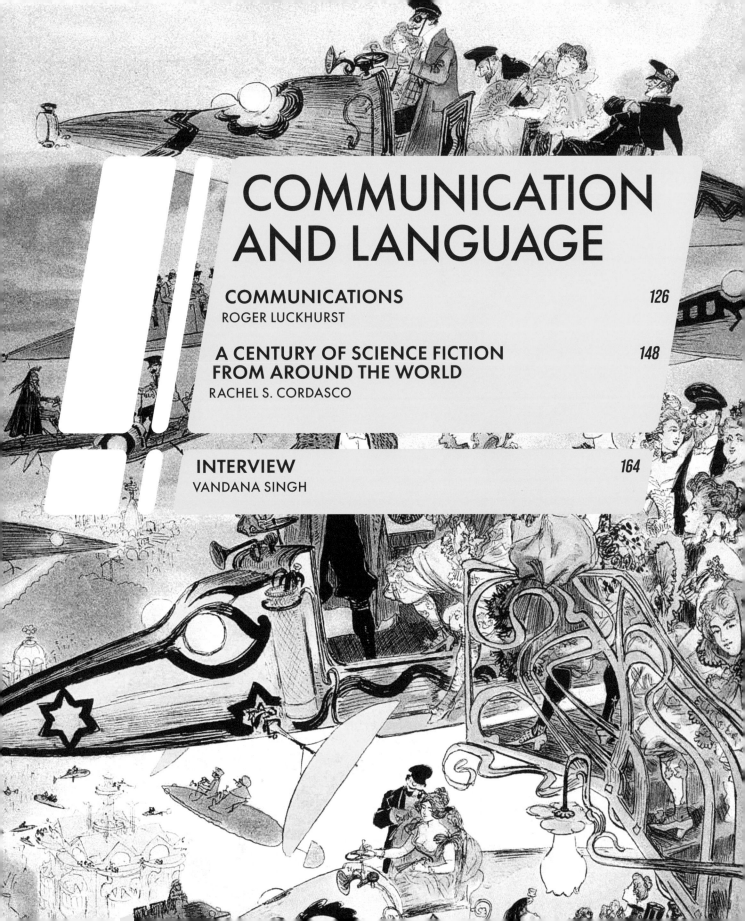

COMMUNICATION AND LANGUAGE

COMMUNICATIONS

ROGER LUCKHURST

← Albert Robida, *A Night at the Opera in the Year 2000*, c. 1882.

1. The 'coffee ring' circular language of the Heptapod aliens in Denis Villeneuve's *Arrival*, 2016.

2. The diagram from the plaques attached to the NASA space probes *Pioneer* 10 and 11. Designed by astronomers Carl Sagan and Frank Drake, they were drawn by Linda Salzman Sagan and launched in 1972 and 1973 respectively.

1

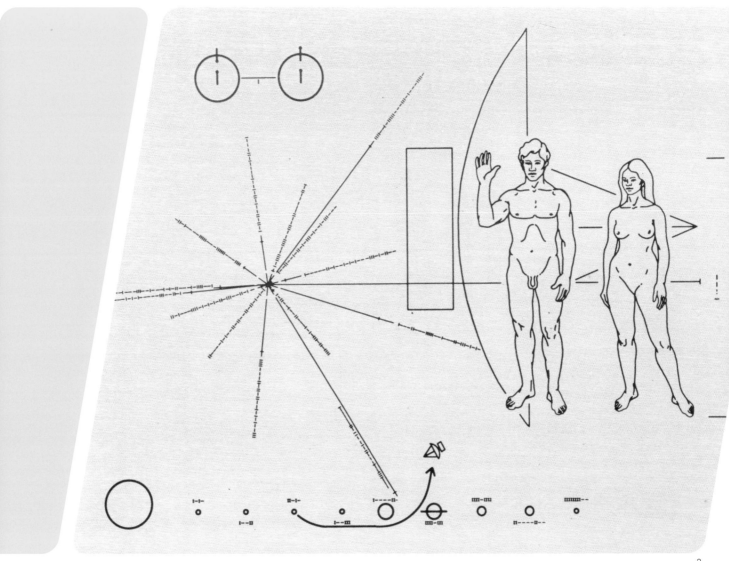

2

The original starship *Enterprise* had only a five-year mission, but encountered a cosmos teeming with weird and wonderful populations. In 1966, *Star Trek* began to air just as earthbound scientists were musing on the unlikely odds and truly profound difficulties of being able to find – let alone contact – alien beings. How could we get in touch with them, or they us, over such vast tracts of space and time? And might this encounter prove not the ecstatic revelation some had imagined, but instead be fraught with unforeseen risk and threats? Science fiction has made a unique and valuable contribution to these reflections on the extension of human communications to the stars.

3

3. *Star Trek*'s Chief Communications Officer,
    Lieutenant Nyota Uhura, played by Nichelle
    Nicholls, was an inspirational figure for many
    Black women, from the actor Whoopi Goldberg
    to the astronaut Mae Jemison.
4. The Babel fish is a fictional creature that consumes
    auditory signals and 'excretes' telepathic signals
    that can be interpreted directly by the human brain.
    In Douglas Adams's fiction, if you put one in your
    ear, you would be able to instantly understand any
    spoken language.

PER ARDUA AD ASTRA!

In 1972, the NASA space probe *Pioneer* 10 blasted off,
bound for Jupiter. It was the first human-made craft
deliberately intended to achieve escape velocity from
the solar system. Bolted to it was a small plaque showing
a set of symbols designed to tell intelligent aliens from
which star system the *Pioneer* originated, and an image
of a naked man and woman. The man was waving.

The opening piece of the American avant-garde artist
Laurie Anderson's epic performance work *United States
I–IV* (1980), called 'Say Hello', ponders:

> In our country, we send pictures of people speaking
> our sign language into Outer Space.
> We are speaking our sign language in these pictures.
> Do you think that They will think his arm is
> permanently attached in this position?

The scientists who designed this message, Frank Drake
and Carl Sagan, both American astronomers yearning
for interstellar contact, aimed for a universal language
embedded in objective scientific laws. Anderson, who
later briefly served as NASA's Artist in Residence, muses
in her work on the potential flaws inherent in any system
of communication, the inevitable snags and slippages
between sender and receiver. Somewhere between
Drake and Anderson lies science fiction.

Sometimes, science fiction invents devices that instantly
erase any problem of transmission and translation. Ursula
K. Le Guin imagined the handy 'ansible' device that sends
and translates messages instantly anywhere in the universe,
similar to James Blish's DIRAC communicator. The ansible
has proved an enduring convenience in science fiction,
cropping up in the works of Orson Scott Card, Neon Yang
and Becky Chambers. Douglas Adams gently mocked
these conveniences in *The Hitchhiker's Guide to the Galaxy*
(1979) with his Babel fish, which swims into the ear and
immediately translates any language: an incredible boon
until, of course, the traveller comes across some Vogon
poetry. But for a lot of science fiction, communication and
its missteps, the habit of language going astray, is a major,
driving concern.

The co-architect of the *Pioneer* plaque, Frank Drake,
was also the creator of an equation that attempted to

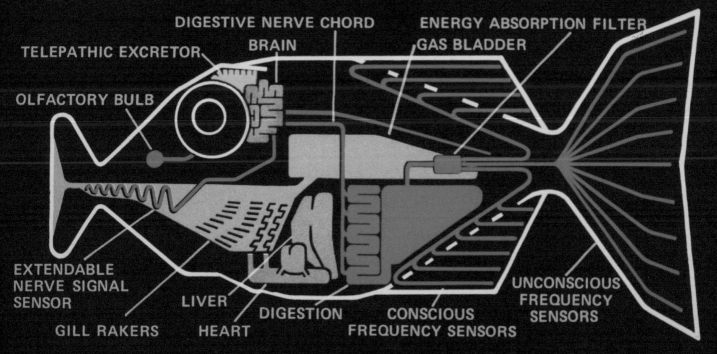

BABEL FISH

DIGESTIVE NERVE CHORD

ENERGY ABSORPTION FILTER

TELEPATHIC EXCRETOR

BRAIN

GAS BLADDER

OLFACTORY BULB

EXTENDABLE
NERVE SIGNAL
SENSOR

LIVER

DIGESTION

CONSCIOUS
FREQUENCY SENSORS

UNCONSCIOUS
FREQUENCY
SENSORS

GILL RAKERS

HEART

THE BABEL FISH IS SMALL, YELLOW, LEECHLIKE,
AND PROBABLY THE ODDEST THING IN THE UNIVERSE.
IT FEEDS ON BRAIN WAVE ENERGY, ABSORBING ALL

5.   Humanity attempts to communicate with visitors from another world
     through the medium of music in *Close Encounters of the Third Kind*,
     directed by Steven Spielberg, 1977.

6.   The Arecibo message. Colour has been added to more easily distiguish
     the different sections of the message, which include representations of
     a number sequence, the elements of DNA and its nucleotides, the DNA
     double helix, a human figure, the Sun and planets, and the Arecibo
     telescope itself.

5

**Just send instructions for your own
rebuilding at the speed of light.**

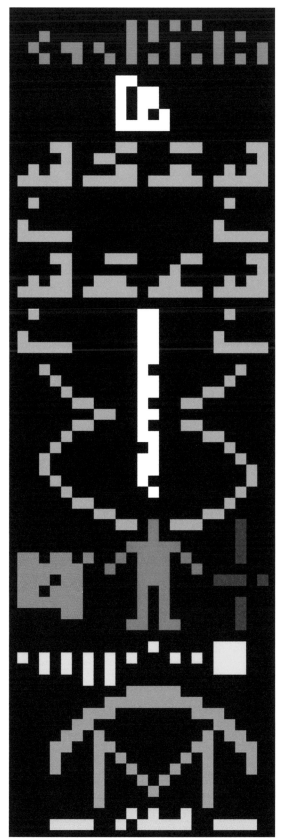

calculate such problems of communication. The speculative Drake Equation seeks to codify the great difficulties humans face in finding evidence for extraterrestrial life. In 1960, Drake was the first astronomer to use time on a radio telescope to scan the stars for communications, starting with Tau Ceti and Epsilon Eridani as possible sources of alien transmissions. He found none. The experiment was named Project Ozma, after the princess in Frank L. Baum's *Oz* books, some of which were framed as radio transmissions beamed down to Earth. Was Drake hoping for a late addition to the series?

Drake later became director of the National Astronomy and Ionosphere Center at Arecibo in Puerto Rico. From the telescope there, he helped to code the 'Arecibo Message', which was beamed out in 1974 towards the star cluster M13 in the hope that it would be picked up by someone or other in about 25,000 light years. This time, the message was in binary code, and contained information about the chemical basis of humans, numerical systems and even an image of the Arecibo dish itself.

This project, like Drake's earlier work with Sagan, displays how speculative science and science fiction often become interwoven. The idea for transmitting the chemical components of human life presumably came from Sir Fred Hoyle and John Elliot's television show and later novel, *A for Andromeda* (1962), where communication is picked up by a new radio satellite receiver in the north of England. The message, in the 'universal' language of binary code, is a set of instructions to design first a computer and then a biochemical machine that will build an alien visitor. Hoyle, a leading astronomer as well as science fiction writer, thought of bypassing the time and effort put into travelling these impossible distances: just send instructions for your own rebuilding at the speed of light. Anyone who has tried to assemble flat-pack furniture using wordless diagrams knows how well this usually turns out, and so it goes in *A for Andromeda*.

Arecibo was also the starting point in Sagan's *Contact* (1985), a novel published just after the establishment of the non-profit organization SETI, or Search for Extraterrestrial Intelligence Institute, which was set up in California with private money in 1984. In the 1997 film version of *Contact*, Jodie Foster's stubborn persistence in the face of the conservatism of 'normal' science in an era of budget cuts

7

7. Drew Barrymore as Gertie shares a tender moment
    with the titular alien in *E.T.: The Extra Terrestrial*,
    directed by Steven Spielberg, 1982.
8. Allen Telescope Array at night, 2011. The Allen
    Telescope Array at Hat Creek in northern California is
    the first radio telescope array to have been
    built specifically for the search for extraterrestrial
    intelligence (SETI).

pays off with another set of instructions beamed out for
yet another alien machine. Foster travels to the Vega star
system through a very expensive wormhole in spacetime,
making first contact with a being that takes the form of her
dead father. It sometimes seems that women are allowed
to be astronauts in twenty-first-century science fiction
films only if they are in mourning, as in *Gravity* (2013),
Interstellar (2014) or *Arrival* (2016).

Drake and Sagan later collaborated again, on a
Golden Record that was sent into space as another side
mission of the *Voyager* 1 and 2 crafts, launched in 1977.
The medium for the message had changed again, this time
taking the form of a disk that contained compressed images
of Earth and sound recordings that included, among other
things, whalesong and the music of Bach, Beethoven and
Chuck Berry (but not The Beatles, controversially). It also
contained a message from the head of the United Nations,
Kurt Waldheim, a figure subsequently disgraced when his
work as a Nazi intelligence officer came to light. Sagan's
young son Nick is heard saying: 'Hello from the children
of planet Earth!' This condensation of human culture was
put together hastily by a group that argued extensively
over its contents (some were appalled that rock music
was included, fearing that aliens would think humans an
adolescent species). It proved easier to send this beyond
the solar system than to release the recordings on Earth,
international copyright law being rather more tangled
than astrophysics. The sound recordings were eventually
released as a two-CD set forty years later, in 2017.

In retrospect, 1977 seems like a significant peak in what
the historian David Nye calls 'the American technological
sublime', a fusion of science, aesthetics and religious
yearning routed through engineering marvels, marked by
a distinct positivity. In the same year that *Voyager* left the
planet, the seminal films *Star Wars* and *Close Encounters of
the Third Kind* were released. George Lucas, the American
director responsible for the former, famously built his space
opera on the supposedly universal language of mythic
archetypes explored by Joseph Campbell in his book *The
Hero with a Thousand Faces* (1949). Steven Spielberg's
vision in *Close Encounters* represents something closer
to Carl Sagan's longing for the sublime encounter with
the Other. At the Devil's Tower, a butte of igneous rock in
Wyoming long believed by Native American communities

8

9

to have mystical qualities, humans communicate with the alien Mother Ship through another supposedly universal language: musical tones.

From the mid-twentieth century, Americans were invited to be inspired by the grand projects of railroads, skyscrapers, dams, freeway systems, weapons stockpiles or rocket ship gantries, but in the years that followed, Ronald Reagan's suspicion of big government led to cuts to NASA's budget, and the *Challenger* space shuttle disaster of 1986 became a traumatic spectacle of the fragility of human life during space flight. Cutesy fictional aliens like E.T. were replaced by darker fantasies of 'little greys' from the Zeta Reticuli star system, who were alleged to have abducted humans for ominous sexual experiments. This story was made ubiquitous by Whitley Strieber's ostensibly non-fictional account of his 'true life' experience in *Communion* (1989) and the unending swirl of conspiracy theories in the television series *The X Files* (1993–2002, 2016–18), in which every communication from the Other is dark,

impenetrable and subject to endless reinterpretation. In *Independence Day* (1996), humans send in a Welcome Wagon to play the cheery *Close Encounter* ringtones to the alien spaceship, only for it to be blasted out of the sky. In several of J. G. Ballard's novels and short stories, Cape Kennedy is a ruin and the astronauts are dead, circling above Earth in decaying orbits.

In the twenty-first century, the space race has ceased to be a spectacular arm of the Cold War and has fragmented into multiple national projects and private industries across the world. There are Indian, Chinese and United Arab Emirates space agencies. Larissa Sansour has imagined a Palestinian space agency across several of her video works and sculptures, while the Angolan artist Kiluanji Kia Henda has produced images, a model and documents chronicling a fictive pan-African space agency that ran parallel to the American and Soviet space programmes. Both offer a postcolonial critique of the space race as a display of the status and power of competing rocket states.

10

9. Kiluanji Kia Henda, *Astronomy Observatory,*
   Namib Desert, 2008.
10. Kiluanji Kia Henda, *The launch of Icarus 13*
   (6:00pm, 25th of May, 2007), 2008.
   In *Icarus 13: The First Journey to the Sun* (2008),
   Kiluanji Kia Henda charts an African space
   mission in images of its (supposed) infrastructure
   and the brilliant green light of a take-off, using
   documentary images to construct a science-
   fictional narrative.

The Japanese artist Mariko Mori, who has created a series
of science-fictional alternative personae including an
interstellar 'cybergeisha' as well as sculptures of UFOs,
uses this space race iconography to critique regressive
gender roles in Japanese culture.

In the twenty-first century, NASA piggybacks on
the SpaceX rockets run by Elon Musk, a transport CEO
with side interests in posthumanism, human-machine
telepathy, cryptocurrencies, satellite technology and digital
immortality. In the West, the space race has come to be
directed by the private wealth of billionaires. The Allen
Telescope Array, which sits in the Cascade mountains north
of the Silicon Valley corporations that privately fund it,
continues the search for extraterrestrial intelligence. This
hyper-capitalized race for the stars feels very different
from *Star Trek*'s 1960s vision of federation and a shared
ethics of knowledge and encounter.

11. Astronauts approach a mysterious alien monolith in
     Tycho crater on the Moon in *2001: A Space Odyssey*,
     directed by Stanley Kubrick, 1968.

TECHNOLOGICAL MAGIC

Arthur C. Clarke's famous Third Law, posited in his *Profiles of the Future* (1974), was that 'any sufficiently advanced technology is indistinguishable from magic'. This rule is particularly helpful when considering the history of communication technologies. The enigmatic black slab found by Dave Bowman on the Moon in *2001: A Space Odyssey* (1968), derived by Stanley Kubrick from Clarke's short story 'The Sentinel' (first published in 1951 as 'The Sentinel of Eternity') is a very good example. But as evidence for Clarke's law, we might point to the fairly continuous way in which electronic communication devices have produced a series of strange and occult doubles – shadowy science fictions – from the very beginning of the electronic revolution in the early nineteenth century.

Scientists and engineers have produced a stream of technological devices that collapse space and time. These were intrinsically intertwined with magical thinking not just in popular sentiment, but by the engineers themselves. Since the nineteenth century, ghosts have appeared on the railway tracks, as in Charles Dickens's unnerving short story, 'The Signalman' (1866). One of the earliest Spiritualist newspapers was the *Spiritual Telegraph*, which compared the messages rapped out by the dead at a séance with the dots and dashes sent by then-brand-new telegraph machines. Cromwell Varley, the celebrated engineer involved in the successful laying of the transatlantic telegraph cable, did so while simultaneously receiving spirit messages from his deceased wife. Alexander Graham Bell's assistant, Thomas Watson, who received the first telephone call, also happened to be a psychic medium, who listened to the crackles on the phone line for messages from beyond the grave or possibly from Mars (he was unable to decide). Father of psychoanalysis Sigmund Freud shrugged off as uninteresting his firm belief in telepathy, a term for 'distant touch' coined in 1882, just six years after the telephone was patented. He compared the two directly and without prejudice, as if they were simply parallel communication devices. Arthur C. Clarke also had a weakness for telepathy, believing it a potential marker of evolutionary advance in humanity, if proven to exist. The gramophone was specifically built to capture and preserve the voice after death, and was used to uncanny effect

> **Any sufficiently advanced technology is indistinguishable from magic.**
>
> Arthur C. Clarke, *Profiles of the Future* (1974)

12

in Arthur Conan Doyle's short story 'The Japanned Box' (1899). Meanwhile, the eminent physicist Oliver Lodge first detected the invisible 'ethereal' waves (now named for Heinrich Hertz) in the midst of attempts to determine the physics underpinning telepathy and possible communications with the dead. Wireless radio waves were intrinsically spooky: Rudyard Kipling's short story 'Wireless' (1902) has a doomed tubercular amateur radio ham picking up sympathetic messages from the poet John Keats, who died of the same disease nearly eighty years before. Born hucksters for their own workshops, Nikola Tesla and Thomas Edison promised photophones and thoughtographs and all manner of incredible devices within a few short years as the electrical revolution accelerated in the 1890s.

The magical effect attending every breakthrough in electronic and digital communications technology has always powered the science-fictional imagination, from Jules Verne's submarines and speedy air balloons or H. G. Wells's rockets, to wireless lunar telegraphy or remote viewing devices. A new world saturated with magical new communication technologies was envisaged particularly vividly by the French illustrator Albert Robida in *The Twentieth Century* (1882). Media haunted by magical elements in this early part of the electronic communications revolution includes the ghosts caught in the chemical film of photographs, spooky communications by telephone and 'electronic voice phenomena' on audio cassettes left running in empty rooms. These uncanny doublings continue all the way up to the haunted spaces of the internet in William Gibson's cyberpunk novel *Neuromancer* (1984), or the deathly infections caught by an entire generation in Japan, from videotapes in the film *Ring* (リング, 1998), to mobile phones in *One Missed Call* (着信アリ, 2003) or networked computers in Pulse (回路, 2001). The ghosts have kept on upgrading their deals with every new telecoms provider.

The science-fictional imagination of writers from the African continent, meanwhile, from Ben Okri to Nnedi Okorafor, frequently acknowledges the culturally very different way of drawing boundaries between natural and supernatural, mundane and spirit worlds in a number of African belief systems. This cannot be easily contained by

12. 'You're all just jealous of my jetpack': a cartoon by Tom Gauld, 2012.
13. An attempt at an early personal flying machine, with two helicopter rotors powered by a backpack mounted engine, on display at the Air and Space Museum at Le Bourget airport, Paris, France.

13

3

a reflector only a few feet across would give a beam so directive that almost all the power would be concentrated on the earth. Arrays a metre or so in diameter could be used to illuminate single countries if a more restricted service was required.

11.   The stations would be connected with each other by very-narrow-beam, low-power links, probably working in the optical spectrum or near it, so that beams less than a degree wide could be produced.

12.   The system would provide the following services which cannot be realised in any other manner:-

        a) Simultaneous television broadcasts to the entire globe, including services to aircraft.
        b) Relaying of programmes between distant parts of the planet.

13.   In addition the stations would make redundant the network of relay towers covering the main areas of civilisation and representing investments of hundreds of millions of pounds. (Work on the first of these networks has already started.)

14.   Figure II shows diagrammatically some of the specialised services that could be provided by the use of differing radiator systems.

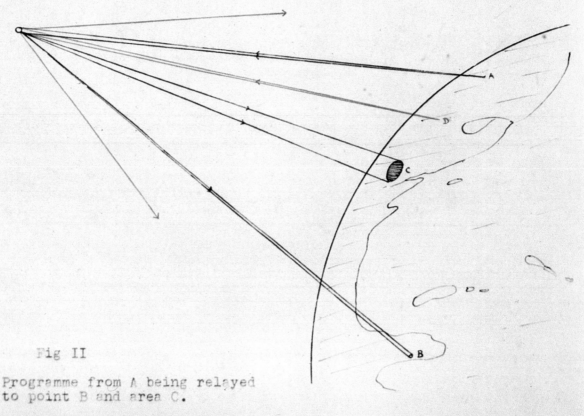

Fig II

Programme from A being relayed to point B and area C.

Programme from D being relayed to whole hemisphere.

15

14. Illustration from *The Space Station: Its Radio Applications* by Arthur C. Clarke (1945). The text and diagrams are used to describe 'the use of a chain of space-stations' in geostationary orbit.

15. The Mir space station was launched in stages between 1986 and 1996. When completed it had a total mass of over 110 tons, making it the largest space station orbited to date.

notions of 'magical realism', but Okorafor has suggested that 'Africanfuturism' might be a useful term for the very different topographies of the imagination at play in fictions that blend such elements with, for example, depictions of futuristic technology.

The magical thinking of these fictions has been criticized, as famously in the many errors detected in the physics underpinning *Hot Tub Time Machine* (2010). But this is to miss the point that new technologies often emerge from that blurry space between fiction and science that has been called the 'SF-nal' (a compression of 'science-fictional') – where advanced technology, shameless boosterism, investor pitches, futurological projections and science fiction deliriously cross-fertilize one another.

Exhibit A: the American tendency to favour the clamshell mobile phone design descends directly from everyone watching *Star Trek* since the 1960s (Motorola called their first clamshell StarTAC in 1996). The iPad, the Bluetooth ear-bud and computer voice activation, if sadly not quite teleportation, all got their test runs in *Star Trek*.

Exhibit B: When making *Minority Report* (2002), Steven Spielberg used a team of futurologists to imagine the technologies at work in the now-familiar everyday of the near future: driverless cars, personalized advertisements, identification by iris, voice-activated homes and gesture-based computing.

Where technological advances push the envelope of our habitual communications, they fall into this temporary phase of seeming nothing short of magical. Science fiction almost routinizes this spooky magic for us. In the era of climate crisis, it has been the ecological sciences that render uncanny the wholly other modes of communication of trees, plants or fungi that scientists are only just beginning to understand, and which has fed into science fiction by Tade Thompson and Aliya Whiteley, among others.

Our irritation that science fiction sometimes gets its predictions for communication technologies completely wrong is summed up in that phrase redolent of all those optimistic post-1945 futures that never came to pass, 'Dude, where's my jetpack?'

16. Leo and Diane Dillon, *Mythic Imagination*, 1990. The husband and wife artists collaborated in such a way that they described a 'third artist' who did things neither of them would do individually.

17. Alphabet and numbers 1 to 10 in Bhaux, an alien language constructed by creative studio Framestore for the 2022–23 exhibition 'Science Fiction: Voyage to the Edge of Imagination' at the Science Museum, London.

IT'S GOOD TO TALK

One of the quintessential science fiction scenarios is, of course, first contact with an entirely alien Other. How would that pan out?

Not always so well. Indeed, we might consider that a lot of Anglo-American 'Golden Age' science fiction is married to social Darwinian conceptions that the human–alien encounter will be driven by the struggle for survival, a vision of nature (actually only intermittently expressed by Charles Darwin himself) that natural selection demands ruthless competition, domination and destruction of rivals, even unto extinction. In the alien invasion genre, it is rare to find the Earth visited by an essentially benign teacher, though we do with Gort in *The Day the Earth Stood Still* (1951). But it is more often instant, implacable warfare from the off: H. G. Wells's Martians skip afternoon tea for a merciless assault on London, that complacent imperial metropole. It is the same assumption in the age of American empire too, from Flash Gordon fighting Ming the Merciless, via Robert A. Heinlein's *Starship Troopers* (1959) and the paranoid B-movies of the 1950s – *Invasion of the Body Snatchers* (1956), or *Earth vs. The Flying Saucers* (1956). Perhaps the purest example is Ridley Scott's *Alien* (1979), where the xenomorph is seen as a perfectly evolved killing machine.

It isn't much of a leap to see this as a colonial mindset, an assumption of asymmetric power and the right, even the duty, to dominate the Other. This set of cultural assumptions has been the subject of critique in the more liberal wing of science fiction. Le Guin, the child of two anthropologists, often focuses on the challenges of encountering radical difference, most classically in *The Left Hand of Darkness* (1969). Octavia E. Butler's fiction explores scenarios in which initial horror at the alien develops into a more complex, uneasy form of coexistence, even symbiosis. In *Adulthood Rites*, the second novel in the *Xenogenesis/ Lilith's Brood* trilogy (1987–89), the human mother, Lilith, tells her hybrid human-alien child:

> Human beings fear difference.... Oankali crave difference. Humans persecute their different ones.... Oankali seek difference and collect it.... When you feel a conflict, try to go the Oankali way. Embrace difference.

Bhaux Standard

Regular

Bold

When you feel a conflict, try to go the Oankali way. Embrace difference.

Octavia E. Butler, *Adulthood Rites* (1988)

Though Butler sees violence and hierarchy as intrinsic human traits, there has, in recent years, been an explosion of availability in science fiction from cultures less embedded in this model of encounter, whether it's Nnedi Okorafor's *Binti* novels, Rita Indiana's *Tentacle* (2017) or Jeff VanderMeer's eco-conscious *Southern Reach* trilogy (2014). In the twenty-first century, science fiction has become distinctly transcultural, the domination of Anglophone science fiction displaced by the wider circulation of translated fiction and films from beyond Hollywood. Science fiction tropes are taken up and transformed in different cultural settings. This can offer radically different understandings of the human-alien encounter, seen from multiple viewpoints outside the violent hierarchy of self and Other.

Some of the most celebrated works of science fiction, though, suspect that communication with the alien will be so difficult, so odd, that readers or viewers are left with only an elusive sense of a missed encounter. Kubrick's *2001* ends in a hallucinatory rush of juxtaposed images that audiences have been trying to understand ever since. In Stanisław Lem's novel *Solaris* (1961), the apparently sentient planet plucks traumatic memories from the astronauts and embodies them, and it remains forever unclear whether this is intended as an act of communication at all. Arkady and Boris Strugatsky's *Roadside Picnic* (Пикник на обочине, 1972) is set after the extraterrestrial visitors have departed Earth, leaving behind strange, inexplicable phenomena. The novel's title comes from the image of humanity as ants picking over the rubbish left behind on a pitstop by a superior species, unable to 'read' what has happened. In Ted Chiang's 'Story of Your Life' (2002), filmed by Denis Villeneuve as *Arrival* (2016), the human linguist is able to translate the written language of the alien Heptapods, but only at the expense of undoing her own linear sense of spacetime. To think in the grammar of the Heptapod language is to experience simultaneity, not past-present-future. Chiang comes to the crucial insight that in the encounter between self and Other, our very sense of being-in-the-world is undone the moment communication begins.

18. The physicist Tom Beddard creates artworks called *Fabergé Fractals,* inspired by both the wonders of mathematics and the creations of Fabergé. This was the writer Nnedi Okorafor's reference image when imagining the mysterious tool, the edan, for her *Binti* series (2015–18).

→ The 1640 feet (500 metre) wide Aperture Spherical Radio Telescope, the world's largest single-dish radio telescope, dubbed the 'China Sky Eye', in Pingtang County, Guizhou Province, southwest China.

A CENTURY OF SCIENCE FICTION FROM AROUND THE WORLD

RACHEL S. CORDASCO

1. Back cover detail of *View from Another Shore*, edited by Franz Rottensteiner (1978).

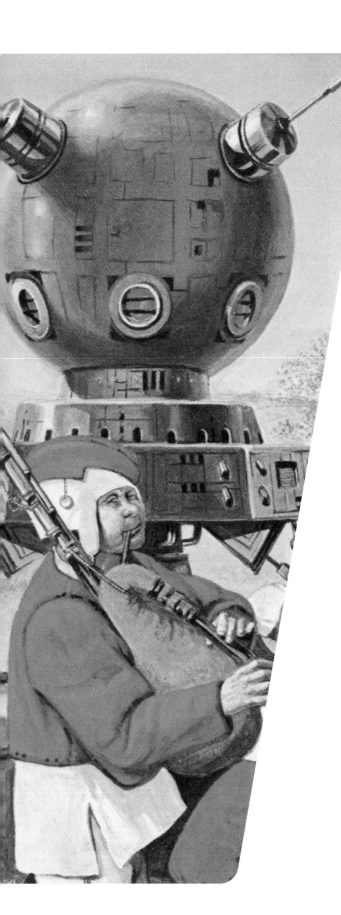

The act of translation and the spinning of fantastic tales both predate the advent of writing in human culture – and each has only become more important with the modern crystallization of genres like science fiction and fantasy since late in the nineteenth century. While Anglophone readers of science fiction in our present time consume more texts originally written in English than in any other language, the twentieth century has witnessed an often robust market for those science fiction texts that have been translated into English (SFT). The dominance of Anglophone science fiction in the world market since the 1940s is well-documented, and translation from English into other languages secured the status of (mostly) American and British texts for decades, often depressing genre markets in countries where they became popular. Nonetheless, the twenty-first century has witnessed a surge of science fiction moving *from* other languages *into* English. Some SFT bypasses English altogether, and has done so since the early twentieth century, with, for instance, Russian speculative fiction being translated into German and Romanian without ever reaching an Anglophone audience.

The increase in science fiction being translated into English may be due to a number of interconnected factors, including the rise of the internet, globalization, trends in publishing, the proliferation of science fiction conventions around the world and the public profile of translation itself. Anglophone readers are now able to read, for instance, Japanese space opera, Chinese hard science fiction (science fiction that roots itself in physics, engineering and mathematics) and Russian dystopia in a way they never could before. Through online magazines, collections, novels and anthologies, these stories enrich readers' literary experiences by reminding them that science fiction is not and never was a solely Anglophone phenomenon. The proliferation of conferences and conventions around the world has also given authors, editors and translators new platforms through which to introduce readers to authors writing in a variety of languages, and the networking that takes place at these events enables authors to connect with translators and publishers more easily than ever before.

The very act of translation is in keeping with science fiction's quest to explore the unknown and discover the

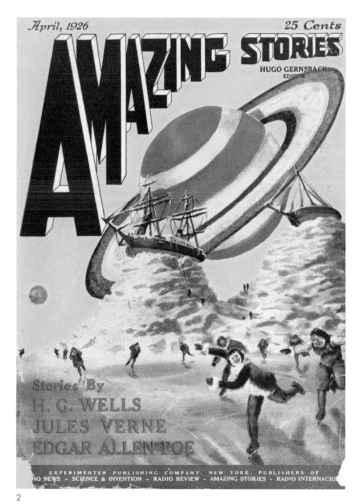

2

Amazing Stories, vol. 1, no. 1, 1926. Hugo Gernsback's pulp magazine *Amazing Stories* marked the birth of American science fiction as a genre. The cover of the very first issue is an illustration of Jules Verne's story 'Off on a Comet' (*Hector Servadac*, 1877), drawn by Frank R. Paul.

3. *Planet of the Apes*, directed by Franklin J. Schaffner, 1968, was based on the 1963 French novel *La Planète des singes* by Pierre Boulle.

unimaginable; it is also a major theme in science fiction literature. Writers like Stanisław Lem, the Strugatsky brothers, Lola Robles, Gustav Meyrink and many others have written about the impossibility of communicating with alien species or the spectral here on Earth. Hampered as we humans are by languages we don't understand, translation gives us a way into other cultures and traditions that we wouldn't have otherwise.

THE EARLY DAYS OF SFT

Since Jules Verne was first translated into English in the latter third of the nineteenth century, the amount of available SFT from certain source languages has shifted over time, depending on geopolitical circumstances. America's close relationship with France since the American Revolution, and its elite's interest in French culture meant that French literature was as in demand as that from England. And while Verne's adventure stories and 'scientific fiction' were originally marketed to adolescents in the US, the Frenchman's particular brand of fantastic literature also heavily influenced what, in 1929, Hugo Gernsback called 'science fiction'. The subsequent proliferation of science fiction and fantasy magazines in the US led to an increasing American dominance in the genre.

An increasingly rich variety of science fiction was also being published in Eastern Europe in the early twentieth century. Yevgeny Zamyatin's chilling dystopia *We* (Мы) was first published in English in 1924, twenty-eight years before it made it into print in Russian, while the Czech author Karel Čapek burst onto the Anglophone scene in 1925 with *Krakatit* (1922), followed by *The Absolute at Large* (*Továrna na absolutno*, 1922; English translation 1927) and *War with the Newts* (*Válka s Mloky*, 1936; English translation 1937). Anglophone readers also had plenty of genre texts to read that were originally written in English, including work from the prolific British author H. G. Wells and the burgeoning American science fiction market. Wells's novel *The Time Machine* was his first to be published in French, as *La Machine à explorer le temps*, in 1895, exporting English-language science fiction back to the country of its great inspiration. These ideas and narratives, moving back and forth over linguistic borders, continued to multiply into the mid-twentieth century, when science fiction truly burst into the mainstream.

4. *Stalker* (Сталкер), directed by Andrei Tarkovsky, 1979, and loosely based on the Strugatsky brothers' *Roadside Picnic* (Пикник на обочине, 1972) is a Soviet-era science fiction masterpiece about a man who takes a writer and academic into a forbidden zone, in search of a room that grants one's innermost desires.

5. A 1993 edition cover of Yevgeny Zamyatin's *We* (Мы). Zamyatin was one of the Russian science fiction writers whose work began to appear outside of the Soviet Union in the 1960s and 1970s, along with the Strugatsky Brothers, Kir Bulychev and Alexander Belyaev.

6. Front cover of *View from Another Shore*, edited by Franz Rottensteiner (1978).

5

6

THE 1960S AND 1970S: FRENCH AND RUSSIAN SFT

Until the Cold War era, science fiction and fantasy written in other languages had only rarely made its way into English. The explosion of SFT in the mid-twentieth century was, unsurprisingly, of French and Russian vintage. Anglophone readers were already familiar with Verne and French literature more generally, and with the rise of the USSR and the space race with the US in the 1950s and 1960s, Russian SFT gained a boost. As the Soviet Union and United States squared off on political and technological issues, writers and readers on either side of the Iron Curtain became more interested in one another's science fiction. Between 1960 and 1979, Anglophone readers suddenly had access to nearly forty works of Russian SFT from some of the nation's best authors, including Zamyatin, Mihail Bulgakov, Arkady and Boris Strugatsky and Kir Bulychev. These authors most often imagined dystopian futures and adventures in outer space, which likely influenced the Anglophone market. This flood of Russian-to-English translations can also be explained by the USSR's political and social liberalization, as well as the rise in English-to-Russian translations of science fiction.

The Moscow-based publisher Foreign Languages Publishing House led the way in Russian-to-English translations in the early 1960s, followed by American publishers such as Macmillan and DAW, who brought on acclaimed science fiction writers like Theodore Sturgeon and Isaac Asimov to write introductions to a number of anthologies. Macmillan's *Best of Soviet Science Fiction* series ran from 1977 to 1986, with a trade paperback edition published by Collier titled *Theodore Sturgeon Introduces New Science Fiction from Russia*.

French science fiction in particular competed with that from Russia during the late 1960s and 1970s, especially after the film version of Pierre Boulle's *The Planet of the Apes* (*La Planète des singes*) premiered in the US in 1968. The work of translators like Xan Fielding, C. J. Richards and Patricia Wolf, and the editor, author and translator Damon Knight, injected French science fiction into the Anglophone consciousness much like Verne had been half a century before. During these two decades, thirty-two works of French science fiction by such authors as Boulle, Pierre Barbet, Robert Merle, Nathalie Henneberg and Gérard Klein were translated into English, often published by Vanguard and DAW.

7

8

But Russian and French SFT were not the only such texts available to Anglophone readers at this time: Chinese, Czech, German, Italian, Japanese, Polish, Spanish and Swedish SFT were also making their way into the Anglophone world. Of particular importance is the role played by Stanisław Lem, who dominated Polish SFT, with nineteen novels and collections published over twenty-four years. Through his fiction and nonfiction, Lem pushed readers to think more deeply about, among other things, what it means to be human and why we seek out alien civilizations – tropes of the genre that continue to be relevant and popular today. His most famous novel, *Solaris* (1961; English translation 1970), was televized in the Soviet Union in 1968 and has been turned into a film twice: first by Andrei Tarkovsky in 1972, and subsequently by Stephen Soderbergh in 2002 (Lem apparently disliked both films).

The celebration of international science fiction truly kicked off in 1970 in Japan. Held in Osaka, the first International Symposium on Science Fiction brought together Japanese, American, British and Soviet writers. A group of major Anglophone science fiction authors subsequently founded the international association known as 'World SF' at the First World Science Fiction Writers' Conference in Dublin in 1976. While its overt aim was to foster the exchange of ideas and scholarship among science fiction authors and scholars, World SF had also been formed to bring together major SF authors from Western and Soviet nations through a professional organization. Major genre writers like Harry Harrison (US), Frederik Pohl (US), Brian Aldiss (UK) and Sam J. Lundwall (Sweden) served as some of its presidents, with Pohl establishing the Karel Award for excellence in science fiction translation.

Magazines and anthologies devoted to promoting SFT sprang up at around the same time, with Pohl's *International Science Fiction* running for two issues (November 1967 and June 1968) and paving the way for Franz Rottensteiner's anthology *View from Another Shore* (1974), the first anthology featuring SFT from multiple countries exclusively. The famed science fiction scholar Darko Suvin published *Other Worlds, Other Seas: Science-Fiction Stories from Socialist Countries* (1970), while Harrison and Aldiss brought out the *7th Annual Best SF 73*, which included Czech, Norwegian and Russian SFT. By the end of the decade, the author, editor and translator

7. Alternative film poster by Victo Ngai for *Solaris* (Солярис) directed by Andrei Tarkovsky, 1972.

8. Stanisław Lem's *Solaris*, 1970 English edition.

9. Original theatrical poster for *Solaris* (Солярис), directed by Andrei Tarkovsky, 1972. Despite Lem's apparent dislike of the film, and Tarkovsky himself regarding it as a failure, the adaptation is widely regarded as a cinematic classic.

10. Poster for *Akira* (アキラ, serialized from 1982–90 and
adapted into a 1988 film) by Katsuhiro Otomo, was
one of the first manga to be translated into English, and
remains a classic of visual science fiction.

11. Cover art detail from Liu Cixin's *The Three-Body
Problem* (三体, 2008), published in English in 2014.

Maxim Jakubowski had put together *Twenty Houses of
the Zodiac* (1979), following Donald Wollheim's *The Best
from the Rest of the World: European Science Fiction*
(1976). With his wife, Elsie, Wollheim had also founded the
publishing house DAW, which championed science fiction in
translation and went on to publish twenty-four works of SFT
in the 1970s and 1980s. By the end of these decades,
SFT was beginning to open up beyond French and Eastern
European literature, and in the 1980s and 1990s the
industry would begin to go truly global.

THE 1980S AND 1990S: JAPANESE SFT AND MORE

By the 1980s, Japan was a rising worldwide economic
and cultural powerhouse. Riding the wave of economic
prosperity and global connectivity that had started in the
1970s, Japanese SFT went from a trickle in Anglophone
publications, like *The Magazine of Fantasy and Science
Fiction,* to over a hundred novels, collections and
anthologies by 2019. Japan's geographical proximity to
Australia allowed Japanese science fiction to find English-
language markets there, and its strong connection to the
US enabled the importation of science fiction along with
American interest in Japanese ideas about education,
corporate culture and advanced technology. Above all,
cultural ambassadors like Judith Merril and English–
Japanese translator teams in the last quarter of the
twentieth century brought high-quality Japanese science
fiction, as well as related genres like surrealism and horror,
to Anglophone audiences interested in another culture's take
on such issues as human–AI interaction and environmental
catastrophe. Major speculative fiction authors such as
Kōbō Abe, Hoshi Shinichi and Haruki Murakami burst
onto the Anglophone stage at around this time, with a
wholly different kind of SFT from that of Russia and France.
While Western SFT had featured thrilling outer space or
underwater adventures before gradually moving towards
more fantastical and absurdist subjects, East Asian SFT in
the 1980s and 1990s was offering a new kind of hard-
science fiction based on technological breakthroughs in
robotics, communications and flight.

The surge in Japanese SFT during these two decades
occurred alongside a more general expansion of
speculative (science fiction, fantasy, horror) fiction
translated into English. While French, Japanese and

12. Cover artwork for Hao Jingfang's novelette *Folding Beijing* (北京折叠), which uses the science-fictional idea of a moving city to think about inequality.

13. Poster for *Nausicaä of the Valley of the Wind* (風の谷のナウシカ) a 1984 Japanese anime film written and directed by Hayao Miyazaki, based on his 1982 manga. With strong use of environmental, anti-war themes and a fascination with flight, the film contains many of the motifs to which Miyazaki returns in his later films for Studio Ghibli, and which mark the director as one of the most influential and important Japanese creators of science fiction and fantasy of the late twentieth century.

14. Cover artwork for Ahmed Saadawi's *Frankenstein in Baghdad*, 2014 (فرانكشتاين في بغداد; first published in 2013). This winner of the International Prize for Arabic Fiction retells Mary Shelley's classic novel in the ruins of a post-invasion Iraq, blending science, magic and religion.

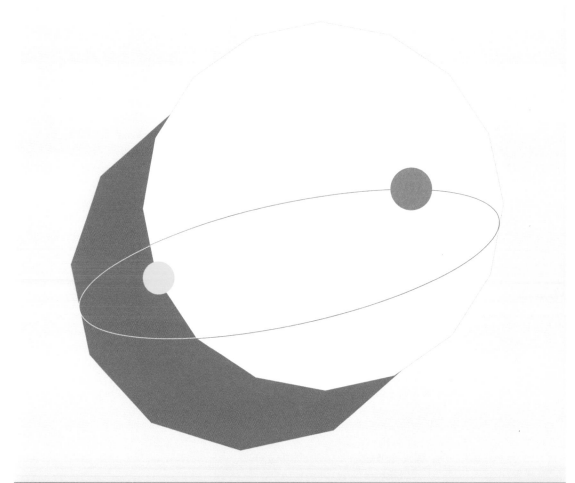

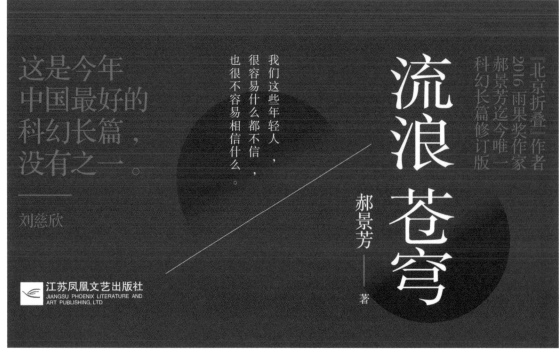

这是今年
中国最好的
科幻长篇，
没有之一。
——
刘慈欣

我们这些年轻人，
很容易什么都不信，
也很不容易相信什么。

「北京折叠」作者
2016 雨果奖作家
郝景芳迄今唯一
科幻长篇修订版

流浪 苍穹

郝景芳——

著

江苏凤凰文艺出版社
JIANGSU PHOENIX LITERATURE AND
ART PUBLISHING, LTD

Russian SFT held the top three spots, Chinese, Czech, Finnish, German, Hebrew, Italian, Polish, Spanish and Swedish SFT were also being published in English, albeit in small amounts. The first work of Hebrew SFT – Amos Kenan's *The Road to Ein Harod* (דרחה ןיעל ךרדה, 1984), published in 1988, was an alternate history about a fascist Israel in the wake of a military coup. Texts like Orly Castel-Bloom's dystopian and disturbing *Dolly City* (יטיס ילוד, 1992; English translation 2010), Hillel Damron's far-future post-apocalyptic *Sex War One* (1982; English translation 2014) and various stories in Sheldon Teitelbaum and Emmanuel Lottem's *Zion's Fiction: A Treasury of Israeli Speculative Literature* (2018) and *More Zion's Fiction* (2021) have followed.

The Finnish author Leena Krohn's *Doña Quixote and the Gold of Ophir* (*Donna Quijote ja muita kaupunkilasia*, 1983, and *Oofirin kultaa*, 1987), the first work of Finnish SFT, was published in translation in 1996, kicking off two decades in which more of Krohn's blend of science fiction and fantasy became available to Anglophone readers. Also at this time, French- and Russian-language SFT underwent a shift from science fiction literature to an increasing number of fantasy texts. Given the rapid growth of the fantasy subgenre in America following J.R.R. Tolkien's *The Lord of the Rings* (1954), it is likely that publishers were looking for less Boulle, Klein or Strugatsky and more Jean Ray or Victor Pelevin.

The 1980s also brought the largest number of SFT anthologies (twelve) to date, with ten more in the 1990s. Along with multi-language anthologies like the two *Terra SF* books edited by Richard Nolane for DAW in 1981 and 1983, and the *Penguin World Omnibus of Science Fiction*, edited by Aldiss and Lundwall in 1986, Anglophone readers could enjoy compilations of Dutch, Russian, Japanese, Spanish, Czech, Francophone and Polish SFT. Long-standing science fiction editors like Nolane and Hartwell were joined in their endeavours by James Gunn, Marjorie Agosin, Roger DeGaris and many others. This laid the groundwork for a true blossoming of SFT in the new century, with writers, editors, translators and readers looking for more diverse stories from all over the world to enjoy and learn from.

THE 2000s AND BEYOND

Shifting geopolitical circumstances have long had a major impact on which speculative fiction is translated and which is not. Overall, the trend toward fantasy and horror is clear

13

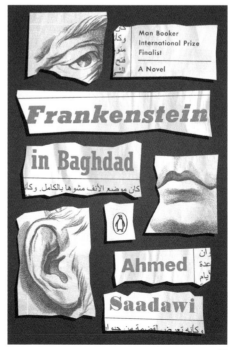

14

across languages including French, Russian, Spanish and Japanese, perhaps signalling a global shift in readers' tastes and the influence of recent movies, streaming television and video games, which, like fiction, tended to be more cynical and fearful around the turn of the twenty-first century. Anxieties over terrorism, biowarfare, genetic engineering and environmental damage appear to be influencing this shift. Sub-genres of science fiction also continue to capture audiences' imaginations. The Second Gulf War, begun in 2003, led to the translation of a number of Arabic-language dystopias, such as the writer, translator and medical doctor Ahmed Khaled Towfik's *Utopia* (2009, يوتوبيا; English translation 2011), Abdel Aziz's *The Queue* (2013, الطابور; English translation 2016) and Ahmed Saadawi's *Frankenstein in Baghdad* (2013, فرانكشتاين في بغداد; English translation 2014).

China's rise as an economic powerhouse at the turn of the twenty-first century has allowed its government to fund and promote science fiction projects that both encourage the genre within the nation and export it to the world – a case in point is Liu Cixin's hard science fiction *Remembrance of Earth's Past* trilogy(地球往事, 2008–10), *Clarkesworld Magazine*'s partnership with Storycom, and the many Chinese science fiction and fantasy anthologies and collections that have appeared just in the last few years. The translator Ken Liu has been instrumental in bringing writers like Liu Cixin, Chen Qiufan and Xia Jia into English for the first time.

In Europe, German-language SFT, represented in particular by Andreas Eschbach, whose novels include *The Carpet Makers* (*Die Haarteppichknüpfer*, 1995; English translation 2005), has come roaring back from a lull in the 1990s, though in the 2000s it competes with an increase in high-fantasy works by the prolific Markus Heitz. Italian-language SFT has had its own renaissance, thanks in large part to the work of the author, editor and publisher Francesco Verso. Verso's own science fiction, including *Nexhuman* (2014), as well as works such as Clelia Farris's *Creative Surgery* (*Chirurgia Creativa*, 2015; English translation 2020) and Paolo Aresi's *Beyond the Planet of the Wind* (*Oltre il pianeta del vento*, 2004; English translation 2016), is gaining attention around the world and taking its place alongside earlier authors such as Italo Calvino and Primo Levi. Spanish science fiction is represented by Sofia

Rhei and Lola Robles's linguistics-focused novels and stories, Cristina Jurado's surrealist science fiction stories and Rodolfo Martinez's cyberpunk novels. Spanish-language science fiction from Cuba has also found its way to Anglophone readers, thanks to Restless Books and its promotion of the contemporary cyberpunk author Yoss's books, such as *Red Dust* (*Polvo rojo*, 2003; English translation 2022).

Despite this significant uptick in SFT available in the Anglophone world, mainstream literary fiction continues to be translated more often than genre fiction. The shuttering of two major publishers of Japanese science fiction in English, Haikasoru and Kurodahan, in 2020, meant that Anglophone readers missed out on some of the best science fiction written in Japan since the 1990s. Haikasoru published translations of Yoshiki Tanaka's award-winning ten-novel space opera series *Legend of the Galactic Heroes* (銀河英雄伝説, 1982–97; English translation 2016–19), Toh EnJoe's *Self-Reference Engine* (2007; English translation 2013) and Taiyo Fujii's *Gene Mapper* (2013; English translation 2015) and *Orbital Cloud* (2014; English translation 2017), while Kurodahan released their 2020 *Speculative Japan* anthologies along with Kitano Yusaku's far-future cyberpunk *Mr Turtle* (かめくん, 2001; English translation 2016) and Yasutaka Tsutsui's absurdist stories in *Bullseye!* Despite these losses, publishers like Vertical and University of Minnesota Press continue to publish classic works of Japanese SFT.

Science fiction continues to develop in fascinating ways around the world, and science fiction readers worldwide continue to demand those stories that infuse the genre with unfamiliar perspectives and imagery and expand what they think of when they look for 'science fiction'. The undeniable interest of readers in science fiction from languages and cultures other than their own means that despite the additional budgetary layer added by translation, publishers continue to move towards including more SFT on their lists. Anthologies proliferated throughout the 2010s and into the 2020s, coming from Mexico, Spain, Romania, Croatia, Russia, China, Japan, Sweden, Denmark, Greece, Israel, South Korea, Iraq and elsewhere. Publications such as Lavie Tidhar's *Apex Book of World SF* and *Best of World SF* series, and Bill Campbell and Francesco Verso's *Future Fiction* anthology demonstrate that the future of world science fiction is bright indeed.

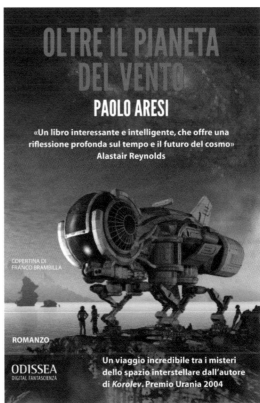

16

15. Cover of Rodolfo Martinez's *Cat's Whirld* (*La sonrisa del gato*, 1995), with artwork by Maciej Garbacz.
16. Cover of *Beyond the Planet of the Wind*(*Oltre il pianeta del vento*, 2004) by Paolo Aresi, with artwork by Franco Brambilla
17. 2017 cover artwork for Yusaku Kitano's *Mr Turtle*, by Mike Dubisch (かめくん, 2001).
→ Ward Shelley, *The History of Science Fiction*, vol. 2, 2009–12.

17

THE HISTORY OF SCIENCE FICTION

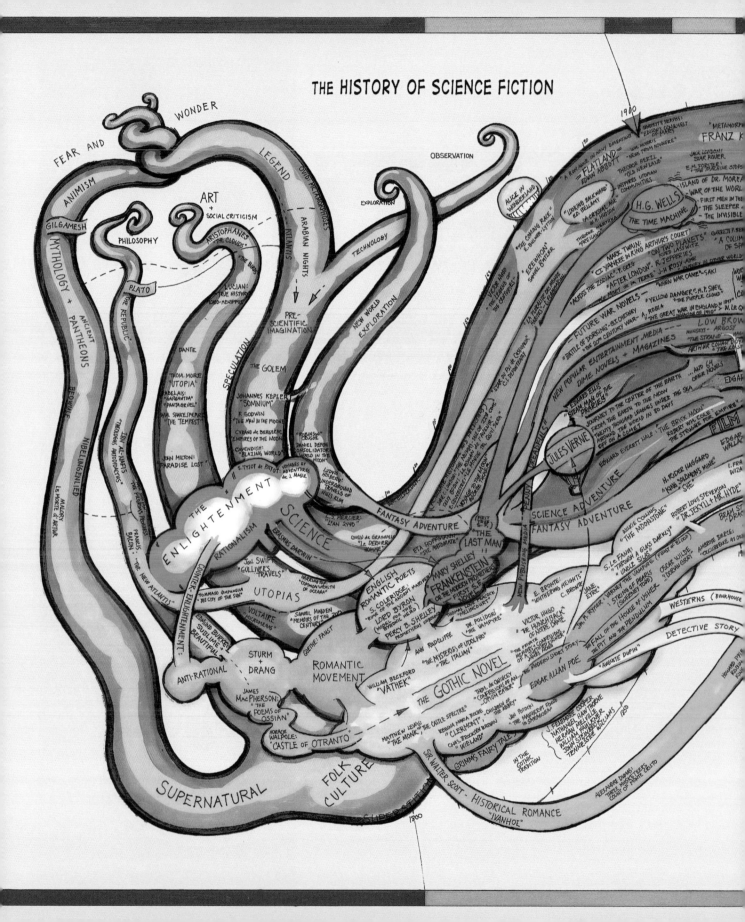

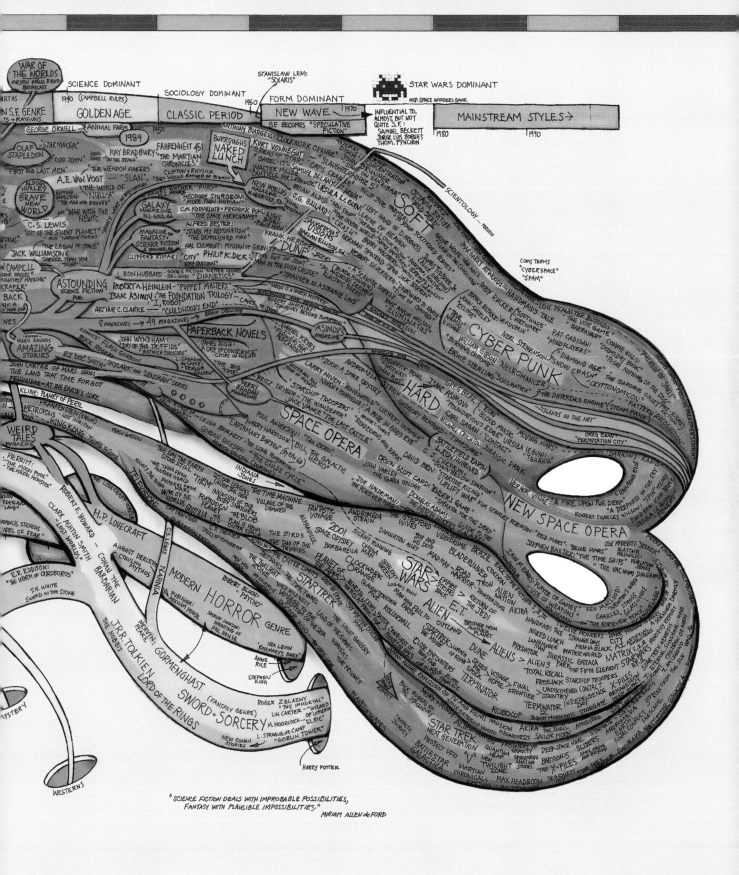

"SCIENCE FICTION DEALS WITH IMPROBABLE POSSIBILITIES,
FANTASY WITH PLAUSIBLE IMPOSSIBILITIES."
MIRIAM ALLEN de FORD

INTERVIEW
VANDANA SINGH

GLYN MORGAN

As well as being a writer of speculative fiction, you are a professor of physics. Do you manage to keep those two hats separate or does your science fiction influence your approach to science and vice versa?

VANDANA SINGH

I always mix hats! My work in academia feeds my fiction, and also the other way around. I've always liked to think outside boxes, and speculative fiction gives me the canvas I need for that. I've had inspiration for stories while setting up a lab for my physics class, for example. And speculating about climate change in fiction has helped me in my current academic work, developing a transdisciplinary climate pedagogy at the intersection of science and society.

GM   Do you have a definition of science fiction that distinguishes it from other speculative fictions?

VS   Well, I don't really worry very much about definitions or categories – I leave that to the scholars! Because when I write a story it goes where it needs to. Much of the time it ends up being science fiction, at other times fantasy or some kind of amalgam. But the way I think of science fiction is really as a story where the science is an essential part of the unfolding of events, and where there's an extrapolation or an alternative to what we know of the universe today (hence the 'speculative' part).

GM   Do you remember how science fiction first captured your imagination? Was there a specific writer or story that hooked you?

VS   I read a lot of fantastic fiction as a kid, from tall tales and fairytales in Hindi to a bunch of trashy science fiction, and when I was around eleven, I found Isaac Asimov and Arthur C. Clarke, and later Ray Bradbury. But apart from books, I was lucky enough to have a childhood where I could develop a sense of wonder about the universe. My brother and I spent time climbing trees, exploring fields and ditches and urban wildernesses. I remember sleeping on the rooftop of my grandparents' house, looking up at the clear night sky full of stars, and wondering whether other life forms were looking back at me. But from my teens to my twenties, science fiction lost its enchantment for me, until I left India to go to the US for my PhD. The experience of being an alien on unfamiliar shores was so startling that it eventually took me back to science fiction. Later I discovered the works of Ursula K. Le Guin, and realized that science fiction could be much more than what

I'd read in my childhood. And it became quite natural to start writing it during a decade-long break from academia.

GM   Who would you say influenced you as a science fiction writer?

VS   I have multiple influences, in and outside science fiction. The classic Hindi writer Premchand, who was a social realist, classic Hindi film songs (a surprising number of them are about space travel!), poets such as Ghalib and Kalidasa and Sahir Ludhianvi. The Bengali writer Premendra Mitra, whom I've read in translation. Rokeya Sukhawat Hossain, who wrote a feminist utopia in 1905. Jorge Luis Borges and José Saramago in translation. In English, my single major influence is Ursula K. Le Guin: I was lucky enough to be among the upcoming writers in whom she took an interest; we corresponded occasionally over the years, and she provided crucial encouragement in my early days as a writer. But although I haven't read very widely in science fiction, mostly due to a lack of time, there are many other contemporary writers whose works I admire, including N. K. Jemisin and Nnedi Okorafor. There's an exciting new crop of writers from South Asia too. We also have many more writers from around the world whose stories are available in translation. It is exciting to be part of a larger and more diverse ecosystem of influences!

GM   Do you think that growing up in India gives you a different perspective on the genre than your American peers?

VS   Yes, growing up in India has definitely influenced my perspective on science fiction, both as a writer and a reader. I have multiple personal and professional ties to India and spend as much time there as I can, even though I have been based on the US for a while. It's hard to describe what a different experience it was for me, growing up in India in the 1970s and 1980s, before globalization changed everything. It was only after coming to the US as a graduate student, where I felt like an alien who had landed on another world, that I could begin to process my experience growing up in Delhi and my home state of Bihar. Among other things, I started to understand how my life had been shaped by colonialism, even though I had been born after Indian independence. I was raised in a large family that was full of stories, not just the oral tales of epics handed down over millennia, but also family stories, such as my grandmother's participation in the Salt Satyagraha, my great-uncle's imprisonment in a British jail. I remember the fervour of nation-building, the sense of service and dedication of my father and grandfather, who were in government; the family culture was about simplicity in the Gandhian tradition, and early on we kids were taught that the caste system was wrong. There were contradictions. I went to an English medium school, for instance, and read a lot of books in English. But stories abounded everywhere, even on a visit to the vegetable market with my mother. People's lives weren't compartmentalized. We lived in webs of interdependence and relationship. I had the chance to run wild as a child, with lots of unstructured time, so I got to know and befriend the local pariah dogs, birds and lizards, and to sense that they had stories too. I wrote painstakingly illustrated stories for my little sister. I don't mean to indulge in uncritical nostalgia – there were many things hidden from view that became apparent to me later – the way caste and class were entrenched in every aspect of life, for example. But growing up in India grew my writer's soul. I doubt I'd be a writer without that experience.

GM If someone reading this wanted to discover more Indian, or South Asian, science fiction literature, what would you recommend?

VS With regard to South Asian science fiction, I'm not an expert, but there are multiple resources now, including translations. I learned near the beginning of my career as a writer that there is a tradition of Bengali science fiction dating back to the 1850s. It's been a wonderfully decolonizing experience for me to discover the roots of Indian science fiction, to have the chance to write back to my own ancestors, so to speak. But also there is much going on in contemporary science fiction in India in multiple languages. In Anglophone Indian science fiction, there are the classic bilingual writers like Jayant Narlikar and Satyajit Ray, then we have writers like Rimi B. Chatterjee, Manjula Padmanabhan, followed by my contemporaries like Anil Menon, being joined by a wave of new talent, for example Indrapramit Das, Mimi Mondal, Gautam Bhatia, Sami Ahmad Khan, to name just a few. But probably the best resource to start with for a bird's eye view is *New Horizons: The Gollancz Book of South Asian Science Fiction* (2019), edited by Tarun Saint, and also Mimi Mondal's 'A Short History of South Asian Speculative Fiction' articles (available on Tor.com), which are a very useful condensed history of South Asian science fiction.

GM Do you think that living and working in the US as an immigrant – an 'alien', as you describe it – informs your writing and your sense of what makes something science fictional?

VS Yes, indeed, being uprooted from one's home makes you look at both the new shores and the place you left behind in a different way. The familiar becomes strange, and the strange, familiar, which is, after all, exactly what science fiction does! You start to notice things you took for granted back home, which were part of the environs and therefore invisible. And in the new place, you are less susceptible to the things people take for granted here, because you know that alternatives exist. So that tension between the familiar and the strange, both of which are changing all the time, makes for a good creative space.

GM Your science background is in physics, specifically in particle physics, and that's perhaps visible in some of your earlier work – in the use of mathematics in your earlier novella 'Distances', for example. In more recent years you've turned your attention more to issues relating to climate change. Can you say a few words about the importance of this change of focus for you as a scientist and how it affects your approach to your work as a science fiction writer?

VS In a way the change in my writing focus might seem to mirror the change in my work in science. I had a brief career in theoretical particle physics, then was in exile from academia for ten years, after which returning to the same field is well-nigh impossible. But through my work at a university where teaching is important,

I began to get worried about climate change, and started my journey of learning climate science, with a view to teaching it in my general physics classes. I learned very quickly that climate science, although endlessly fascinating, does not by itself motivate people to the right kind of action. So it led me to a reconceptualization of climate change through a transdisciplinary lens, centred on justice. This work is at the intersection of science, pedagogy and activism. Since science fiction is transdisciplinary by definition, it is natural to play with ideas related to climate change and other social-environmental problems through story.

But it's not as though I've abandoned the kinds of fiction where physics or mathematics is the main focus. In my 2018 collection, *Ambiguity Machines and Other Stories*, there are a couple of reprints, 'Sailing the Antarsa' and 'Peripeteia', both of which involve a creative play of ideas in the realm of theoretical physics. I will never lose interest in my original field!

GM   Some people consider science fiction to be 'escapism'. I'd like to know your thoughts on a label like that and whether you think science fiction can offer meaningful contributions to our approaches to the scientific and social problems that face our societies.

VS   I believe it was Ursula K. Le Guin who said something to the effect that when our imagination is imprisoned, if we value freedom, then we have a duty to escape and to take as many people along with us as possible (from her collection of essays, *The Language of the Night*, 1979). There's such a thing as 'anaesthetizing the mind', which is what we do when we binge watch or binge read meaningless drivel, and then there's *escape* from the realities of life under the globalized criminal conspiracy that has brought us climate change and pandemics and the destruction of biodiversity, not to mention the plodding, humdrum, grinding nature of existence for most people not privileged by the current system. While speculative fiction often reproduces the status quo, at its best it can take the imagination to places outside the epistemological garrison, where we might experience, if only for a moment, other possibilities. It is this subversive undermining of the current default reality that is speculative fiction's greatest potential. If we just stop at the temporary, personal escape through story, we are unlikely to make a difference in the real world, but sometimes that experience of alterity can inspire meaningful change. After all, our paradigms are shored up by narratives, and different narratives, if powerful enough and viral enough, can at the very least inspire us to rebel.

GM   If you were going to direct people to one story you've written, which would it be?

VS   I wouldn't! I write across a spectrum of interests and concerns, so the reader would not get much of an idea of my work through just one story. So how about a compromise? I'll name three, without any pressure to read all three (or even one): 'Ambiguity Machines: An Examination' (2015), 'Requiem' (2018), 'Widdam' (2018).

ALIENS AND ALIENATION

ALIEN SPECULATION: SCIENCE, FICTION AND THE FUTURE

AMANDA REES

Are we such apostles of mercy as to complain if the Martians warred in the same spirit?

H. G. Wells, *The War of the Worlds* (1897)

← Illustration by Alex Andreev, *Solaris*, 2016.

1. *District 9*, directed by Neill Blomkamp, 2009, depicts aliens forced to live in a compound in Johannesburg, in a metaphorical analogue to the segregation and dehumanization of people of colour in apartheid South Africa.

The strangest thing about twenty-first century aliens is that they are so often considered to be strange. Believing in aliens is frequently taken as the mark of an unsound mind or a disordered imagination: a signal that someone need not be taken seriously, or has an unhealthy absorption in fringe media. But the existence of extraterrestrial life – even of extraterrestrial intelligence – is something that many scientists take very seriously indeed. Aliens play an extremely important role in the human imagination. They are, and have been, central to the philosophical and empirical investigation of the world around us, and they tell us more than we might like to know about the limits of our own humanity.

The War of the Worlds, H. G. Wells's account of alien invaders landing in the heart of London's commuter belt, first appeared in 1897. It has never been out of print, and has inspired numerous sequels (authorized and illicit), radio, television and film adaptations, comic books and at least one album. It was one of the first alien invasion stories to catch the public imagination, and it can be read on a number of levels. On the one hand, it is a cautionary tale about natural selection and 'survival of the fittest'. The Martians are militarily and cognitively superior to their helpless human opponents, who are wholly incapable of fighting back; human survival is ensured only by the lucky chance that Martian biology is susceptible to Terran bacteria. On the other, it's a warning against complacency about national security and a resource for technological innovation. Wells's descriptions of Martian weaponry, for example, prefigure many twentieth-century developments in military technology, and the story is known to have inspired the young Robert Goddard, who went on to become a crucial figure in the development of rocketry and crewed space travel.

At the heart of the book, though, is one simple question, echoed across science fiction – Liu Cixin's *Remembrance of Earth's Past* trilogy (地球往事, 2008–10) is just one recent example, the shattered ruins of New York City in the video game *Crysis 2*'s post-alien invasion future another. In the opening pages, Wells's narrator reflects on the motives of the invaders, and concludes:

> Before we judge of them too harshly, we must remember what ruthless and utter destruction our own species has wrought, not only upon animals, such as the vanished bison and the dodo, but upon its inferior [sic] races. The Tasmanians, in spite of their human likeness [sic], were entirely swept out of existence in a war of extermination waged by European immigrants, in the space of fifty years. Are we such apostles of mercy as to complain if the Martians warred in the same spirit?

Aliens, in this reading, are a threat quite simply because they are powerful enough to treat white Europeans as they have treated other communities. Rather than equal participants in negotiated debate or diplomacy, humans are at best irrelevant, at worst a hindrance to alien plans for the Earth. In some cases, such as Andre Norton's early twentieth-century military science fiction, Tanya Huff's *Confederation of Valor* series (2000–) or the *Half Life* video games (1998–), humans are permitted to live on as mercenaries, cannon fodder or servant populations in alien wars. In others, from Raccoona Sheldon's 'The Screwfly Solution' (1977) and Octavia E. Butler's *Xenogenesis/ Lilith's Brood* trilogy (1987–89) to Tade Thompson's *Wormwood* series (2016–19), the alien future is one that is decidedly posthuman. Often, as with Liu's Trisolarian aliens, alien extermination of humanity can be seen as just retribution for the crimes some human cultures have committed against others – not to mention against the rest of the planet.

By the time Wells was writing, Mars and its (potential) inhabitants had already been the inspiration for much scientific speculation. In 1877, during a 'planetary opposition', or close approach between Earth and Mars, the Italian astronomer Giovanni Schiaparelli was able to observe a series of 'canali' on the planetary surface.

3

2. Brazilian artist Henrique Alvim Corrêa's illustrations for H. G. Wells's *The War of the Worlds,* for the French translation published in 1906.
3. *Mars Attacks!,* directed by Tim Burton, 1996.

What, after all, are all those lights in the sky actually for?

At a time when American and European governments and businesses were closely engaged in significant imperial engineering projects (including both the Suez and the Panama canals), it was taken for granted that any civilized society would be both willing and able to reconfigure the natural world to meet their own needs. Understandably, perhaps, the next planetary opposition in 1894 saw vastly increased public interest in the possibility that these channels were actually irrigation canals, taking water from the Martian ice caps to the drier equator to support agriculture there. Percival Lowell, an American mathematician and astronomer, did much to develop this theory in a series of three books published from 1895 to 1908, which argued explicitly for the existence of life on the red planet.

Wells was not the only writer to explore the nature and extent of Martian life in the early twentieth century – nor the only one to assume that life on the red planet was older, more evolved and more powerful than humanity. In *Stowaway to Mars* (1936), John Wyndham described the red planet as populated by intelligent machines, built by an ancient Martian race to support the next stage in the evolution of their species. Robert A. Heinlein's *Red Planet* (1949) and *Stranger in a Strange Land* (1961) showed a Martian civilization that had advanced so far beyond any human moral or technological achievements that inter-species communication was impossible. But by the 1970s, NASA's Mariner programmes had shown the Martian surface to be dry and barren: the adventurers in Heinlein's later book, *The Number of the Beast* (1980), had to travel to an alternate dimension to find life on Mars. Writers soon adapted to the new normal, and in the 1990s novels by Ben Bova, Kim Stanley Robinson and Gregory Benford explored ways in which humans could colonize and terraform Mars. Intriguingly, however, these later accounts often turned on the same themes of imperialism, exploitation and alienation that had characterized the earlier stories of Wells, Heinlein and Dick and which, in video games like *Red Faction* (2001), led to revolution and wars of independence.

Even in that earlier period, some scientists were clear that the 'canals' were just optical illusions. But belief in life on Mars in the early twentieth century was strong and widespread. In 1899/1900, the Pierre Guzman prize was established – 100,000 francs was on offer to the person

4. Mars as seen by the Hubble Space Telescope (right), compared with a map of Mars (left) based on French astronomer Eugene Antoniadi's observations in 1894. Antoniadi later concluded that what he had thought were Martian canals are an optical illusion.

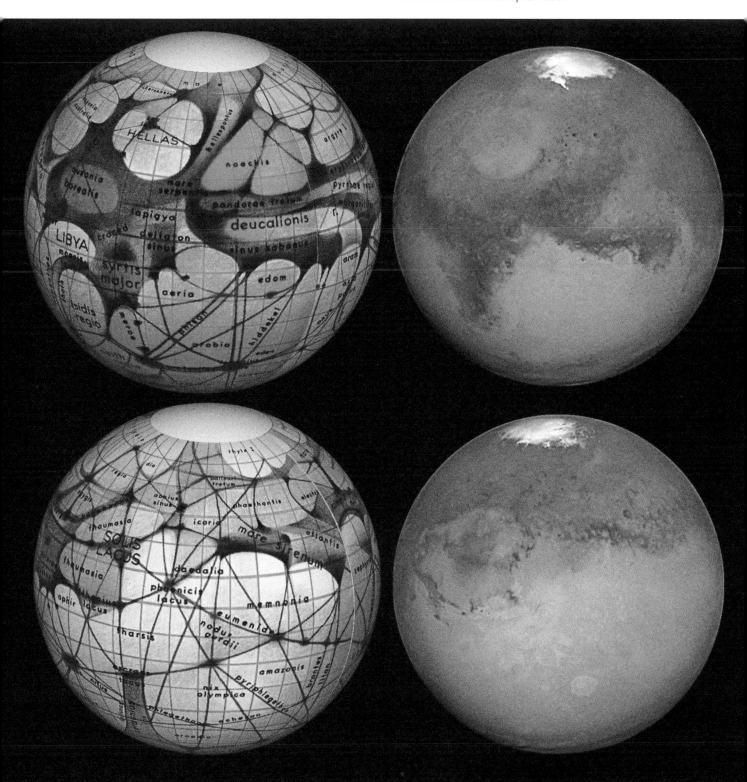

5. In *Close Encounters of the Third Kind*, directed by Steven Spielberg, 1977,
    the UFO is first encountered in the back roads of Indiana, flying so close
    as to burn the face of the electrician Roy Neary.

who could first succeed in making contact with a celestial body. Communication with Mars, however, didn't count. The planet was specifically excluded from this competition, since the existence of life there was taken for granted: the real question was whether there was life elsewhere. Two decades later, during the 1924 opposition between the two planets, a 'National Radio Silence Day' was declared in the United States. Radio stations nationwide would shut down for five minutes every hour on the hour for a thirty-six-hour period, so that a team from the US Naval Observatory, perched in a dirigible 2 miles (3.2 kilometres) up, could listen for and — with the aid of the Army's chief cryptographer — interpret Martian signals. Aliens were not the province of fantasists or fanatics; they were the focus of serious, sustained scientific and military attention.

A PLURALITY OF WORLDS?

This pervasive belief in alien existence did not appear out of thin air. The existence of life beyond Earth has been a critical aspect of scientific imagination for at least the past two-and-a-half millennia. What, after all, are all those lights in the sky actually for?

Many Greek philosophers believed that other worlds like our own were likely to exist. In fact, this concept of a plurality of worlds was fundamental to their conception of an infinite universe. The Pythagoreans and the Stoics both argued from the principle of plenitude (that what can exist, must somewhere exist) to show that in an infinite universe, there must be many worlds like ours. If such worlds exist, they argued, then they too must be populated by intelligent beings. They would, after all, not exist without a purpose. Augustine of Hippo's integration of the Aristotelian universe with Christian theology might have had little space for the existence of a plurality of worlds, but the Copernican Revolution, which placed the Sun, rather than the Earth, at the centre of the universe, once again opened the door to the possibility of extraterrestrial life. Galileo's observations of the mountains on the Moon and the moons of Jupiter demonstrated that, close-up, extraterrestrial bodies did, in fact, resemble the Earth. Johannes Kepler believed that the other planets were inhabited by other creatures, albeit creatures inferior to humankind.

6

7

By the early eighteenth century, belief in the existence of many populated worlds was well-established in both scholarly and public discourse. Books such as Bernard De Fontanelle's *Conversations on the Plurality of Worlds* (1686), Christian Huygens's *The Celestial Worlds Discover'd* (1698) and William Derham's *Astro-Theology* (1715) became bestsellers, to the point where opponents of organized religion like Thomas Paine could use the existence of extraterrestrial life as a stick with which to beat believers. If God had really become incarnate and sacrificed himself to save a sinful Earth, a sarcastic Paine pointed out, he would presumably have to do the same for all of the other worlds, travelling in never-ending cycles of birth, martyrdom and death. In response, the Scottish theologian Thomas Chalmers rather forlornly suggested that perhaps only on Earth was intelligent life sinful – a notion explored in depth by C. S. Lewis in *Out of the Silent Planet* (1938) and again by James Blish in his 1958 novel *A Case of Conscience*. Blish, in particular, considers the implications that contact with an alien race, who enjoy perfect morality despite having no connection to God, would have for Christianity. Conversely, Michael Bishop examined the other side of the argument – what would happen if Christ was not unique, and if each world had its own Saviour? – in his multiple-messiah novella 'The Gospel according to Gamaliel Crucis' (1983). The existence of extraterrestrial life was absolutely taken for granted in such debates.

Similar assumptions were made throughout the nineteenth century, despite the best efforts of key thinkers such as William Whewell and Alfred Russel Wallace to challenge them. Whewell pointed out that the existence of intelligent life was the exception, not the rule, for much of Earth's history – so why assume that intelligence or civilization must currently exist elsewhere? Wallace stressed the sheer number and complexity of the coincidences that had produced first life, and then intelligent life, on Earth – what were the odds, he asked, that these millions of modifications could have occurred twice, let alone again and again? In response, other scholars pointed (again) to the principle of plenitude and the infinity of the universe: in infinite space, anything is possible. But by the early twentieth century, a new theory about planetary origins was starting to take shape – one that seemed to place a limit on the numbers of possible inhabitable planets.

6. Cover art by Peter Curl for James Blish's *A Case of Conscience*, part of a small sub-genre of science fiction centred on Jesuit priests – in this instance, a priest who travels to an alien world and encounters an intelligent species who, despite having no concept of religion, have a perfect and innate sense of morality.

7. The Wardenclyffe Tower, Long Island, pictured here in 1908, was an early experimental wireless transmission station designed and built by Nikola Tesla.

8. The Andorians, one of *Star Trek*'s many alien species, who in 2161 became founding members of the United Federation of Planets – promoting equal rights for all sentient life.

8

9.　Robert Ruthven, *Sand Triangle* mixed-media collage print, 1998.
　　Digitally print for the set *Improbable Events*. Collaged from the artist's
　　paintings and photographs and NASA photographs from the Hubble
　　telescope, including nebulae, the series explores theories of complexity
　　and probability in the universe.

THE DRAKE EQUATION

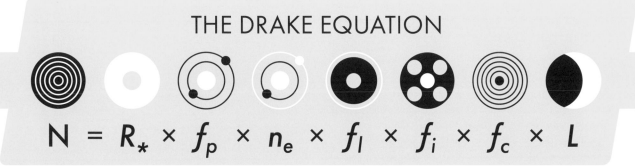

$$N = R_* \times f_p \times n_e \times f_l \times f_i \times f_c \times L$$

N The number of civilizations in the Milky Way galaxy whose electromagnetic emissions are detectable.	R_* The rate of formation of stars suitable for the development of intelligent life (number per year). f_p The fraction of those stars with planetary systems.	n_e The number of planets, per solar system, with an environment suitable for life. f_l The fraction of suitable planets on which life actually appears. f_i The fraction of life-bearing planets on which intelligent life emerges.	f_c The fraction of civilizations that develop a technology that produces detectable signs of their existence. **L** The average length of time such civilizations produce such signs (years).

The nebular hypothesis, whereby the solar system was thought to emerge out of a spinning cloud of dust, was the generally accepted theory for planetary formation during the nineteenth century, but in the early twentieth century the collision hypothesis began to gain ground. This theory speculated that planets had formed as a result of the close approach by some other star to the Sun – an event that would logically make extra-solar planets, and hence aliens, a fairly rare phenomenon.

The trouble with all of these debates, though, was that they were almost wholly theoretical. The existence of alien life might well be a taken-for-granted aspect of scientific world-views and paradigms – but could humans actually make contact with them? Nikola Tesla, the electrical entrepreneur expert in wireless technology, had in fact claimed in 1901 that he had heard signals through his telegraphic equipment, that 'had their origin in no mind native to this planet'. While the media had been fascinated by this prospect, few scientists took him seriously. But by the mid-twentieth century it seemed that, if scientists wanted to know what, or who, was out there, then they too needed to start listening.

ARE THEY OUT THERE? OR ARE THEY ALREADY HERE?

By the mid-twentieth century, the scientific status of extraterrestrials was shifting rapidly. No longer the focus of theoretical speculation, they were now firmly in the realm of empirical investigation. Tesla notwithstanding, 'National Radio Silence Day' had failed to detect any radio signals from Mars; but in 1959, Giuseppe Cocconi and Philip Morrison argued that it was not only possible, but likely, that alien civilizations had 'long ago...established a chain of communication' and were waiting patiently for 'answering signals from the Sun'. They published a paper in *Nature*, 'Searching for Interstellar Communication', which set out the frequencies that should be investigated.

In the years that followed, scholarly and public fascination with extraterrestrial life intensified sharply. In 1961, Frank Drake formulated the 'Drake equation', aiming to approximate the number of extraterrestrial civilizations that could potentially exist in our galaxy. Two years later, the BBC's time-travelling science-fiction series *Doctor Who* began broadcasting. Its apparently British hero is in actuality a Time Lord from the planet Gallifrey, who battles to protect humanity from the ultimate mechanical evil, the Daleks, among other existential threats. Also in 1963, Ohio State University's 'Big Ear' radio telescope, designed by the astronomy

10. A selection of classic *Doctor Who* villains, from left: a Wirrn, a Sontaran, a Super-Voc robot, a Zygon and, of course, a Dalek, wait in line for a US passport with the fourth Doctor, played by Tom Baker, and his robotic dog companion K-9, in 1978.

and engineering professor John D. Kraus and built by student labour to reduce costs, began listening for radio signals.

Cocconi and Morrison had, of course, initially suggested that aliens might also be listening out for us. By the early 1960s, many people in the US and Europe had gone a step further, and believed that aliens were not just monitoring but also visiting the Earth. In 1966, John Fuller hit the bestseller list with his book *The Incident at Exeter*, in which he described multiple sightings of an Unidentified Flying Object (UFO) near the town of Exeter, New Hampshire, by highly reputable witnesses. In the immediate aftermath of the Second World War, a new class of aerial phenomena seemed to be emerging. From the 'foo fighters' seen in Scandinavia to the 'flying saucers' observed by Kenneth Arnold in Washington State, more and more people were reporting seeing strange and unidentified objects in the sky. The Roswell incident of 1947, where the US Airforce was allegedly able to capture a flying saucer and its crew, is probably the most famous of the UFO encounters in North America – it is certainly the one that has resonated most in Western popular culture, from *The X Files* (1993–2002, 2016–18), to *Independence Day* (1996), to *Indiana Jones and the Kingdom of the Crystal Skull* (2008). But in the 1950s, it seemed that aliens were not just visiting – they had come with a purpose. What remained unclear was whether their purpose was to communicate with humans, or to harvest them.

The earliest widely publicized abduction event also happened in New Hampshire, where in 1961 Betty and Barney Hill claimed to have been abducted by little grey aliens (the same type of alien linked to Roswell). Although they reported the incident at the time, their case did not become well known until John Fuller wrote it up as *The Interrupted Journey*, the 1966 follow-up to his Exeter bestseller. The Hills became the archetypal victims of alien abduction: following them, later victims reported having no direct memory of the experience, but through hypnotic regression eventually recalling that they had been taken aboard a spacecraft and used for medical and reproductive experiments. The only direct evidence of the encounter was a period of unexplained 'missing time', as explored by the artist and ufologist Budd Hopkins in *Missing Time: A Documented Study of UFO Abductions* (1981).

11. Alien autopsy exhibit at the Roswell UFO Museum, New Mexico. In 1995, a 17-minute tape purporting to show an alien autopsy being undertaken by US government officials was released to great controversy. Its makers, Ray Santilli and Gary Shoefield, later executive-produced the comedy *Alien Autopsy* (2006) about the events.

The UFO phenomenon and the methodologies for investigating it had expanded rapidly. In 1972, the astronomer J. Allen Hynek had classified UFO sightings according to the amount of empirical evidence available – ranging from visual observation to radar confirmation, and including physical impact on the observers (paralysis, heat, scorched grass, dogs barking, electric lights failing). By the late 1980s, hypnosis and a sense on the part of the participants that they had been profoundly personally transformed by their experiences had become central to the story.

This was precisely the point explored by Steven Spielberg's 1977 film *Close Encounters of the Third Kind*. Science fiction films had for many years been eagerly engaged in considering the consequences that alien life might have for the human future – sometimes as a means of examining the relationship between technology and ecology (1976's *The Man Who Fell To Earth*), sometimes in relation to the threat that the military-industrial complex itself posed to human survival (*E.T.*, 1982, and later films such as *Contact*, 1997, and *Arrival*, 2016). Some films simply took alien intelligence as a given (the *Star Trek* and *Star Wars* franchises, for example), although these aliens often seemed profoundly human in their approach and appearance. Others – *Alien* (1979), *Predator* (1987) and their sequels – were absolutely clear that aliens posed an immediate threat to humanity. Still others (*Spaceballs*, 1987; *Earth Girls are Easy*, 1988) treated the whole subject as essentially ridiculous. But regardless of its precise role in the plot, by the late 1970s and 1980s, extraterrestrial life was playing an increasingly significant part in Western public culture.

At the same time, direct scientific interest in alien life was becoming rather more cautious. In 1971, NASA's Project Cyclops had designed an ambitious search for extraterrestrial life: this project was ultimately shelved on the grounds of cost. This didn't mean that NASA had ended its involvement with alien contact – the long-range space exploration missions of the 1970s were both sent out with messages to potential contactees (the *Pioneer* plaque and the *Voyager* Golden Records). Ohio State's 'Big Ear' had its Eureka! moment in 1977 when a very strong and unexplained signal was detected – but while the signal's origins remain unexplained, the event was not repeated.

In 1980, Carl Sagan and others founded the Planetary Society as a non-profit, private organization to support space exploration and the search for extraterrestrial life, and the concept of extraterrestrial life has continued to inform scientific research. James Lovelock's 'Gaia' hypothesis, for example, emerged from NASA's efforts to identify inhabited planets, in response to discussion of the kinds of signals a life-bearing planet would send though its biosphere, and how humans might go about detecting them.

PLANNING FOR ENCOUNTERS?

NASA funding for SETI (Search for Extraterrestrial Intelligence) was cut in 1993 – ironically the year after the existence of the first exoplanet was confirmed. Launched in 2009, the Kepler space telescope identified more than two thousand of these exoplanets before it was deactivated in 2018, and the search for signs of life within the solar system (on Mars, Europa, Enceladus – even Titan) using robot probes continues to this day. There are now established scientific disciplines such as astrobiology and space archaeology, complete with peer-reviewed journals and degree programmes, if not yet academic departments, devoted to extraterrestrial life. The identification and investigation of planets similar to Earth, along with the consideration of the environmental conditions that might permit life to emerge, is one of the key themes of the European Space Agency's Cosmic Vision 2015–25.

Extraterrestrial life and the related question of alien intelligence continues to be an important topic of scientific debate, as a meeting held at London's Royal Society in January 2010 demonstrated. This gathering explicitly discussed the current status of the search for life beyond Earth – and considered, in some depth, the consequences that its detection would have for both the sciences and for society more generally. The scholars assembled discussed chemical and kinetic strategies for identifying extraterrestrial life, as well as strategies for investigating Earth's 'shadow biosphere' – that is, the possibility that life on Earth might have evolved more than once – as a strategy for investigating the hypothesis that life is a cosmic imperative. They also considered the implications of first contact. Clearly, encountering alien life would involve some rearrangement of both scientific and religious worldviews – but more practically, what should humans

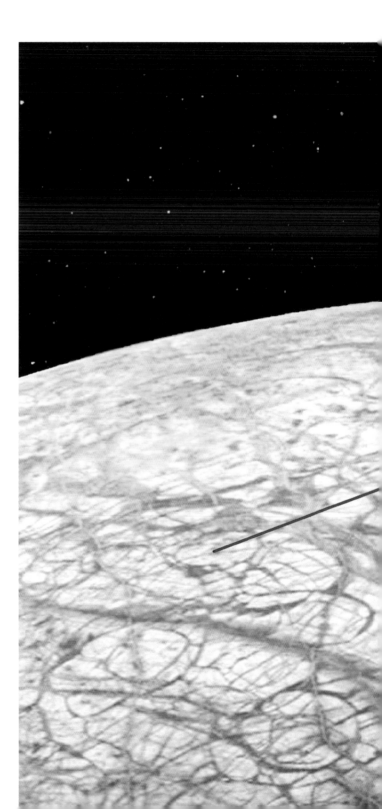

actually do if they meet aliens? Would there be worldwide
panic? Would decades of science-fictional depictions of
aliens as threat (*Mars Attacks!* – or even *The War of the
Worlds*) make it impossible for the threat to be assessed
dispassionately? Or would the news of microbes on
Europa be met with a shrug and no more than momentary
interest? In 2002, the astronomers Iván Almár and Jill
Tarter proposed the Rio scale, along similar lines to
the Richter scale, intended to measure the likely social
consequences of contact with extraterrestrial intelligence:
in London, writing with Margaret Race, Almar put forward
a revised version of the scale, classifying projected events
according to type of phenomenon, distance and means
of discovery. The London scale's focus was primarily on
assessing the scientific significance of a potential alien
contact; its secondary consideration of risk concentrated on
biohazard. The question of whether – or how – one might
try to actually *talk* to an alien intelligence was left open.

The issue of how one might achieve interstellar
communication (as opposed to contact) has been a
matter of debate since the mid-twentieth century, that
heyday of alien abductions. In a lecture given to the British
Interplanetary Society in the early 1960s, Lancelot Hogben,
an eminent zoologist and statistician, proposed using
numbers and shapes as the basis for a new language –
Astroglossa. His position was that one could be reasonably
confident that mathematics would represent a shared set
of referents both on and beyond Earth; twenty years later,
Carl Sagan similarly used prime numbers in his novel
Contact. But by and large, efforts to signal or otherwise
contact alien civilizations have tended to concentrate on
demonstrating to the aliens that intelligent, scientifically
and technologically engaged life exists on Earth. The 1974
'Arecibo message', which contained basic mathematical,
chemical and biological information, as well as graphical
depictions of the (male) human body and the solar system
itself, was just one of several attempts to do this. The two
'Cosmic Call' (1999 and 2003) messages, organized by
the Russian astronomer Aleksandr Zaitzev and broadcast
from Yevpatoria, Ukraine, similarly contained a mixture of
information about the natural world and humanity, while
the 'Teen-Age' message (2001), created by a group of
Russian teenagers under the guidance of Zaitzev (who felt
that art must be part of any interstellar message) was set

12. NASA's *Europa Clipper* is a satellite that will perform a close fly-by of Jupiter's icy moon, Europa, in 2030; the next step in determining whether it can support microbial life.

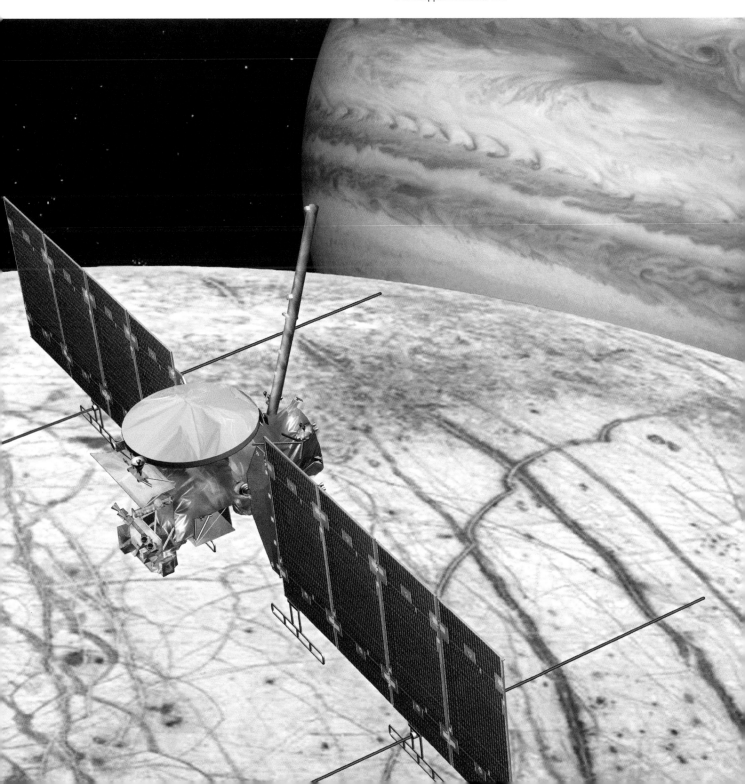

13. *The Man Who Fell
to Earth*, directed by
Nicholas Roeg, 1976,
based on the 1963 novel
by Walter Tevis. David
Bowie played Thomas
Jerome Newton, an
extraterrestrial who
comes to Earth to find
water to save the people
of his home planet,
who are experiencing
a catastrophic drought.
To achieve his aims and
to blend into human
society, Newton patents
his advanced technology,
becoming head of a
powerful company.

Sensory tendrils around ears, eyes, mouth and breathing slits on throat (closed during speech). These are tough fibres that protect delicate openings and intensify sensory input.

Octavia E. Butler, notes made for the Oankali, 1980s

out in three parts – including information delivered using a musical instrument, the theremin. In each of these, scientific information is used as a communication 'Rosetta Stone' to aid the aliens in interpreting and responding.

It's ironic that this dependence on the cryptographic capacities of aliens in many ways reflects the efforts by scientists to communicate with non-human intelligences on Earth. Also in the mid-twentieth century, zoologists and psychologists devoted considerable time and effort to teaching great apes and cetaceans to 'talk' to humans. In fact, intriguingly, one of the scientists at Frank Drake's inaugural SETI meeting in 1961 was John C. Lilly, who was in the process of becoming (in)famous for his work with dolphins. The trouble with many of these approaches, however, was that they took human language as the standard, and tried to find ways of enabling non-humans to approximate communication within it. In a similar way, the key plot element in David Brin's *Uplift* series (1980–98) was the fact that humanity had successfully 'uplifted' dolphins and chimpanzees to the level of human intelligence.

But what if we could imagine a more-than-human intelligence? Other approaches – Laurance Doyle's work with humpback whales, for example, or Dorothy Cheney and Robert Seyfarth's observations of vervet monkeys – have sought to identify patterns in non-human communication. That is to say, rather than focusing on what non-humans might want to say to humans, these research projects try to understand the signals that other species of sentient beings give to each other. In the case of Doyle, it's hoped that this project might have direct implications for the kinds of signal to look for in SETI programmes.

ALIENS AND ALIENATION

It is undeniably difficult to imagine non-human intelligence. One of the best examples of this in fiction can be found in William Golding's *The Inheritors* (1955), which explores an imagined first encounter between early human beings and a group of Neanderthals. Golding's depiction of the kinaesethetic, hyper-communal intelligence of these quasi-human beings is disturbing and difficult: how much more distressing might it be to conceive of a wholly alien way of being? And what would communicating, empathizing, with something so alien do to our own humanity?

But there is another way to think about aliens, both in terms of science and science fiction. H. G. Wells deliberately used a story about alien invasion to reflect on the morality of European treatment of the people they sought to colonize. The film *District 9* (2009) focused on the forced ghettoization of alien refugees by the South African government, using the non-human in order to raise questions about the historical context of apartheid and dehumanization, while itself being heavily criticized for its stereotypical portrayals of Black South African characters. In the same year, James Cameron's *Avatar* drew on the history of European imperialism to explore the relationship between capitalism and environmentalism.

One of the strangest things about regarding aliens as strange or strangers is the fact that most fictional explorations of aliens in fact reflect relationships between human communities. *Star Trek* was famously conceived by Gene Roddenberry as a living demonstration that humanity could eventually mature beyond racial tensions, although again, the extent to which this was achieved is controversial. The translator and communications officier Lieutenant Nyota Uhura, born in the United States of Africa, was a constant and very visible presence on the bridge; in the role, Nichelle Nichols was praised by Dr Martin Luther King Jr for her visible demonstration that Black professional women had a future. As Whoopi Goldberg (herself to star in *Trek*'s *The Next Generation*) put it, 'There's a Black lady on TV, and she ain't no maid!' But the original crew still had a tendency to encounter alien communities that looked an awful lot like early colonial depictions of indigenous people – as in, for example, the episode 'The Paradise Syndrome' – and to casually depict them as non-technological, 'undeveloped' societies in much the same way as indigenous communities were caricatured as 'backward' and marginalized by Euro-Americans.

Star Trek's stories about alien life in the far future are, according to its creators, intended to make the audience confront uncomfortable truths in the human present. The show has also raised some interesting questions about the nature of alien communication – see, for example, the aliens who speak only in culturally specific memes in the Next Generation episode 'Darmok' (1991) – 'Darmok and Jalad at Tanagra!' – as well as making the key point that, if aliens do come calling, as in 'The Voyage Home', then out of all the species on Earth, why do we assume that they'd want to talk to us, as opposed to humpback whales? Would they value our 'intelligence'? Or would they, as in Octavia E. Butler's *Xenogenesis/ Lilith's Brood* trilogy, despise our hierarchical tendencies? The Oankali are described in Butler's notes for her series as having 'sensory tendrils around ears, eyes, mouth and breathing slits on throat (closed during speech). These are tough fibres that protect delicate openings and intensify sensory input.' They are clearly similar enough that interspecies communication is possible, but alien enough that Lilith Iyapo, Butler's lead character, is at first repulsed by them. In the post-nuclear world of the books, they are busy harvesting the last resources from a dying Earth. Surviving humans have been sterilized by the aliens: their next generation can be produced only by sharing genetic information with the Oankali. In this trade, the aliens will eugenically prune the human characteristics they consider dangerous (the lethal combination of intelligence and hierarchical aggression) and keep the elements they value (our 'talent' for cancer). Biological hybridity is our only hope for the post-human future.

And who is 'we' in all of this? Lilith is clearly a Black woman – but Warner Books's initial cover art for the first book in the trilogy, *Dawn* (1987) depicted two white women. So many of these alien narratives derive from Euro-American sources, a culture with a long and inglorious history of treating other communities as non-human, of literally alienating them from their lands, their resources and their languages. Putting the study of extraterrestrial aliens in the context of imperial histories can make for very uncomfortable thinking, for Western audiences – as, indeed, H. G. Wells intended back in 1897. Perhaps, as cartoonist Bill Watterson once put it, 'the surest sign that intelligent life exists elsewhere in the Universe is that none of it has tried to contact us'. Or perhaps anyone engaged in planning for alien contact might be best advised to seek out new narratives.

→ Humpback whales (*Megaptera novaeangliae*) socializing. The astrophysicist Laurance Doyle, lead researcher at SETI, uses information theory and statistical analysis to try to understand the languages of Humpback whales, with the intent of broadening our understanding of how languages work in other species so that we may be better equipped to recognize an alien language if we ever receive a transmission.

14. *District 9*, directed by Neill Blomkamp, 2009.

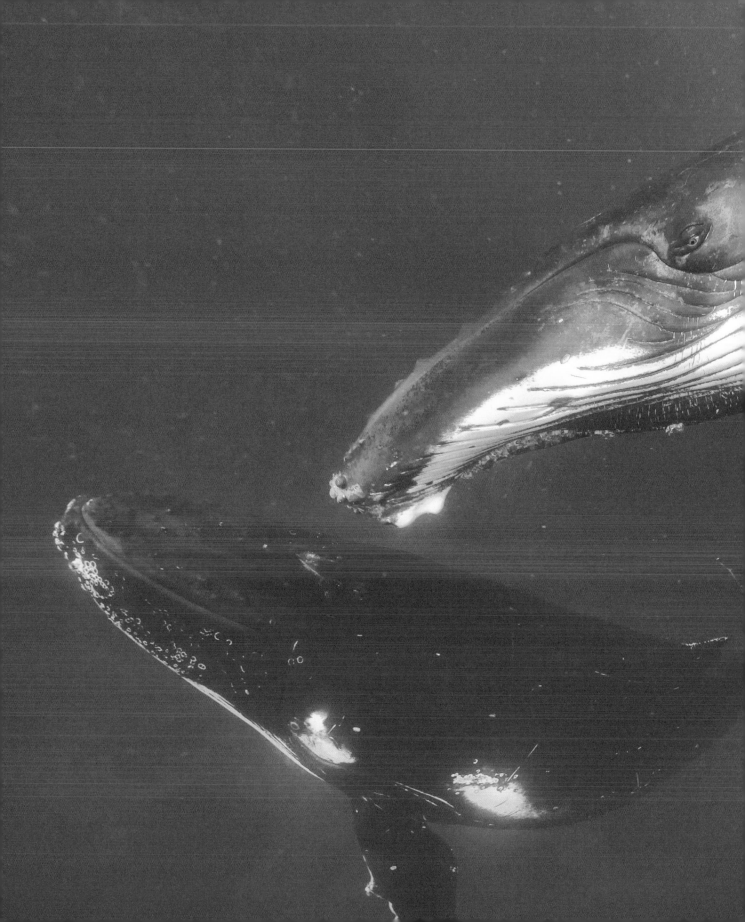

INFINITE DIVERSITY: PLEASURES OF THE UNKNOWN

GLYN MORGAN

1. The microscopic world has continued to be a source of both fascination and horror, as in this 1842 cartoon by J. J. Grandville in response to the second cholera pandemic of 1829–49, which is believed to have caused more deaths more quickly than any other disease in the nineteenth century. Grandville depicts a microscopic menagerie of creatures, overpowered and devoured by the monstrous *Cholder vibrio*.

What does it mean to be or, indeed, not to be? I am a singular organism, a mammal, a human. Like most other living things I take in air, water and nutrients to metabolize energy and I dispose of the waste products. I do this to continue to live, to exist, to thrive. And yet, like you, reading this, I am more than a single being.

Each of us is an ecosystem, a microbiome for a vast array of bacteria, fungi, viruses and other tiny organisms on our skin, in our gut and other organs; all generally kept in balance, but too many or too few and we become unstable. We are reliant on those miniscule organisms to perform the basic functions of our existence.

Scientific interest in the miniscule began in earnest in the seventeenth century, with the publication of the first scientific bestseller, Robert Hooke's *Micrographia*, by the Royal Society in 1665. This opened up an entire new realm of observation for what was then called 'Natural Philosophy', a smaller world beyond our natural perceptions. At the same time, advances in telescope technologies were opening up the vastness of space; in 1668, Isaac Newton, later a president of the Royal Society, constructed the first working reflecting telescope, offering unparalleled clear views of distant planets and moons.

The work of the Royal Society laid some of the foundations for modern science, but it was also subject to criticism. The writer, poet and natural philosopher Margaret Cavendish, a contemporary of Hooke and Newton, was the first woman to be admitted to attend Royal Society lectures and experiments (albeit not as a member). Depending on how one defines science fiction, she may be able to lay claim to being the first writer in the genre, preceding Mary Shelley by some 150 years. Her novel *The Blazing World* (1666) engages with the ideas of contemporary natural philosophy and sees its protagonist

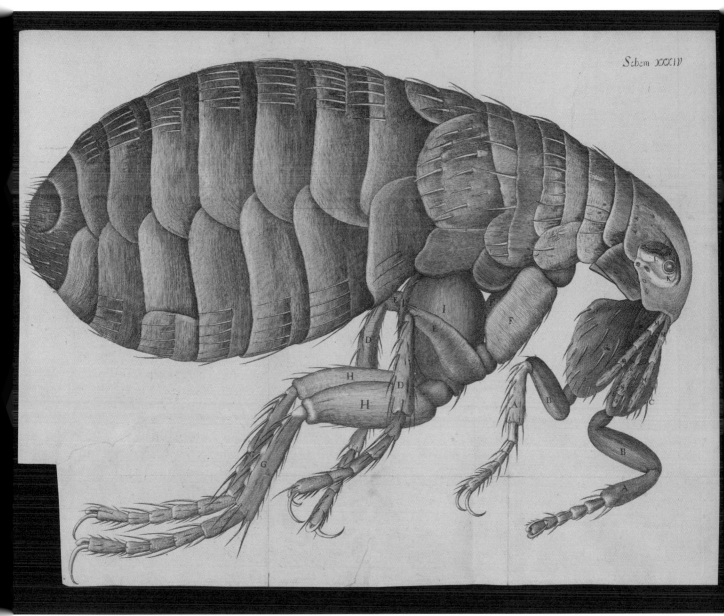

Schem XXXIV

2. Robert Hooke's *Micrographia* (1665) introduced a world on another scale; perhaps the most famous of its illustrations is his diagram of the anatomy of a flea.

3. Portrait of Margaret Cavendish in the frontispiece to her *Grounds of Natural Philosophy* (1668). The image is also used as frontispiece to some editions of *The Blazing World* (1666).

travel to another world accessible from ours only at the pole. This world is filled with anthropomorphic animals who see the narrator as divine and make her their Empress. Each creature specializes in different skills: the spider-men are mathematicians, the bear-men natural philosophers, the parrot-men orators, and so on. Each group shows her the greatest advances in their fields and she passes judgment on them all. In one scene, the bear-men attempt to use telescopes to observe celestial bodies:

> [T]hese Telescopes caused more differences and divisions amongst them, then ever they had before... the Empress began to grow angry at their Telescopes, that they could give no better Intelligence; for said she, now I do plainly perceive, that your Glasses are false Informers, and instead of discovering the Truth, delude your Senses; Wherefore I command you to break them, and...trust only their natural eyes, and examine Celestial Objects by the motions of their own Sense and Reason.

The Blazing World was written as a companion piece to Cavendish's Observations Upon Experimental Philosophy, included in order to expand her audience, because 'most Ladies take no delight in Philosophical Arguments'. Combined, the two books show that she was greatly dismissive of the observations recorded by Hooke and his fellows, feeling that advances in microscopes and telescopes had placed too much emphasis on observing the surface of things and not enough on understanding their hidden inner (often spiritual) depths.

Similarly critical, but more openly satirical, is another famous piece of proto-science fiction: Jonathan Swift's novel Gulliver's Travels, or Travels into Several Remote Nations of the World (1726), better known simply as Gulliver's Travels. Now perhaps best remembered as a staple of abridged children's classics, this satire takes square aim at topics from religion to the travel and exploration writing of its day. Among Swift's targets are the men of the Royal Society. The famous scenes of tiny Lilliputians and gigantic Brobdingnagians are themselves likely extrapolations of the observations of men like Hooke and Newton, but the truly biting satire comes in the less commonly recalled third part of the novel,

3

The Empress began to grow angry at their Telescopes, that they could give no better Intelligence.

Margaret Cavendish, The Blazing World (1666)

4

in which Gulliver visits the flying island of Laputa and from there travels to the Academy of Lagado. While the nation in which it sits is desperately poor, the Academy of Lagado is lavishly funded in its pursuit of knowledge, with experiments ranging from the extraction of sunbeams from cucumbers, changing faeces back into food, and work on 'The Engine' a large calculating machine and proto-computer that pre-dates Charles Babbage's Difference Engine by a century. Needless to say, none of the experiments produced any results or benefitted anyone in any way.

Despite these early instances of scepticism, science and science fiction have not lost their fascination with scale. One has only to think of the powerful ending of the 1957 film *The Incredible Shrinking Man*, the script adapted by Richard Matheson from his own novel *The Shrinking Man*. Having been exposed to a combination of rare chemicals and nuclear radiation, Scott Carey finds himself shrinking a few centimetres a day. Despite all the efforts of modern medicine, doctors and scientists are only able to slow the process. After a series of mishaps involving a house cat and then, still smaller, a spider, Scott is missing, presumed dead by his family. Overcoming his despair, he realizes that he has a unique opportunity to see things no human has ever witnessed, as he shrinks beyond visible perception, beyond even the domain of matter:

> [I]n that moment I knew the answer to the riddle of the infinite. I had thought in terms of man's own limited dimension. I had presumed upon nature. That existence begins and ends is man's conception, not nature's. And I felt my body dwindling, melting, becoming nothing. My fears melted away, and in their place came acceptance. All this vast majesty of creation, it had to mean something. And then I meant something too. Yes, smaller than the smallest, I meant something too. To God, there is no zero. I still exist.

The 'quantum realm' has continued to play a pivotal plot role in some of the biggest box-office movies ever made, thanks to the shrinking powers of the superhero Ant-Man (created by Stan Lee, Larry Leiber and Jack Kirby in 1962) and his role in the Marvel Cinematic Universe. Sometimes it seems that the more we learn about the universe, whether the very small or the incredibly vast,

4. Extracting sunshine from cucumbers is just one of the activities that occupies the careers of the researchers at the Academy of Lagado in *Gulliver's Travels* by Jonathan Swift (1726).

5. Difference Engine No. 2, designed by Charles Babbage, 1847–49. This engine was built by the Science Museum, completed in June 1991.

6. Grant Williams in *The Incredible Shrinking Man*, directed
   by Jack Arnold, 1957.
7. Sketch for Cthulhu by H. P. Lovecraft, 1934.

the more questions are raised. Science fiction sometimes tries to address these questions with hypothetical answers, tying up solutions with neat narrative bows. But sometimes, too, it can accept that not everything is comprehensible to the human mind – or at least not yet.

A common criticism of aliens in science fiction is how relatable they are. The creatures in the cantina sequence in *Star Wars* were a revelation in 1977 for how strange they all looked, but ultimately they are nearly all bipedal, with two arms and two eyes. Even when the limb numbers change they generally conform to a certain level of familiarity. After all, one relatively small bar is capable of stocking suitable drinks and entertainment for all of them. The irony of this chapter's title is that 'infinite diversity in infinite combinations' is the basis of philosophy for *Star Trek*'s Vulcan race, who, despite their pointy ears, green blood, pon farr reproductive cycle and adherence to logic, are themselves very close to being human – certainly closer than most Vulcans would be happy to admit. Need alien life be so familiar?

The terror of unknowability is territory well staked out by the horror genre, perhaps most iconically in H. P. Lovecraft's Cthulhu mythos. But in science fiction the unknown can just as easily be a source of wonder. Arthur C. Clarke's *Rendezvous with Rama* (1973) depicts humanity in the 2130s as a spacefaring multi-planet civilization with colonies on the Moon, Mars, Mercury and elsewhere. The novel focuses on the arrival of an object from outside the solar system, too perfectly formed to be natural. As it comes closer, it becomes obvious that it is the artificial product of another civilization, and humanity's first proof of intelligent life elsewhere in the cosmos. A crew is scrambled to intercept the object, given the name Rama after the Hindu aspect of Vishnu (astronomers having exhausted the Greco-Roman pantheons as they catalogued the solar system), as it races through the solar system on a trajectory that will see it tightly orbit the Sun and then race out into interstellar space once more. The book received a resurgence of interest in 2017 when the Haleakalā Observatory in Hawai'i detected object 1I/2017 U1, which was eventually named 'Oumuamua, from the Hawaiian word for 'scout' (the name Rama was proposed but not accepted). 'Oumuamua was the first interstellar object

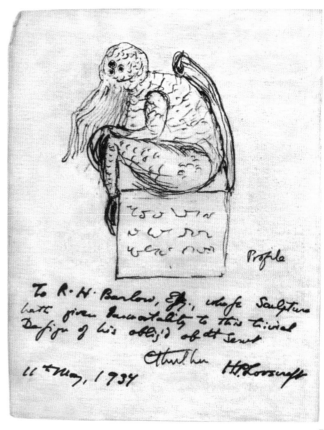

7

Science fiction has always existed in a delicate balancing point between explaining the world, and leaving enough mystery.

ever identified visiting our solar system; like Rama, it entered our neighbourhood and exited it so quickly that we barely had time to study it, and astronomers cannot be certain of its origins or composition.

In Clarke's novel, the human astronaut–explorers successfully dock with and penetrate the interior of Rama, discovering a vast hollow space of unknown metallic materials that resemble cities and plains, but whose actual purposes remain inscrutable. The interior gradually comes to life as Rama approaches the Sun, with peculiar biomechanical organisms beginning to emerge and perform various functions, but the crew's insights into what is going on remain limited. As Rama passes perihelion, its closest point to the Sun, and begins its exit from the solar system, the humans have to depart and the interior activity returns to a state of inactivity, without the explorers ever having definitively worked out the purpose of anything – including Rama itself. This may seem narratively unsatisfying, but Clarke manages instead to create an overwhelming feeling of awe in the face of the unknown. The mystery is the point, and it does not need to be solved (sequels notwithstanding).

Science fiction has always existed in a delicate balancing point between explaining the world, and leaving enough mystery to suggest a wider world beyond the confines of the narrative. Prior to *Prometheus* (2012) the colossal 'space jockey' corpse of the pilot in the original *Alien* (1979), completely unexplained in the film or its sequels, had been a fan favourite, not least because of the iconic and rich character design work of H. R. Giger.

The Polish writer Stanisław Lem produced one of the archetypal examples of this kind of mystery alien in his novel *Solaris* (1961), in which the titular planet is being studied by humans on an orbiting space station. The ocean that dominates the planet's surface is a living entity capable of forming shapes and forms, even drawing them from the minds of the observer through a psychic connection. While the human characters draw their own conclusions based on their interactions with these simulacra of both people and places, the true meaning and intent (if any) of the alien ocean is deliciously ambiguous. *Solaris* is a rebuke to the anthropomorphic and familiar science fictional alien, but it's also a challenge

8. Artist's concept of the asteroid 1I/2017 U1 ('Oumuamua), discovered in 2017. This asteroid is the first to be confirmed as having originated around another star.

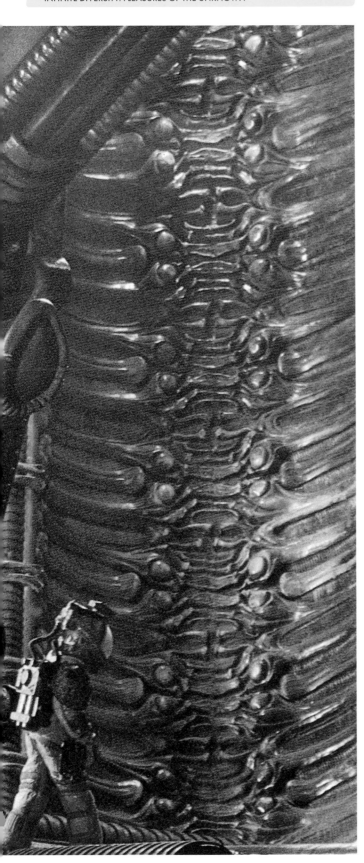

9. The pilot corpse from Ridley Scott's *Alien* (1979), designed by H. R. Giger.

to our collective ego: 'How do you expect to communicate with the ocean', asks one character, 'when you can't even understand one another?'

More recently, Kameron Hurley's *The Stars Are Legion* (2017) features alien life forms known as 'worlds', vast organisms that are both the ship and progenitor of everything they contain: when the ship needs a new crew member, one is born from the ship; when the ship needs a new gear, a crew member becomes pregnant and gives birth to a gear. A completely single-sex society (all-female) exists on the worlds in a delicately balanced ecosystem. For all the politicking and personal struggle of the human protagonists, the worlds remain more complex and unknowable than they can fully comprehend. In the video game *Control* (2019), the strangeness is reflected back onto our own world through a secret government agency, the 'Federal Bureau of Control', who gather devices and objects from around the world that are imbued with strange properties and powers. The Bureau is overseen by a mysterious, heterogenous entity known only as 'The Board' that resides in a separate plane of existence from our own. The rich game world, which draws heavily on modernist architecture styles and juxtaposes brutalist order with geometric chaos, posits a multidimensional reality of which, iceberg-like, we are only able to observe a small proportion.

What common frames of reference might we have with a creature that exists as a space-faring world, or a planet-scale ocean? Or with a species capable of manipulating matter, time, or the dimensions of reality in ways we can't even understand? Why do we presume that these aliens would be any more interested in us than most of us are in entomology? This latter question is explored in a number of science-fictional works, including the pilot episode of the original *Star Trek*, 'The Cage' (1965), in which the captain of the *Enterprise* – Pike, not yet Kirk – is imprisoned to be studied by the large-brained, psychic and emotionally cold Talosians. In the psychedelic French-Czech animated film *Fantastic Planet* (*La Planète sauvage*/ *Divoká planeta*, 1973), the humans, or 'Oms', are kept as pets and fauna by the gigantic, blue-skinned Traags. Another famous example is the protagonist of Kurt Vonnegut's semi-autobiographical novel *Slaughterhouse-Five* (1969), Billy Pilgrim, who is kept in a zoo on an

10. Alex Chinneck's melting house *A Pound of Flesh for 50p*, shown as part of Merge Festival, London, 2014. In *Roadside Picnic* by Arkady and Boris Strugatsky (Пикник на обочине, 1972), the 'Zones' that have been visited by aliens are irreversibly altered and changed in ways that defy our understanding of science.

11. *Fantastic Planet (La Planète sauvage/Divoká planeta)*, directed by René Laloux, 1973.

10

11

alien world by the hand-shaped Tralfamadorians, who later bring him a companion, the pornographic film star Montana Wildhac.

The Tralfamadorians of Vonnegut's novel perceive time differently to humans, and their study of Billy and Montana is an attempt to understand humans' point of view in the same way as we might study animal behaviour. We perceive time as a line, with the future in front of us and the past behind us. The Tralfamadorians perceive time as happening all at once, with no beginning, middle or end; thus, 'When a Tralfamadorian sees a corpse, all he thinks is that the dead person is in a bad condition in that particular moment, but that the same person is just fine in plenty of other moments.' These aliens are a tool to express the post-traumatic stress syndrome experienced by Billy Pilgrim, and by Vonnegut himself, as a result of his experience as a Second World War veteran and a survivor, while a prisoner of war, of the fire bombing of Dresden by British-American forces in 1945. Inspired by Vonnegut, the Heptapod aliens in Ted Chiang's 1998 'Story of Your Life', adapted by Eric Heisserer and Denis Villeneuve as the film *Arrival* (2016),

are also enigmatically imperceptible, less because of their seven limbs than because they, too, experience events simultaneously, allowing the linguist Dr Louise Banks to glimpse her own future as she begins to learn their language. At the end of the story, the aliens leave with no reason given for their departure or, indeed, their arrival.

In many respects we derive our sense of self from our perception of 'now' (itself formed of a perceived history and anticipated future). We are culturally, perhaps even biologically wired to perceive time linearly. Yet physics seems to suggest that time is far more malleable, fluid and subject to change than we are capable of naturally experiencing, beginning with Einstein's theory of special relativity and developing with ideas of quantum mechanics. In this respect, while Vonnegut's Tralfamadorians and Chiang's Heptapods might seem almost impossibly strange to us, they may in fact be more reflective of the true nature of time – a reminder that 'alien' is a relative term and it may be humanity that is the oddity. One might look to the angel described by the philosopher Walter Benjamin, who, like Vonnegut, was more than familiar with traumatic experiences:

A [Paul] Klee painting named *Angelus Novus* shows an angel looking as though he is about to move away from something he is fixedly contemplating. His eyes are staring, his mouth is open, his wings are spread. This is how one pictures the angel of history. His face is turned toward the past. Where we perceive a chain of events, he sees one single catastrophe which keeps piling wreckage and hurls it in front of his feet.

At one point in Greg Egan's *Diaspora* (1997), beings are encountered who perceive a greater number of dimensions than humans, and whose frame of reference is so different that communication seems impossible until a chain of interpreters is created: modified human consciousnesses each slightly closer to the alien perspective, who pass communications up and down the chain. Adam Roberts explores a similar concept in *The Thing Itself* (2015), which brings together Kantian philosophy and John Carpenter's *The Thing* (1982) to suggest one solution to the Fermi Paradox (named for the physicist Enrico Fermi), which asks 'Where are the aliens?' In *The Thing Itself*, Roberts explores the idea that we can never perceive the truth of the universe because we are inside the universe, but that other beings might not have the same restrictions of perception. One proposed solution is to build an AI capable of thinking outside our limited scope.

From the miniscule to the gigantic, science fiction is resplendent with aliens that challenge our sense of normalcy and thus our ideas of identity, self and our place in the universe. But this is not to say that these aliens are better than Klingons or Wookiees, those more anthropomorphic, human-scale aliens. We certainly have no data against which to measure which category is more 'realistic'. Familiarity is itself a powerful tool. The behaviour of the 'greyfellas' who settle on Earth in *Terra Nullius* (2017) by Claire G. Coleman, an indigenous Wirlomin-Noongar writer, is deliberately analogous to the behaviour of white European settlers in Australia. The novel offers a compelling account of Earth's colonization from the point of view of the colonized. Indeed, science fiction has increasingly become a space in which writers and artists can undermine the manners in which they have been historically rendered 'Other' or alien, and thus

13

12. Paul Klee's *Angelus Novus*, 1920, was cited by the philosopher Walter Benjamin as a reference for the 'angel of history' who perceives time differently to mere humans.
13. Physicist Enrico Fermi, famous for creating the world's first nuclear reactor in 1942, is associated with the Fermi Paradox, which highlights the apparent paradox between the high probability that there is other life in the universe, and the fact we have never discovered evidence for it.

We are culturally, perhaps even biologically wired to perceive time linearly. Yet physics seems to suggest that time is far more malleable, fluid and subject to change.

unimportant or disposable, by European colonial powers or capitalist power structures. Thus, for example, Gerry William (of the Spallumcheen Indian Band, Enderby, British Columbia) wrote a space opera, *The Black Ship* (1994), in which time is experienced as a cone or spiral, in common with Okanagan First Nation traditions, and offers a presentation of new worlds that wholly rejects the idea of empty land awaiting colonization. 'Water', a novella by Yugambeh writer Ellen van Neerven (from their 2014 collection *Heat and Light*), is set in a near-future Australia where resources are being poured into building on new land – a form of reparations to Aboriginal communities, but one that in turn requires the displacement of sentient 'plant people' who live in the mangroves and are both 'startlingly human' and 'alarmingly unhuman'.

In the afterword to his novel *Far From the Light of Heaven* (2021), Tade Thompson writes about how he includes elements of Afrospiritualism for the alien species in his spaceship detective novel 'because reality is more fluid than we think'. This blending of spiritualist or traditional beliefs with science fiction challenges some preconceived notions about the very nature of the genre, while powerfully expressing a sense of wonder and a wider view of the universe. Nonetheless, the presence of the alien in science fiction is one of prime importance. Science fiction invites us to think differently about aliens in all their multiplicities, from the telepathic beings inhabiting the atmosphere of a gas giant who cannot conceive of a flightless life in James Tiptree Jr's *Up the Walls of the World* (1978), to the structures of an intelligent spider civilization whose web architectures and technologies are born of creatures with no regard for anything as simple as 'up' and 'down' in Adrian Tchaikovsky's *Children of Time* (2015). Each of these encounters leaves our own minds a little expanded, a little stranger, and perhaps makes us feel a little more familiar towards each other. We are humbled by the vast expanses of what we don't know about the universe and its possibilities, by just how strange the cosmos is, and so we are encouraged to see ourselves in the alien and to find strange new ways of being together.

14. Jason Coulthard, *Urtli Yuratu* (*Star Woman*), 2020. Coulthard's pen and ink drawings seek to encourage indigenous cultures to learn and preserve their own stories and knowledge.

→   *Control*, 2019. The mysterious 'Board' of the Federal Bureau of Control manifests in the game only through the Black Pyramid, which communicates through telepathic broadcasts. These are frequently scrambled or ambiguous, perhaps signalling the difficulty of communication with something so completely alien as the Board.

INTERVIEW
TADE THOMPSON

GLYN MORGAN
How did you first become interested in science fiction?

TADE THOMPSON
Through Stan Lee and Jack Kirby's *Fantastic Four* comics. Apparently the only thing I wanted to read as a small child was comics. Kirby's images just burst off the page. In particular the Human Torch, this human being who is on fire! It's so energetic, so immediate! It was also things on television like *The Six Million Dollar Man* (1974–78), Adam West's *Batman* (1966–68), and *Space: 1999* (1975–77). I got into pulp and anthology magazines as well. Then the Robert A. Heinleins, the Isaac Asimovs, all of that, and Ursula K. Le Guin really cemented me in what I would call a 'higher form' of science fiction: a more feeling and emotional and philosophical type of science fiction. Magazines like *Starburst* steered me towards things that maybe we were too young to see, like *Alien*. Something else I wasn't supposed to see was *Heavy Metal* (*Métal hurlant*). Somehow I got access to the original French version, where I encountered people like Moebius.

GM I'd like to pick up with Le Guin and that almost humanistic science fiction. Do you see Le Guin's fingerprints in the way you approach writing?

TT Obviously the people you admire find their way into your work, but I couldn't say there's any conscious attempt to write like her. My influences come from everywhere because the problem when I think about my writing is that everything speaks to it, so films I've seen, books I've read. Comics definitely feature in there because they were the first storytelling medium that I had. But I think that in terms of style I owe more to pulp crime novels. If you can imagine people like Le Guin, their style is quite dense and introspective. As someone who started writing at fifteen, my thoughts were not that dense, I didn't have the life experience. I could never have mimicked Le Guin at that age, but I could mimic the pulps because they tend to have a more immediate style, a quicker way with sentences. I read those and I thought 'I could write like that', very conversational. There's a way I think writing should be done, which is essentially: thoughts, feelings and actions. As you are writing, it's about thinking 'what started it, what actually happened and what is the aftermath'. Pulp doesn't do that, it probably tells you 'this happened and then this happened', so actually I was able to curate these new skills. I started in a pulp style and then added other layers.

GM Do you think your childhood love of science fiction gave you an interest in or an enthusiasm for science that led to you becoming a doctor?

TT   Strangely, not at all. What I wanted to do was be a comic book artist. I wanted to draw. But my parents are Nigerian – you don't tell Nigerian parents you want to be a comic artist. So I said I wanted to be an architect! I'll be training myself to write comics while I'm studying architecture. Then it turned out that I didn't really like the precision of technical drawing at all – it's too confining. I realized I did well on standardized tests, I definitely didn't want to be a lawyer, so I was going to become a doctor or something. Even in medical school, I couldn't actually imagine myself at the end of it as a doctor. I could not imagine myself in a white coat. It wasn't until fourth year, when you have a synthesis of a lot of the things that you were learning before, that I got truly interested. So it wasn't that science fiction sparked an interest in science. It might have subconsciously led me in that direction, and obviously the desire to be like *Star Trek*'s Spock was definitely in me: I liked the idea of a person who had the scientific answers to problems. And of course *Fantastic Four*'s Reed Richards was a scientist. So I can't say it wasn't anything to do with it, but it wasn't directly on my mind.

GM   Do you think that medicine as a scientific discipline is handled well by the genre, compared to, say, engineering and space science?

TT   I think it's handled poorly in general, because I have a vantage point. But I also figure that other people's specialties may be handled in an equally bad way, but I'm less aware of it. I also realized that you have to simplify things in order to tell a story. So, if you don't have specialist knowledge and you've done your research, you still have to strip away that research to tell the story you're trying to tell. The other thing is that something like medicine is a whole bunch of different disciplines that are smushed together, and if you're just researching it without the practical element, you can't really understand it. It's very difficult to understand a doctor's point of view from the outside, especially if yours has always been as a patient. You can't read to understand what it means to stand in front of a person and be their only hope. And it's not just knowledge – the person may just not like you and therefore not be able to tell you everything that they should for you to figure out the problem. Or you may have a problem in the environment that is stopping you from fully understanding what's going on. Or you may know what to do but might not have the resources to do it. And yet somehow you have to sell what you *are* going to do to the person in front of you, even though you know that there is something better. It's incredibly difficult.

GM   Do you have a favourite science fiction doctor?

TT   It would have to be *Star Trek*'s Leonard McCoy, a.k.a. Bones, played by DeForest Kelley. I can't think of anybody else who looms larger than him in my imagination.

GM   You wrote about the expediency of plot versus researched facts in the afterword to *Far From the Light of Heaven* (2021), but I want to talk first about your debut novel, *Rosewater* (2016). How much research did you do for that book and its series? Were you looking into mycology and the science of fungi?

TT   Well, the good thing is that I'd already done that in medical school, so I didn't have to do much new research. There was some interesting new stuff, like a lot of the research on cordyceps (the so called 'mind-control fungus'), and the radiotrophic fungus that grows on nuclear reactors. But other than that, I had enough background knowledge to know that I could use a fungus for this particular purpose. There's also the network of fungal communication that trees use through their root system. That was new to me, and very interesting, but I always have to be careful because I get lost in the science. I love interesting things, and it can stop me from writing!

GM   Do you have to be constantly on guard for that? Because science fiction has a tendency, or a risk, of information-dumping – whole paragraphs of stuff the writer found interesting and has dropped in. How do you reconcile your deep research and love of the facts with that streamlined narrative?

TT   Never let the facts get in the way of a good story. That's one of my maxims: if there is a fact, and there is fiction, you're writing fiction, stick with the fiction. A second maxim: when I'm writing something, I don't watch films except documentaries, and I read non-fiction but I don't read any fiction. And I don't actually do research immediately while I'm writing. What I do is I write the story that's in my head, then I go and do research and modify the story based on what I find. What I've found is that the research becomes a reason not to write. It actually slows me from finishing the story.

GM   Torpor or stasis sleep pods are important in *Far From the Light of Heaven*, but this isn't like researching fungus, which is out there in the world and people can research it. This is a technology that doesn't exist, but is something that NASA, ESA and their partners are working towards. How does that change your research approach?

TT   Human biology is human biology, right? That's not going to change. One of the problems that I've had with a lot of space travel in fiction is that they just freeze the people in 'cryosleep' and then they arrive, and everybody's fine, they basically just defrost. That will never work. There's a reason our body temperature is this body temperature. Our enzymes work within a particular range of temperature, pH and everything. And we are seventy or eighty per cent water, roughly. When you freeze water, unlike most fluids, its volume expands (anomalous expansion of water). Then you get destruction of cells in the body. You're not going to be the person you were when they froze you, even if they could keep you alive, which is not even theoretically possible right now. I couldn't do that, some of my doctor colleagues are going to read my books and be like 'what the hell have you just done there?!' So the body was going to have to be kept at normal temperature. It might be cooled a little bit, which is something we do now, for example, if you're having cardiac surgery.

The other part of it is that the body produces waste and that's another thing you don't see in cryosleep, there's no system for bringing in nutrients, taking out waste, any of that. So I decided there would be fluid balance, with IV tubes, catheters and all of that connected, which is one of the reasons why it would take a while to come out of this long-term sleep. Plus, your muscles haven't been used for over ten years, so you're going to have to have machines stimulating the muscles. You can't just wake people up and have them say: 'I'm awake and I'm cognitively OK. I'm psychologically OK. I'm ready to start flying the ship'. Equipment is going to fail, so you need to have robots tending the equipment. Otherwise you're going to set off for a ten-year mission and by the time you get there, maybe only twenty per cent of the people will survive. My cryopods are maintained, the people are anaesthetized, because you can't just wait for ten years in a lying position. And boredom makes human beings dangerous. If you send people on a ten-year mission in a spaceship, many of them will crack up before they get there. Never underestimate the danger of bored humans. They'll be messing with airlocks, you know? All kinds of things will happen, so they have to keep them occupied. So basically you put them to sleep.

GM   I thought your use of it was really good. As you say, the technology may one day exist and we may use it to go to Mars, but it's going to be so much messier and more involved than the way it's often portrayed.

TT   It's the human factors, you know. There's actually an entire specialism called space psychology and space psychiatry. And the idea that seeing the Earth is a thing that maintains sanity. Like, not seeing the Earth can make you psychotic, for example. Even the idea of sending people to Mars has huge potential psychological problems. Do you send couples? Do you send people who are not couples? Do you say, whatever happens in space stays in space, and that sexual matters will not be discussed after you get back? We get the sanitized version of space travel. Also there's no room, so privacy is a problem. It all has to be figured out. Astronauts are screened for psychological problems. But if your psychological problem is going to stop you from going, then you lie about it. And then you go into space and it's amplified because space amplifies all your personality. It makes you your worst self. All of that is just really fascinating, but it adds to the danger of being in space. We really cannot be glib about it and treat space like air travel, which is what happens in a lot of science fiction. Even the idea of a space battle – from everything I've read, it would be incredibly difficult to fire on another ship because both crews know how dangerous space is, how expensive it is, and that it could be dangerous to them. There are so many different variables in space. Getting into a battle increases the odds of you getting blown up into space and not knowing where you are. Part of the problem is that I think the pedigree of science fiction movies and stories has been from a post-war period, which used the dogfights from the war as a kind of template.

GM   You see those 'making of' featurettes from *Star Wars* where they show dogfight sequences from classic films and newsreel, then you see the special effects clip and the X-Wing does exactly the same manoeuvre. I love the cinematic action, but they are nonsense from a space science perspective.

TT   Yeah, I mean I get it. But spaceflight is expensive. If battling during the Second World War was massively expensive, a space battle will bankrupt entire planets. The training that goes into one astronaut and then you're going to risk them...?! Honestly, if you crunch the numbers, I don't see how space battles can become a thing. The USSR had a space cannon on one of their space stations, they fired it once and never did it again. Now, we don't know why they didn't do it again, but there are obviously many problems, like the reaction force after you fire a weapon. How do you maintain accuracy? The point is, space fighting doesn't make sense to me. Space diplomacy makes more sense.

GM   One of your nonfiction pieces that stuck with me was 'Please Stop Talking About the "Rise" of African Science Fiction' for *Lithub*, where you talk about how African science fiction has been around for ages and what we are seeing is more of a growing awareness of it in white Western culture.

TT   Yeah, but even that is due to a kind of selective amnesia of white Western culture. The only thing I can compare it to is that whole idea that comics are for kids, where every so often someone says 'oh wow, comics are not for kids anymore'. People have been saying that since the late 1970s. There's this amnesia, right? Do you want to know how long someone like Nnedi Okorafor has been winning prizes and working on the scene for, right? There are decades of work out there and then all of a sudden when someone writes a new thing, they say, 'wow, African science fiction is rising!' Shut up! It's not, it's there, you just haven't been looking or you've decided to kind of forget about it. Every time I see that kind of article I get irritated because it shows they haven't done their research. Because Africans in particular – *and* African Americans – but Africans in particular have always had to imagine a future. One of the reasons is because literature from Africa was deliberately funnelled into a particular direction. For example, Chinua Achebe deliberately suppressed science fiction. And I understand why he did it, because that generation of African writer, their thing was, 'We need to talk about colonialism', right? People like Achebe felt like science fiction was frivolous. I understand that they might not have that broadness of thought to accept that science fiction stories are actually quite relevant, that they may be even *more* relevant. The idea of trying to imagine a future is of equal importance to trying to articulate a past and a present. So the idea of trying to *imagine* a future where we were never colonized. What would that lead to? That is as important, you know. Or even if it doesn't have any function – even if it's just a flight of fancy – that's equally important because the brain needs a rest from everything else that's going on. You know, stories have many different forms and purposes, and they're all valid, so I think it is partly because people like the Wole Soyinkas, the Achebes, the Ngũgĩ wa Thiong'os, they were all respected and they were the foundations of contemporary African literature and most of them kind of suppress science fiction and fantasy. It was artificial, it was always going to break through, because imaginative writing has been in Africa almost from the beginning of any oral tradition; the stories that we tell each other are fantastical in nature. They involve people transforming into animals, or spirit travel, stuff like that. To deprive or to impoverish a particular form of literature is another kind of oppression, although I understand why. But we also need to use our imagination. We need to imagine futures. We need to imagine different ways of doing things.

GM   Within science fiction, there's sometimes snobbery about the rigorousness of the science. Some of the things I see as an outsider in fiction coming from the

African continent, including yours, are the incorporation of traditional cultural and spiritual influences, which are not what purists might call 'hard science fiction'. Could you speak about the influence of fantastical storytelling on your work?

TT   The moment someone says 'hard science fiction' I'm immediately out, because it is not *sometimes* wrong, it is *always* wrong. Let's talk about the big fundamental concept of science: to do science you have to ignore certain things. You have to start from initial conditions – like when we're doing chemical reactions, we say 'in stp' – 'standard conditions of temperature and pressure', which don't exist in day-to-day life. To perform an experiment, you take some parameters, and you say I'm going to fix these parameters so I can test these two things, and then I'll test the other things. You ask someone, at what temperature does water boil? They'll tell you 100°C, but the answer is it is 100° under particular conditions, but it's not always 100°. You ask people what the speed of light is and they tell you, but actually there's a doctrine of variable speed of light right now. People who talk about 'hard science fiction' talk as if certain things are fixed, but even in physics those things aren't fixed, they're not even fully understood. It's why people will tell you that if you're a person who says you understand quantum physics, then you don't understand it. And most of the time when we talk about it, we're talking mostly about it in metaphor. I don't understand it. I've been reading it for years. Things like spooky action at a distance, they really interest me. Even Einstein really thought quantum physics was a bit dodgy. So in my opinion, in many parts of the universe the rules are not actually understood, and many of them can lead to very strange phenomena indeed and in order to write hard science fiction, you have to ignore the strangeness. That's bullshit. I write what is scientific, but I keep the strangeness in, especially the human experience. Because even if you assume that the physical phenomena of the world are fixed, it is highly subjective. Even as I'm talking to you, your brain is sorting out different interpretations of what I'm saying, and it is choosing one. The realities that we create are varied. The access to those alternative realities, or like alternative understandings, alternative perceptions is also varied. Some people perceive more, some people are not able to do that kind of sorting out and therefore appear to be psychotic; some people have more limited versions of what they're perceiving. All of that is going to lead to one of the things we call the spirit realm. You have to ignore it deliberately to say it doesn't exist. It requires you to ignore the fact that people are subjective. And we don't do that. How we deal with the subjectivity differs in different cultures. Maybe we have a particular way of conceptualizing that subjectivity and that's kind of what comes out through the spiritualist parts you're talking about. So, for example, we don't know what happens to the energy of a person when they die. All the knowledge you acquire when your body stops working, we don't know where all of that goes to. And maybe it just switches off, and maybe it just dissipates. I don't know, you don't know either, right? So I'm allowed to speculate on that and it doesn't make what I'm doing any less scientific. It may not be as measurable, but it doesn't make it any less scientific. This world of the cold equations doesn't exist, people only wish it would. In all of those books that are called hard science fiction, at some point they deviate anyway because a lot of what they're talking about really can't be followed through.

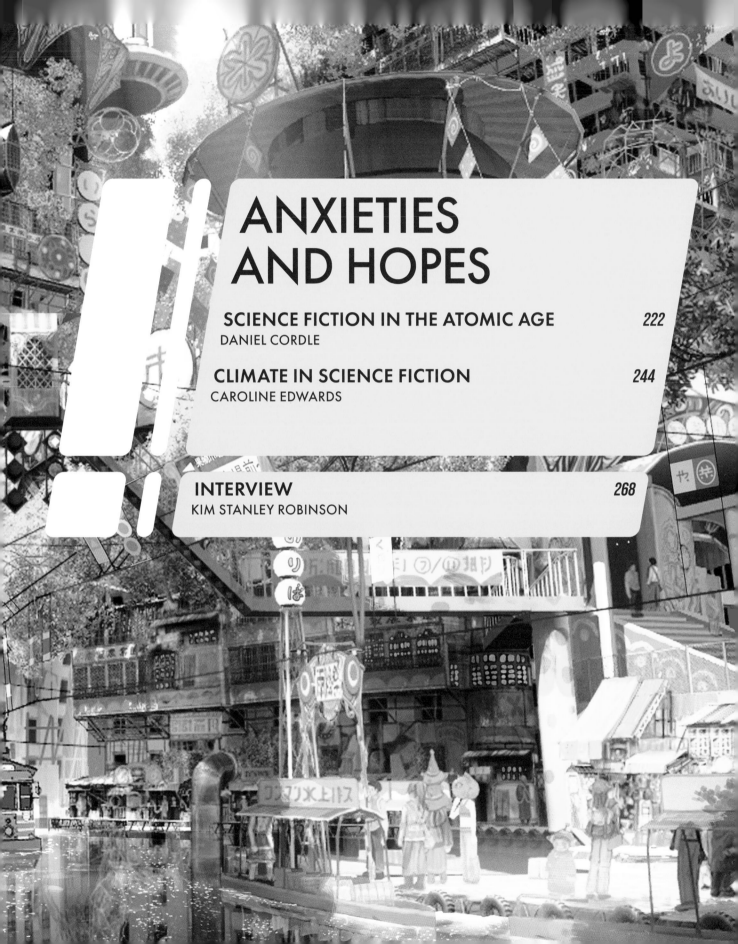

ANXIETIES AND HOPES

SCIENCE FICTION IN THE ATOMIC AGE

DANIEL CORDLE

← Teikoku Shounen, a.k.a. Imperial Boy
(帝国少年) *Solar Punk City*, 2008.
1. 'We Maintain the Union of Science and
Labour', a poster from the Soviet Union
celebrating atomic energy, 1966.

A few minutes before dawn on 16 July 1945, at the top of a 100-foot (30.5-metre) steel tower in the New Mexico desert, a new sun, about twenty times brighter than our own, flashed suddenly into existence. For the first time, rising rapidly to a height of 7.5 miles (12.1 kilometres), a mushroom cloud from an atomic explosion blossomed before human eyes. This was the Trinity Test of a weapon that worked on the principle of fission: the splitting of atoms. William L. Laurence, the only journalist present, said he 'felt as though he had been privileged to witness the Birth of the World – to be present at the moment of Creation'. For George Kistiakowsky, who'd been part of the Manhattan Project that built the bomb, it brought to mind not beginnings, but endings, for it was 'the nearest thing to doomsday that one could possibly imagine...at the end of the world – in the last millisecond of the Earth's existence – the last man will see what we have just seen!'

A few weeks later, atomic attacks on Hiroshima and Nagasaki, the culmination of six terrible years of fighting during the Second World War, unleashed enormous destruction, killing between 150,000 and 240,000 people. Since the raid on Guernica in 1937 during the Spanish Civil War, the world had got used to the bombing of civilians, but the new equation introduced by atomic weapons – a single bomb for a single city – introduced fresh horror. The development of ever more powerful hydrogen bombs from 1952, the proliferation of nuclear arsenals during the Cold War and, later, the means to deliver them rapidly around the globe using intercontinental ballistic missiles meant that civilization-ending, perhaps even species-ending or world-ending nuclear war has continued to trouble the human imagination since the second half of the twentieth century. There was, too, something peculiarly disturbing about the idea of radioactive fallout: invisible to the senses,

2

2. First US edition of H. G. Wells's *The World Set Free* (1914). Wells dedicated the book to the atomic physicist Frederick Soddy, whose work inspired the book.
3. The mushroom cloud rising from the explosion of the atomic bomb in Hiroshima, 1945. The blank spots on the image were caused by the effect of radiation on the photographic film.

it promised an uncanny haunting or hidden inhabitation of the environment or the body until it manifested in radiation sickness.

Projections of nuclear futures proliferated from the mid-century onwards. During the Cold War, conventional science fictions were in dialogue with a multitude of other kinds of speculative fictions, which proliferated in civil defence pamphlets and drills, war games, anti-nuclear campaign leaflets and scientific models of the Earth's climate and ecosystems after nuclear war. In the 1950s, New Yorkers took shelter during annual citywide drills for an atomic attack, with sirens sounding, planes roaring overhead and smoke-pots simulating burning buildings. American schoolchildren did 'duck and cover' exercises under their desks. In so doing, they were participating in dramatizations of nuclear futures. When concerned – or, frequently, incredulous – British citizens read about how to 'Protect and Survive' in the 1970s and 1980s, they were imagining their homes after the bomb had dropped. When, in the absence of concrete experience of global thermonuclear war, strategists 'war-gamed' military scenarios, they were telling stories about the future, preparing for unknown potential outcomes. And when scientists modelled nuclear winter in the 1980s, they were predicting our post-nuclear ecosystem. All these were speculative future narratives, comprising 'science' and 'fiction' to various degrees.

As a future-oriented genre, science fiction was, then, particularly well placed to try to make sense of the new atomic age. While some of its engagements were sensationalist, there was also much nuance and sophistication. There were many dimensions of nuclear culture, but depictions of nuclear war, disaster and radioactivity-induced mutation were also recurring preoccupations for writers and filmmakers.

The prospect of atomic war gave rise to a science fiction that became nuclear over thirty years before the invention of actual atomic bombs. In *The World Set Free* (1914), H. G. Wells imagines atomic technology releasing the energy bound up in matter and transforming human existence. In the prelude, 'The Sun Snarers,' he tells the human story as one of 'progressive attainment of external power,' beginning with the discovery of fire. The more recent exploitation of mineral resources like coal, and the

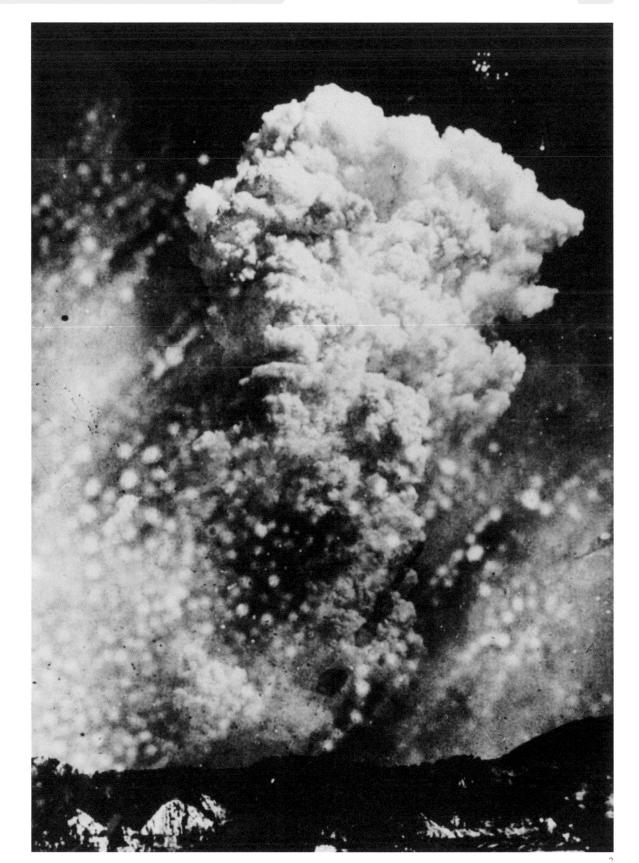

4. Peter Kennard, *Protest and Survive*, 1981. A skeleton reads the 'Protect and Survive' leaflet, the official guidelines issued by the UK government on how to survive an atomic attack. The photomontage artist Peter Kennard used his work to campaign for nuclear disármament and to highlight the absurdity of nuclear weapons and survival strategies.

5. Atomic Brand flashlight crackers, dating from between 1930 and 1950. The exploding nuclear bomb mushroom cloud was designed to catch the attention of children.

development of steam and electric power, are continuations of this history. Human mastery over the world culminates, in Wells's story, with atomic power, when the Sun is finally 'snared.' This thinking about our deep past occurred to many when atomic energy was tapped in reality. Laurence, the journalist present at the Trinity Test, equated the moment of the test with the discovery of fire:

> In that infinitesimal fraction of time...during which the first atomic bomb converted a small part of its matter into the greatest burst of energy released on Earth up to that time, Prometheus had broken his bonds and brought a new fire down to Earth, a fire three million times more powerful than the original fire he snatched from the gods.

In Greek mythology, Prometheus, one might note, was punished for his hubris: each day an eagle tore out his liver; each day it grew back so that he might suffer again.

The explosions of Wells's bombs, powered by a fictional new element, Carolinum, and heaved manually out of airplanes, are different to the sudden, shuddering impact of actual atomic weapons. They burn slow and hot, producing 'a miniature active volcano', a 'boiling confusion of molten soil and superheated steam' that 'remained spinning furiously and maintaining an eruption that lasted for years or months or weeks according to the size of the bomb'. Still, they threaten the end of everything. In a foreshadowing of the contradictory responses atomic energy would later produce, the crisis produced by these bombs results in a transformation of global society. The horror of atomic war 'shook men out of cities and businesses and economic relations,' Wells writes, out of 'lightly held beliefs and prejudices,' and the result is a World Republic modelled on Wells's socialist principles. With war unthinkable in an atomic age, the world finds peace. Such utopian projections found a real-world corollary in 1945. Perhaps, some thought after Hiroshima and Nagasaki, the prospect of future wars would be so terrible as to make them impossible. Indeed, some dreamed that global cooperation – even world government – would emerge.

Wells holds up, too, the prospect of the atomic age as one in which new industrial and domestic technologies will

5

The prospect of atomic war gave rise to a science fiction that became nuclear over thirty years before the invention of actual atomic bombs.

transform society. His narrator describes a 'tremendous
dawn of power and freedom'; the science that releases
atomic energy stands 'like some bountiful goddess over
all the squat darknesses of human life, holding patiently in
her strong arms...security, plenty, the solution of riddles,
the key of the bravest adventures'. This dream, too, flowered
briefly in the mid-century. In 1954, Lewis Strauss, the
Chair of the Atomic Energy Commission, said that civilian
nuclear power promised energy 'too cheap to meter'. *A is
for Atom* (1953), an animated promotional film sponsored
by General Electric, imagined atomic power through the
figures of giants doing human bidding, rather like Wells's
'bountiful goddess'. But later science fiction writers were, on
the whole, rather less optimistic about humans' capacity to
reorganize in the interests of mutual benefit. The overriding
fear of was nuclear destruction.

ENDINGS AND BEGINNINGS

The World Set Free's vision of history is a linear one:
powered by increasing technological sophistication, human
society moves forward and, eventually, having scraped
through the atomic crisis, enters a state of maximum
material plenty and harmonious social organization.
For some writers, though, nuclear war locks humans into
a cyclical history by precipitating the end of civilization.
Walter M. Miller's *A Canticle for Leibowitz* (1959) plunges
the reader into a future dark age in which monks dedicate
their lives to preserving the few scraps of knowledge that
survived the 'Simplification', a vengeful destruction of
culture and learning after the catastrophe of the 'Flame
Deluge' of nuclear war. Later sections of the book jump
forward in history to chart a renaissance, the rise of a
new, technologically sophisticated civilization and the
rediscovery of atomic energy. Are humans condemned,
the book asks, to repeat previous mistakes, or can they
break the cycle of violence?

A similar question is posed in the short story
'The Crystal Goblet' ('O Copo de Cristal', 1964) by the
Brazilian writer Jerônimo Monteiro, in which a journalist,
Miguel, finds a beautiful crystal goblet with a 'radiant
glow'. As he looks at it he sees visions of men marching,
battles and people fighting desperately for food.
To Miguel's horror, his son-in-law Lazlo spots amidst
the goblet's visions a sign saying 'Drink Coca-Cola',

6. A blue and white porcelain bowl retrieved from Hiroshima after the atomic bomb explosion on 6 August 1945.

How do we contemplate
a world not only in which
everyone is dead, but in
which there is no one left to
conceive of this absence and
mourn their passing?

and realizes they're seeing images not of the past, but of a possible future (this revelation is unconsciously echoed in the famous final scene of the 1968 film, *Planet of the Apes*, when the astronaut George Taylor, played by Charlton Heston, makes a shocking discovery half-buried in the sand on the beach). The two men argue about what this means: Miguel assumes atomic war is inevitable, but Lazlo disagrees and holds that the 'future of mankind will be happy'.

One of the most sophisticated versions of this cyclical vision of history, with nuclear war resetting the clock of human civilization, is Russell Hoban's *Riddley Walker* (1980). Set in an England long after nuclear war, its eponymous narrator is part of a nomadic group of hunter-gatherers being squeezed by the re-emergence of settlement and agriculture. The novel's great achievement is its sophisticated portrayal of the persistence of fragments of our culture, both in folk tales of the 'Bad Time', and, strikingly, the shattered language in which the child protagonist Riddley thinks and writes. For example, the stories Riddley's people tell feature a trickster, 'The Littl Shynin Man the Addom,' whose name evokes both the Adam of Genesis and the 'atom' split (we're told he was '[p]ult in 2 lyk he wuz a chicken') necessary for the bombs that have produced this devastated world. The nuclear age is not merely a technological phenomenon here: it is a cultural and social one, shaping thought and belief thousands of years after it has passed. Riddley is heartbreakingly aware both that a far better world has been lost and that it can't easily be resurrected. Denis Johnson's inventive novel *Fiskadoro* (1985) pulls off a similar trick, as does the post-apocalyptic video game *Fallout* (1997–). Both works are strewn with relics of the old world: records, car parts and fragments of the man-altered landscape. In *Fallout* gameplay, an 'atompunk' soundtrack of mid-century classics by Louis Armstrong and The Ink Spots plays out over the Californian nuclear wasteland through which the player must journey.

Of course, all projections of the future also encode the times in which they're written and read. For example, while Judith Merril's *Shadow on the Hearth* (1950), about a woman's struggle to hold her family and home together after a nuclear attack on New York, is about fear of nuclear war, it also interrogates American domestic culture.

7.   Poster with graphics created by Malik, 1982, publicizing the Washington DC Nuclear Weapons Freeze campaign, part of a national 'call to halt the nuclear arms race' between the US and USSR.

Published in a country on the brink of suburban housebuilding and baby booms, the novel shows its protagonist, Gladys, beginning to feel twinges of dissatisfaction with the 1950s version of the American dream. In the context of domestic routine, childcare and cleaning the home, Gladys struggles to defend her family from an array of external threats, including radiation, looters and unwanted sexual advances from a civil defence worker. Yet for all its horror about what lies outside the home, one shocking scene reveals the key danger inside the house. While speculating on the consequences of nuclear aggression by another country, the book also explores, through a subplot about a persecuted schoolteacher, how America's National Security State might treat its own citizens. Some later women's science fiction, published during a period of heightened Cold War tension in the 1980s, resonates with the concerns raised by the feminist campaigners who helped reinvigorate the anti-nuclear movements of the 1980s at protests like the Greenham Women's Peace Camp in Britain and the Women's Pentagon Action in the United States. Vonda N. McIntyre's *Dreamsnake* (1978), Sherri S. Tepper's *The Gate to Women's Country* (1988) and Louise Lawrence's *Children of the Dust* (1985) all imagine devastated post-nuclear worlds in which militaristic values are contested by female protagonists.

Lawrence's novel is a fine example from a significant body of 1980s young adult fiction dealing with nuclear disaster. It is striking, upon reading the depictions of nuclear war and its aftermath in *Children of the Dust* or Robert Swindells's *Brother in the Land* (1984), or of the social upheaval after a reactor accident in the German writer Gudrun Pausewang's *Fallout* (*Die Wolke*, 1987), to realize how pressing nuclear worries were for some adolescents in the 1980s. Writers were surprisingly open with their young audience about the potential death of family members and the collapse of society.

For some writers, of course, the nuclear age introduced a new twist to the long history of the end of the world. Instead of a Day of Judgment – a cosmic vision of religious reckoning – nuclear war seemed to promise the end of the species as a somewhat arbitrary event. This is, perhaps, most clearly captured by Stanley Kubrick's bleakly hilarious film *Dr Strangelove: Or, How I Learned to Stop Worrying and Love the Bomb* (1964), in which nuclear war

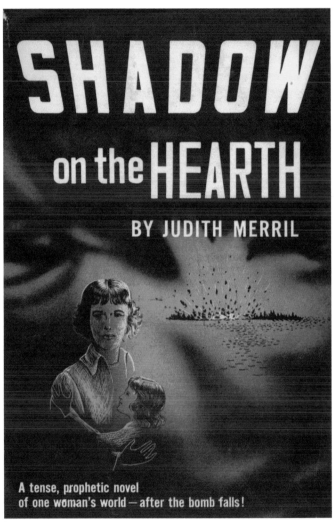

8

8. Cover art by Edward Kasper for Judith Merril's *Shadow on the Hearth*, 1950.

9. Still from *Threads*, directed by Mick Jackson, 1984. The first film depiction of a nuclear winter, *Threads* imagines the aftermath of a nuclear attack in Sheffield in chilling, documentary style. Here, a woman who has survived the bombing cradles her child, who has been killed.

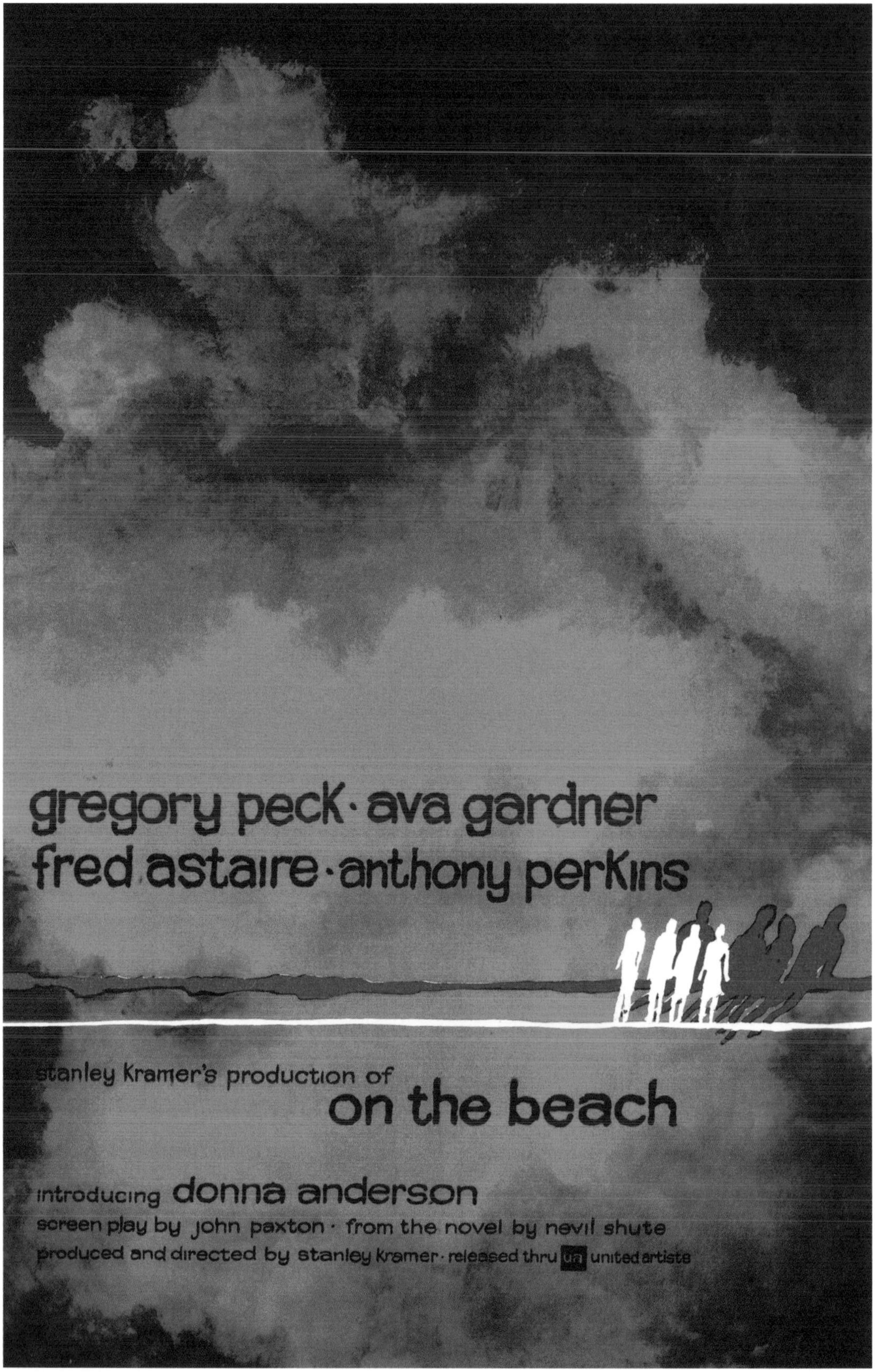

10. Poster for *On the Beach*, directed by Stanley Kramer, 1959.

is an absurd joke, the product of belligerent, paranoid patriots and the failure of complex fail-safe systems.

One of the most influential visions of a nuclear ending is Nevil Shute's *On the Beach* (1957), made into a Hollywood film in 1959. Imagining a group of Australians as they await a cloud of deadly radioactivity from a nuclear war that has destroyed the northern hemisphere, it tries to grasp the near future absence of humans from the planet, its central image the haunting, affecting vision of the empty city. For some, Shute's apocalypse is too tidy and sentimental; Helen Clarkson even wrote a fabulous, if bleak, novel, *The Last Day: A Novel of the Day After Tomorrow* (1959), as a rejoinder to it. But the quietness of Shute's post-nuclear Earth is perhaps precisely the point: how do we contemplate a world in which not only is everyone dead, but no one is left to conceive of this absence and mourn their passing?

A similar point might be made about Ray Bradbury's exquisite short story, 'There Will Come Soft Rains' (1950), in which the family who inhabited a futuristic, automated house remains only in the blast silhouettes their bodies cast on its outside wall as a nuclear explosion incinerated them – an image Bradbury takes from the notorious shadows left by some Hiroshima and Nagasaki victims. The house merrily continues frying up bacon and eggs, reminding the family of their appointments, dealing out cards and reading them poetry (Sara Teasdale's beautiful First World War poem, 'There Will Come Soft Rains,' from which Bradbury takes his title), but no one sits for breakfast or a game of cards, no one has an appointment to keep anymore and there is no one to hear the poetry. What does it mean to be alive, the story asks? Can the absence of humans mean anything in the absence of humans?

Strikingly, though, some of these visions of future wars are also – as in the predilection for new societies to emerge in post-nuclear adventure narratives – fantasies of renewal. Even a novel like Pat Frank's *Alas, Babylon* (1959), which depicts the privations of a Florida town as a warning about nuclear war's horrors, is seduced by the possibilities the scenario opens up for Americans to escape the perceived corruption rife in the mid-twentieth century, and return to the frontier lifestyle mythologized in their culture.

SUPERHEROES, GIANT ANTS, RADIOACTIVE DINOSAURS AND ALIENS

Science fiction also responds imaginatively, and often with considerable artistic license, to the features of nuclear energy and radiation. Often these are imbued with almost supernatural properties. In Isaac Asimov's epic *Foundation* series (1942–93) about the rise and fall of galactic empires, atomic gadgets are repeatedly used by those shaping history to dazzle less technologically advanced peoples, to whom such things seem to be magical. An atomic priesthood even emerges. In superhero narratives, atomic energy carries the power of transmutation. Famously, in a 1962 edition of the comic *Amazing Fantasy*, it is a spider accidentally irradiated in a public science demonstration that bites Peter Parker and turns him into Spider-Man. In Alan Moore and Dave Gibbons's brilliant *Watchmen* (1986–87), meanwhile, Jonathan Osterman is turned into Dr Manhattan as a result of a nuclear lab accident.

Monster movies of the 1950s also think creatively – if rather speculatively – about radioactivity, many of them projecting the anxieties of the period onto the monsters they create. In *Them!* (1954), giant ants, mutated by radiation from the Trinity Test, stalk the New Mexico desert. While surely no viewers really believed that giant ants, hellbent on destroying the American way of life, could be produced by nuclear weapons testing, such films provide a safe medium through which to express (and to some extent assuage) the feeling of threat to which the idea of radioactive contamination gives rise. The ants evoke, too, fears of the 'red menace' of communism in the McCarthy-era US. When a scientist briefs people in Washington about ant society – they are, he says, common in American backyards, but have an 'instinct and talent for industry, social organization and savagery', they attack other colonies and 'make slave labour of the captives they don't kill' – he could be describing the threat many in the US thought that communism posed both at home and abroad. The proliferation of seemingly identical ants – and their sheer number – makes them potent symbols of the supposed communist threat to individualism.

That same year, in Japan, the first of many *Godzilla* films (ゴジラ, 1954) was released, in part a response to Japan's complex and traumatic nuclear history. Deep in the Pacific Ocean, a dinosaur who has survived since

11

the Jurassic period is disturbed by the testing of hydrogen nuclear weapons and becomes radioactive, acquiring a sort of atomic breath from the tests, and wreaks havoc. Scenes of the aftermath of Godzilla's attack on Tokyo – an onslaught that can't be prevented by conventional defences, and that leaves the city burning and flattened – recall the erased cityscapes produced by the bombing of Hiroshima and Nagasaki only a decade before. The film's opening scenes, in which merchant ships disappear after a mysterious flash of light and disturbance in the ocean, also recall an incident involving the *Lucky Dragon 5*, a Japanese fishing vessel contaminated earlier in 1954 with fallout from an unexpectedly large blast from a nuclear test on Bikini Atoll. The crew, one of whom died, became ill with radiation sickness, and this well-publicized news story crystallized concerns about nuclear testing.

Both the perpetrator of atomic-scale destruction and victim of American atomic testing, Godzilla is a more complex monster than the ants of *Them!*, and space is made, in the melancholy scenes of his demise, for the viewer to empathize with him. More sophisticated still in its engagement with monstrosity is Octavia E. Butler's *Dawn* (1987), the first novel in the *Xenogenesis/Lilith's Brood* trilogy. Here the 'monsters' are not produced by atomic energy, but instead rescue Lilith and other human survivors of nuclear war. The novel explores relationships and reproduction across species. Of course, the point is that, though appearing monstrous, the Oankali are not monsters; but the novel eschews a bland resolution, and the surviving humans, struggling with the Oankali's physical and moral alienness, cannot easily accept them. Exploring the relationship between biological and social constructions of identity, the book allegorically broaches issues of racial, sexual and gender identity, but it also engages more broadly with the negotiation of Otherness, and with the operations of power.

NUCLEAR LITERATURE IN THE TWENTY-FIRST CENTURY

What, might we ask, does nuclear science fiction have to say to us now? Why should we read or watch it in the twenty-first century? After all, the Cold War did not turn hot. Nuclear technologies continue to feature frequently in twenty-first century science fiction, but although there have been some notable images of nuclear disaster –

12

11. *Godzilla* (ゴジラ), directed by Ishirō Honda, 1954.
12. *Them!*, directed by Gordon Douglas, 1954.
13. *Frankenstein Conquers the World*
    (フランケンシュタイン対地底怪獣バラゴン),
    directed by Ishirō Honda, 1965.

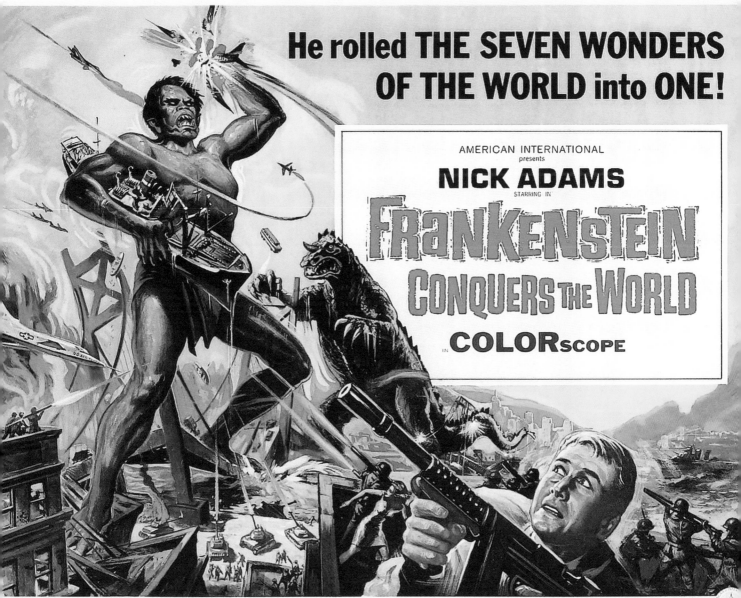

13

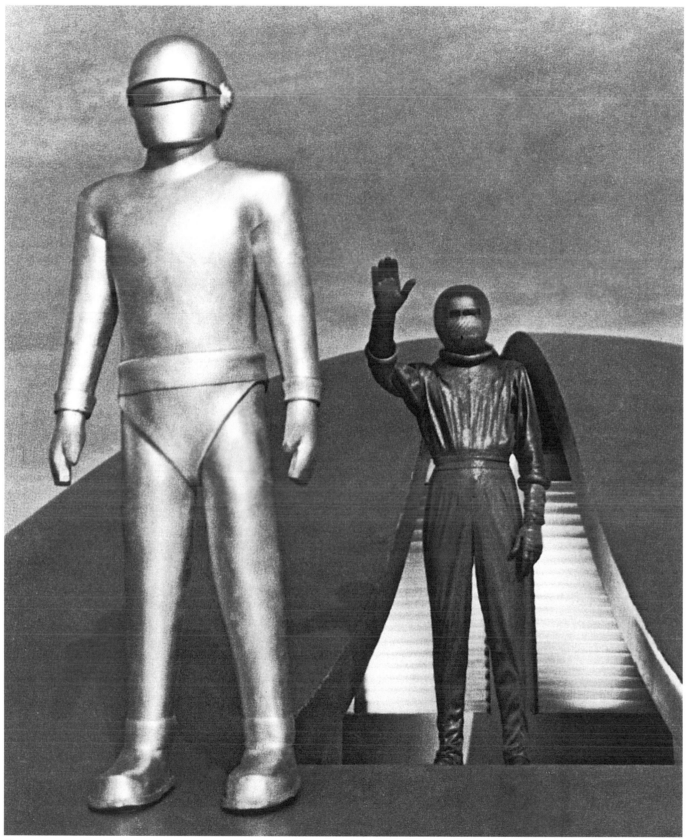

14. The alien Klaatu and the robot Gort come to Earth to warn against nuclear aggression in *The Day the Earth Stood Still*, directed by Robert Wise, 1951.

15. *The Road*, directed by John Hillcoat, 2009, based on the 2006 novel by Cormac McCarthy.

15

for example, the potent images of planetary nuclear destruction in the first and last seasons of the rebooted *Battlestar Galactica* (2004–9) – these are more the exception than the rule. When they do appear, nuclear weapons feature almost casually, as in the series *The Expanse* (2015–), where they are one of many sets of armaments with which Earthers, Martians and 'Belters' might confront one another (though the 'protomolecule' – an all-powerful, transformational biotechnology – takes on some of the qualities previously associated with nuclear weapons).

One reason for reading or viewing nuclear fictions now is simply that many are very good indeed. There is a rich archive of nuclear culture that deserves attention. Another is that these fictions are not only, or even predominantly, about nuclear issues. They address much else besides. A third is that the nuclear issues with which they deal have not disappeared. The terrifying armoury of nuclear weapons that remains in the world could still wreak human and ecological havoc as at Chernobyl in 1986, and this is perhaps most dangerous when it is normalized. Deterrents and fail-safe systems might have worked in the past, but that does not guarantee their success in the future. Nor have we yet worked out what to do in the long term with the highest-level radioactive waste, which will be toxic tens of thousands of years into the future. Science fiction can't solve any of these issues, but it can keep them in our minds and prompt us to continue to think about them.

A final answer is that nuclear culture speaks to the big challenges of the twenty-first century. Over the last decade, there has been a growing interest in the Anthropocene, the proposal that the human impact on the planet is so great that the present moment might be considered a distinct, human-inflected geological epoch. Nuclear technologies are bound up with this to the extent that, although they haven't caused the Anthropocene, the radioactive legacy of nuclear weapons testing is one candidate for the signature of the Anthropocene in the geological record. Perhaps more significantly, though, by addressing human endings, nuclear fiction often prompts us to think precisely about the questions the Anthropocene raises: about deep time and our place in the history of the planet, and about the relations between humans, their technologies

Nuclear fiction often prompts us to think precisely about the questions the Anthropocene raises: about deep time and our place in the history of the planet, and about relations between humans, their technologies and the environment.

and the environment. For instance, J.G. Ballard's short story 'The Terminal Beach' (1964) reimagines a Pacific nuclear test island as a geological relic of the future:

> The series of weapons tests has fused the sand in layers, and the pseudo-geological strata condensed the brief epochs, microseconds in duration, of thermonuclear time.... The island was a fossil of time future.

It might remind us, too, that by imagining atomic explosions as continually erupting volcanos, H. G. Wells was drawn to geological ideas. In the imagery with which they are rendered, the most dramatic nuclear events and materials resonate with fundamental planetary processes, and with the fraught Anthropocenic sense of humans poised between the deep past and deep future.

Nuclear science fiction is, too, frequently an environmental literature that might speak to contemporary climate emergencies. Science fictions depicting a devastated post-nuclear world are precisely about the human impact on the ecosystem. The legacy of the nuclear age lives on, too, in contemporary climate fiction. The source of the catastrophe that is killing the Earth in Cormac McCarthy's *The Road* (2006) might not be clear, but McCarthy's imagery – a sudden flash of light, burned cities – emerges from a cultural history shaped by the nuclear imagination.

The very best nuclear fictions often confront us with what to do in the face of an uncertain, perhaps frightening, future. How, they ask, should we act in the face of powerful forces that seem beyond our control? We end on a stunning, scandalously little-known example: M.K. Wren's novel *A Gift Upon the Shore* (1990). Two women, Rachel and Mary, have survived nuclear war. They might even be the only survivors. Yet, in her imagination of an apocalyptic future, Wren focuses not so much on the fight for survival as on the women's decision to dedicate themselves to the longer task of cultivating a sustainable human future, by collecting and preserving the books that remain. The novel describes the women making two important choices: first, during the horror of nuclear winter, they make 'a choice to survive' by refusing to lay down and die. But it is the second choice, an existential one, that is crucial. By labouring to preserve an archive of books,

to build something beyond themselves, they make a 'choice to live, not just survive; to live as human beings.' There is no certainty of survival, and the novel confronts us with the mortality of both individual humans and of the species. Nevertheless, by saving the books, Rachel and Mary invest in the hard choice of hope. They commit to struggle to live on, and ultimately more gently in harmony with, the Earth. While the novel is set in the imagined catastrophe of nuclear war, the women's choice surely also speaks to how we might choose to face, not simply survive through, the twenty-first century's anxious futures.

16. The Runit Dome, on the Enewetak Atoll, part of the Marshall Islands in the Pacific Ocean, seen from above alongside a crater from the testing of a nuclear weapon. The dome attempts to contain radioactive waste from the tests, but is now cracked and leaking, as well as being threatened by rising sea levels.

CLIMATE IN SCIENCE FICTION

CAROLINE EDWARDS

As the turn to climate catastrophe narratives reflects, our environmental and climate systems are out of kilter.

← John Martin, *The Destruction of Sodom and Gomorrah*, 1852. This picture illustrates the biblical story of Sodom and Gomorrah, two cities destroyed by rains of fire and sulphur as punishment for the immorality of their people.

1. Carbfix domes at the Hellisheiði power plant, near Reykjavik, Iceland. The plant sucks carbon dioxide from the air and sequesters it in rock. This technology remains controversial: environmental concerns include leakage and the debate over whether its use as a tool for climate mitigation in fact legitimizes the continued use of fossil fuels.

Science fiction has a long tradition of engaging with climate issues. The genre's emergence in the late nineteenth century coincides with growing awareness of the impacts of industrialization, such as smog, air pollution, flooding and poor sanitation. Since then, generations of science fiction writers have investigated environmental concerns through a diverse variety of science-fictional climates: from alien invasions that disturb Earth's hydrological systems to futuristic tales of deluge and rising sea levels; from narratives of drought and desertification to petrochemical pollution, grain blight and famine; and from visions of resource scarcity to ongoing coastal erosion, dwindling biodiversity and the end of life as we know it.

As a genre, science fiction is uniquely suited to imagining all kinds of non-humans – whether aliens, robots, artificial intelligence, animals, sentient rock or bioengineered plants – and these non-human perspectives might help us confront the challenges posed by our current era of climate emergency. Science fiction narratives question received assumptions about human superiority or exceptionalism, asking us to reflect upon our hubris in thinking that we are better than, or entitled to exploit, the animal, vegetal, microbial and oceanic worlds around us. As the turn to climate catastrophe narratives reflects, our environmental and climate systems are out of kilter. We have entered what earth scientists call the Anthropocene – a new geological era in which human activity has fundamentally, and irreversibly, altered the Earth system.

What is urgently required is a shift in how we understand humanity's relationship to the environment. Science fiction can help us on this journey.

During the second half of the nineteenth century, the efforts of urban reformers to raise awareness about air pollution, specifically the coal smoke pumping out of

2

smokestacks and chimneys, led to the emergence of early environmental activism. The dramatic presence of London fog in literary works such as Charles Dickens's *Our Mutual Friend* (1864) or Arthur Conan Doyle's *Sherlock Holmes* novels (1887–1927) took on an increasingly sinister role as the so-called 'aerial sewage' moved to the centre stage of near-future dystopian projects. William DeLisle Hay's *The Doom of the Great City: Being the Narrative of a Survivor, Written A.D. 1942* (1880) presents an 'eyewitness' account of 'the greatest calamity that perhaps this Earth has ever witnessed', in which 'fog had drawn over midnight London an envelope of murky death' and only those with access to portable oxygen-generating machines survived.

London pollution did not inspire only dire visions of dystopian and apocalyptic calamity. A number of late-Victorian stories used the smog as inspiration for imagining cleaner industrial worlds, powered by electricity and hydroelectric power. As William Morris describes in *The Earthly Paradise* (1868–70), contemporary Londoners 'dream of London, small, and white, and clean / The clear Thames bordered by its gardens green'. These utopian visions frequently involved extraterrestrial trips to Venus or Mars to see how advanced alien civilizations had tackled the issue, moving through their own periods of heavy industry into smoke-free futures thousands of years more advanced than on Earth.

The Polish-English vicar W. S. Lach-Szyrma's *Aleriel, or A Voyage to Other Worlds* (1883) transports its protagonist to Mars in a car fuelled by a hypothetical clean energy derived from aether. Readers are treated to a city of tree-lined boulevards, electric cars, ubiquitous roof gardens and living walls, liberated from all of the industrial problems associated with smog back home. We find another utopian image of renewable electricity in Alice Ilgenfritz Jones and Ella Merchant's *Unveiling a Parallel: A Romance* (1893), in which the human narrator experiences 'the cleanest city I ever saw' on Mars. Returning to Earth, H. G. Wells's *A Modern Utopia* (1905) similarly powers his utopian society with clean and renewable energy sources, including electric tramways, bicycles and a large network of footpaths to encourage walking. Wells's later novel, *Men Like Gods* (1923), offers an even more impressive programme of hydroelectric engineering, transforming the utopian landscape into a series of lakes

2. A man covering his mouth with a handkerchief, walking through a smoggy London street in the nineteenth century.
3. Yao Lu, *Passing Spring at the Ancient Dock*, 2006. Part of his *New Landscapes* series, Lu uses photographic collage techniques to create images that evoke the paintings of past masters, but which use piles of rubble and netting encompassing mountains of waste instead of rolling hills of grass.

4. In *Pumzi* (2009), a short film written and directed by Wanuri Kahiu, climate change-driven drought has caused a devastating Third World War over water. The film's protagonist is Asha, curator of the Virtual Natural History Museum in the Maitu community, which is sealed off from the supposedly dead outside world.

5. James Lovelock in his laboratory at Coombe Mill, Devon, in the 1980s. Lovelock's Gaia hypothesis argues that Earth functions as a self-regulating 'superorganism', on which all living things collectively maintain the conditions needed for life to continue.

4

and dams supplying 'great batteries of water-turbines' with renewable power. The perils of industrialization and its impact on Earth's climate systems was explored in a parallel strain of science fiction in the late nineteenth and early twentieth centuries that imagined catastrophic flooding. The best-known example is Richard Jefferies's *After London* (1885), which thrilled readers with its futuristic vision of an apocalyptically deluged neo-feudal England. The cause of the flooding is attributed to repeated failures to dredge the Thames river properly, leading to a disastrous rise in the water table that reshapes the English landscape into a network of vast lakes.

A more galactic context underpins the question of flooding in 'The Second Deluge' by the American astronomer Garrett P. Serviss – a story so popular that it was republished several times after its original appearance in *Cavalier Magazine* in 1911. Earth has passed through a 'watery nebula' in space that precipitates a series of devastating storms. In one memorable scene, the White House is struck by lightning: 'as if that had been a signal, the flood-gates of the sky immediately opened, and rain so dense that it looked like a solid cataract of water poured down upon the Earth'. Sydney Fowler Wright's *Deluge* (1928) obliterates the global map with perhaps less drama, but no less chilling a sense of the casual power of seismological forces. 'To an observer from a distant planet the whole movement would have appeared trivial,' Fowler writes, 'India was no more, and China a forgotten dream'. Volcanic fissures trigger a global deluge that almost instantaneously wipes out human civilization; pathetic attempts to flee are likened to the struggles of insects.

Early science fiction publications such as *Amazing Stories*, *Wonder Stories* and *Weird Tales* were full of comet collisions impacting Earth's gravitational and environmental systems, near-future narratives of melting ice caps and rising sea levels, and alien invasions that transformed the planet's climate. Accompanied by lurid cover art, these pulps posed a serious question: how do the estranging non-human perspectives of science fiction, with its other planets, alien worlds and apocalyptic climate futures, challenge ideas of human superiority over environmental systems? George R. Stewart's proto-environmentalist apocalyptic novel *Earth Abides* (1949) addresses this question through the narrative conceit of a deadly plague of measles.

5

How do the estranging non-human perspectives of science fiction, with its other planets, alien worlds and apocalyptic climate futures, challenge ideas of human superiority over environmental systems?

6. Liam Young, *Planet City*, 2020–. Young, an architect, collaborated with a range of science fiction writers, artists and designers to create this conceptual work that explores the productive potential of intense densification. It imagines a future where all of humanity lives in a single, dense mega-city created by mining and recycling all existing cities. The self-supporting super-structure would be approximately the size of an average US state, leaving the rest of the planet to rewild and regenerate.

The novel's protagonist is an ecologist and views the unfolding disaster of mass depopulation as an interesting chance to conduct his research into the impact upon natural cycles once humanity's dominance has been wiped out.

Stewart's sympathy for the non-human environment anticipates the arguments of deep ecologists by nearly twenty-five years, illustrating the frequently prescient speculative power of science fiction that engages with climate issues. Frank Herbert's interstellar epic *Dune* (1965) offers another approach to the science-fictional critique of human exceptionalism. On the desert planet of Arrakis, an indigenous community of Fremen reveal their adaptation to the extreme environment of the planet's challenging ecology, as opposed to the imperial Atreidis regime that plunders its resources of the highly valuable drug melange.

Another popular idea employed by science fiction writers imagining threats to Earth's climate is the theme of rampant over-population and resulting food shortages. John Christopher's *The Death of Grass* (1956) offers a sober vision of environmental disaster caused by a grain blight that destroys the world's staple crops. The spread of this highly contagious virus produces an eco-apocalypse that is blamed on the overuse of pesticides and over-production. *The Death of Grass* prefigured Rachel Carson's environmental bestseller *Silent Spring* (1962), which documents the toxic impact of pesticides such as DDT (dichloro-diphenyl-trichloroethane) upon birds, insect life and the food chain. With its science fictional opening – 'There was once a town in the heart of America where all life seemed to live in harmony with its surroundings.... Then a strange blight crept over the area and everything began to change' – *Silent Spring* demonstrates the power of speculative storytelling to underscore the urgency of ecological crisis. Carson's book has been widely credited with igniting the environmental movement, at a time when awareness of climate change was rapidly gaining momentum (as seen in the formation of political parties on an environmental platform).

The impact of *Silent Spring* on science fiction in the 1960s and 1970s can be seen in the shift towards themes of over-population, precarious food production and the consequences of our over-reliance on fossil fuels.

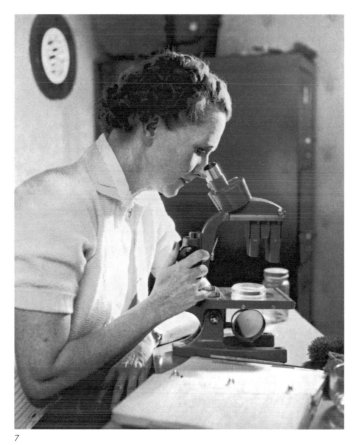

7

The fragility of food security is the central theme of Harry Harrison's eco-dystopian novella 'Make Room! Make Room!' (1966), adapted into the influential 1973 film *Soylent Green*. Inspired by projected population growth figures for the United States, Harrison imagines an unforgettably claustrophobic vision of New York City in 1999. With its abandoned cars, rotting container ships and skeletal population, the crumbling state is reduced to producing synthetic food from plankton and petrochemicals. Published in the same year as Paul Ehrlich's Malthusian bestseller *The Population Bomb*, John Brunner's multiple award-winning dystopian novel *Stand on Zanzibar* (1968) offered an experimental literary approach to these questions that characterized New Wave science fiction of this period. Following Anthony Burgess's *The Wanting Seed* (1962), Brunner's novel offers a similarly crowded vision of over-population; and this theme was further explored in his later *The Sheep Look Up* (1972) as well as Robert Silverberg's *The World Inside* (1971). While these novels drew on Paul and Anne Ehrlich's argument that economic prosperity in America was forged at the expense of the biosphere, they also walked a fine line between environmentalism and eugenics and racism, a point forcefully conveyed to Ehrlich himself on stage at a 1972 convention of the Zero Population Growth (ZPG) movement.

Arguably the most influential science fictions dealing with climate change at this time were J. G. Ballard's 1960s environmental disaster novels. The second novel in this quartet, *The Drowned World* (1962), is perhaps Ballard's most successful novel from this period and offers a powerful vision of a post-deluge future, when much of the world has been flooded, its iconic cities submerged beneath a jungle-like series of lizard-infested swamps and lagoons. Looking back at the series, it is interesting to note that the third, *The Burning World* (1964; published in the UK as *The Drought*), is the only one to explain the environmental disaster as having been caused by human activity: petroleum-produced industrial wastes have been pumped into the sea and have created an oceanic membrane that stalls evaporation, halting the water cycle.

This anthropogenic climate change, which we have seen prefigured in late-nineteenth-century narratives of air pollution, was given a new name in 1969: the eco-catastrophe. Inspired by the record-breaking Santa Barbara

Arguably all literature that considers itself to be realist should now include the issue of climate emergency.

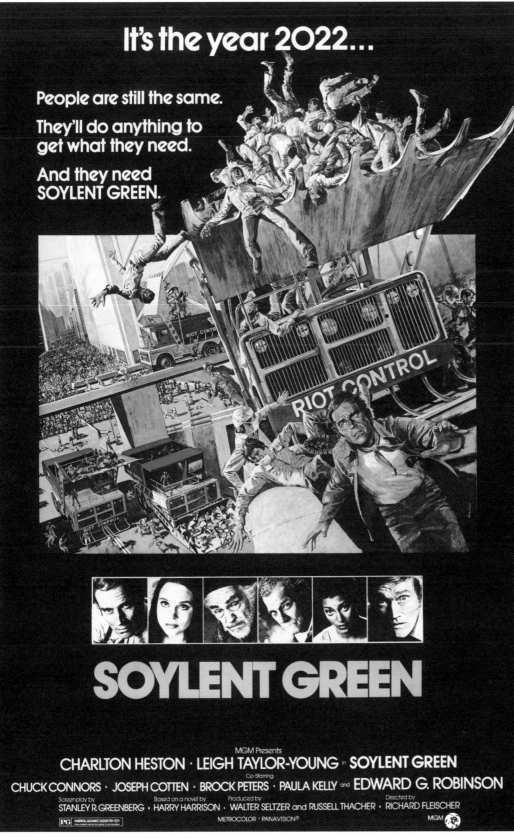

7. Rachel Carson in her laboratory, 1951.
8. Poster for *Soylent Green*, directed by Richard Fleischer, 1973, based on the 1966 novel 'Make Room! Make Room!' by Harry Harrison.

9. Simon Stålenhag, *Rising Tide*, 2016, part of a quartet of works created for the Radical Ocean Futures project led by Andrew Merrie at the University of Stockholm, which explores the use of science fiction prototyping as a method of modelling future scenarios.

10. Logging in the Borneo rainforest, Malaysia. As well as accelerating climate change, loss of wildlife habitat is also likely to lead to an increase in new diseases transferring to humans, potentially leading to new pandemics.

10

oil spill, in which between 80,000 and 100,000 barrels of crude oil washed up across 35 miles (56 kilometres) of Californian coast, the term was coined by Paul Ehrlich to describe 'the most spectacular of man's attacks on the systems which sustain his life'.

Amid growing public awareness of the link between environmental issues and climate change exemplified in the eco-catastrophe, science fictions of alien and vegetal horror retained their appeal throughout the 1960s and 1970s. In Brian Aldiss's bizarre science fantasy *Hothouse* (1962), the Earth ceases rotating around the Sun, leading to irradiated hothouse conditions on half of the planet. The novel raises questions about the future impact of greenhouse gases through the surreal vision of an alien species of murderous omnivorous plants. Joan Slonczewski builds on ideas of plant sentience in the symbiotic relationship between an all-female human colony and an alien maritime environment in *A Door into Ocean* (1986).

Slonczewski, an American microbiologist, weaves her professional interest in the interrelations between the human and microbial worlds into her fiction, blending ecological, pacifist and Quaker principles of non-violent resistance in this narrative about empathic women living symbiotically upon a watery planet.

Not all science fictions about climate change imagined dystopian or apocalyptic outcomes for humanity. Some offered hope of future utopian societies emerging from the rubble of capitalist crisis. California and the Pacific Northwest feature heavily in this strand of science fiction. Looking backwards to the pastoral visions of Henry Thoreau and William Morris, Ernest Callenbach's bestseller *Ecotopia: The Notebooks and Reports of William Weston* (1975) features the secession of northern California, Oregon and Washington State to create an independent nation galvanized by ecological ideals. Callenbach's San Francisco draws heavily on the hippie spirit of Haight-Ashbury's Summer of Love in 1967 for its utopia. Meanwhile, Ursula K. Le Guin's 'The Word for World is Forest' (1972) brings into sharp focus the relationship between colonial conquest and ecological destruction. Written in the final years of the Vietnam War, Le Guin's novella thrilled readers with its tale of indigenous resistance to an interstellar imperialism that has colonized the forest planet of Athshe and set about stripping its pristine arboreal reserves for timber. This resource extraction, which echoes the logging of ancient redwoods on America's western frontier and its accompanying logic of settler colonialism, is radically defamiliarized as an act of ecocide, as well as genocide, through the novel's focus on the rebellion of a race of furry humanoids. Le Guin's later novel *Always Coming Home* (1985) expands on this environmentalist worldview. Presented as a pseudo-anthropological document, it follows the tribal Kesh people in a future California. Its richly conceived world includes music, artworks and poetry written in the Kesh language, invented by Le Guin, each of which illustrates the ecological sense of interconnectedness between people and place that runs through Kesh culture.

Another ecotopia that looks towards a futuristic Pacific Northwest is Kim Stanley Robinson's *Three Californias Trilogy* (1984–90). Renewable energy powers the utopian townships featured in *The Wild Shore*, *The Gold Coast* and *Pacific Edge*, and human physical labour is privileged as an alternative form of transport. Resonant scenes of erotically charged athletic bodies pumping pedal-powered light aircraft or customized bicycles through the Californian landscape offer a forceful counterweight to the clogged arterial networks of decaying highways. *The Fifth Sacred Thing* (1993), meanwhile, reworks the idea of the ecotopia along pagan principles, reimagining San Francisco after a nuclear apocalypse. Written by Starhawk, an influential ecofeminist and neopaganist associated with the Goddess movement, the novel presents an ecotopian city of abundant green commons where everyone has more than enough to eat.

These notable Californian ecotopias were somewhat overshadowed by the more dramatic science fictions dealing with the issue of peak oil. When oil production peaked in the US in 1970, following petroleum production spikes elsewhere in the 1960s, science fiction turned its attention to imagining near-future worlds ravaged by deprivation. George Miller's post-apocalyptic film *Mad Max* (1979) stages the disaster in the Australian outback. Followed by *Mad Max 2* (1981, released in the United States as *The Road Warrior*), *Mad Max Beyond Thunderdome* (1985) and *Mad Max: Fury Road* (2015), the Mad Max franchise offered an iconic dieselpunk fantasy in which resource scarcity (first petroleum, but later, as in *Fury Road*, water) leads to warring, leather-clad gangs. Driving improbably (yet enjoyably) customized cars, these anarcho-primitive tribes eke out a precarious existence as salvagers amid the post-apocalyptic ruins.

Alex Scarrow's thriller *Last Light* (2007) offers a more restrained, mimetic account of the end of oil production, in which an oil engineer stranded in Iraq witnesses the rapid collapse of global infrastructure when Middle Eastern oil production is abruptly halted. Meanwhile, Omar El Akkad's *American War* (2017) combines a similarly realistic imagining of post-oil life reframed around global heating – signified by frequent flooding, federal outlawing of fossil fuels and an intensification of climate-induced migration to the American South, to escape the rapidly disappearing Gulf of Mexico. Moving the action to a post-oil Bangkok, Paolo Bacigalupi's award-winning biopunk novel *The Windup Girl* (2009) extrapolates the biogenetic fallout of patented seed sterility amid a collapsing ecosystem of disrupted weather, sea-level rise and famine.

Margaret Atwood's *MaddAddam* trilogy (2003–13) is another relevant example of bioengineering gone awry. While not strictly speaking a peak-oil science fiction, the story is set in a hyper-capitalist world dominated by the Church of PetrOleum, whose religious zeal is matched by that of their corporate gas-guzzling sponsors. In Atwood's frequently satirical near-future America, climate change has already caused a mass extinction event, and the techno-fix of genetic engineering ultimately leads to a manufactured plague wiping out humanity, which leaves a lone survivor – in a nod to Mary Shelley's *The Last Man* (1826) – drunkenly staggering about. His only company are a transgenic species of new humans called Crakers, whose iridescent blue skin and various animal traits bring to fictional life the bioluminescent rabbits and mice made possible by the gene editing tool CRISPR.

Anxieties about the pollution and destruction of forests and pristine landscapes during Japan's post-Second World War construction boom were incorporated into the popular genres of anime and manga. Hayao Miyazaki's *My Neighbour Totoro* (となりのトトロ, 1988), for instance, references Shinto-inspired pantheism in the giant camphor tree that houses the mythical totoro creature; a tree that, Satsuki and Mei's father tells them, 'has been around since long ago, back in the time when trees and people used to be friends'. Miyazaki co-founded the animation studio Studio Ghibli, which has been releasing feature films since 1986 and has helped establish the global popularity of ecologically informed anime, in narratives that explore questions of environmental balance, precarity, industrial pollution and human–non-human relations. In *Nausicaä of the Valley of the Wind* (風の谷のナウシカ, 1984), the eponymous princess Nausicaä struggles to save her woodland community from the twin existential threats of humanity and the Toxic Jungle. Incessant wars have led to the globe becoming infested with poisonous plants and insects that pollute the biosphere, and the remaining pockets of civilized humanity attempt to destroy the Jungle to control the epidemic. Nausicaä's ecological message reminds audiences that nature is essential to human wellbeing, and her ability to empathise with the non-human natural world brings together the traditional Japanese ideals of feminine *yasahii* (meekness or kind-heartedness) and masculine *bushido* ('the way of the warrior').

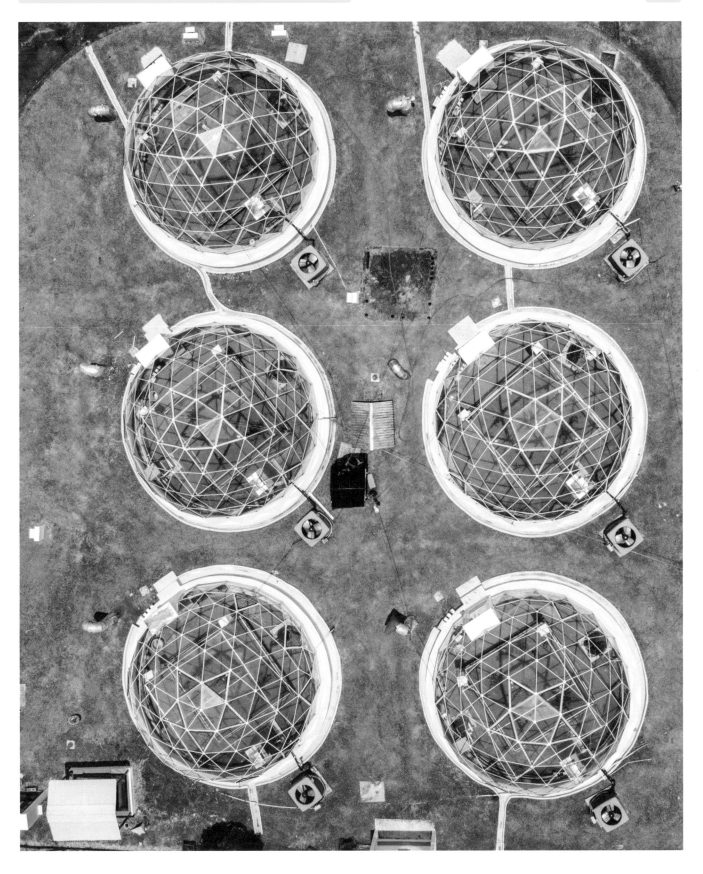

← The Smithsonian Tropical Research Institute, Gamboa, Panama. Extreme climate scenarios are simulated inside each of these tropical domes, to study how tropical vegetation behaves under different circumstances.

12. Poster for *Silent Running*, directed by Douglas Trumbull, 1972. In this eco-minded film, a fleet of spacecraft preserves the last examples of Earth's flora.

13. Wyvern driftwood sculpture by James Doran in the Flower Dome, Singapore, the largest greenhouse in the world. Spectrally selective glass allows in maximum amounts of light while minimizing solar heating, helping to maintain a 'cool-dry' Mediterranean climate within the greenhouse.

13

The historical fantasy *Princess Mononoke* (もののけ姫, 1997), the first of Miyazaki's Studio Ghibli films to receive a major cinematic release in the US, brought environmental themes to a global audience, and *Spirited Away* (千と千尋の神隠し, 2001) offered a post-industrial alternative to the excesses of mass consumption in the era of globalization. The film revives the pre-modern Shangri-La of *The Peach Blossom Spring* (桃花源記), a Taiyuan fable from the Chinese Jin dynasty written by Tao Yuanming in 421 CE that explicitly criticizes Western notions of technological progress. *Ponyo* (崖の上のポニョ, 2008) approaches questions of ecological precarity through a gentler story about the friendship between a young boy, Sōsuke, and the eponymous fish-turned-human girl, Ponyo. Wrestling with her father, a magician, Ponyo accidentally releases a powerful elixir into the ocean, causing a tsunami that reanimates long-extinct prehistoric fish and knocks the Moon out of its lunar orbit. Balance is eventually restored by Gran Mamare, the sea-dwelling Goddess of Mercy, who eradicates marine pollution and allows Ponyo to remain human.

Contemporary Chinese-language science fiction is similarly concerned with the ecological relations between humans and non-humans. As scholars like Mia Chen Ma

and Regina Kanyu Wang suggest, ancient belief systems such as Confucianism, Buddhism and Daoism have survived into this modern Chinese eco-consciousness. While male Chinese science fiction writers such as Liu Cixin, Wang Jinkang and Han Sung have become internationally recognizable, a younger generation of women, transgender and non-binary writers including Nian Yu and Congyun 'Mu Ming' Gu are returning to pre-modern ideas to explore ecological themes. In Gu's untranslated story 'The Heart of Time' (时间之心, 2018), inter-species collaboration is required between symbiotic species in order to survive in an alien world, recalling the balance between yin and yang.

Many science fiction writers have chosen to frame stories about climate crisis by foregrounding social and economic inequality. In George Turner's *The Sea and the Summer* (1987), rising sea levels reveal the unevenness of climate change's catastrophic impact on people's lives in Melbourne in the 2020s. In Octavia E. Butler's eerily prescient *Parable of the Sower* (1993) and *Parable of the Talents* (1998), it is an African American teenager who inspires the hope of a small utopian community in a near-future California laid waste by global warming, religious fundamentalism, widespread homelessness and a drug-induced plague of pyromania that incinerates the last remaining fortified suburban compounds.

We must search to find collaborative strategies for survival – and this requires a radical rethinking of the category of the human and its embeddedness within non-human networks of matter, energy and agency.

14. Abeer Seikaly, *Weaving a Home*, begun in 2013. Architect Seikaly's initial aim was to create 'a portable, dignified shelter for displaced communities', with sustainability and community as central values. Combining traditional Bedouin practices with contemporary science, the material of her tents captures moisture in internal reservoirs for drinking and washing, while soft solar panels allow power for light and charging portable devices.

The protagonist Lauren Olamina's religious system of Earthseed draws on a long African American ecoliterary tradition to produce a syncretic blend of Christian theology and indigenous ecological knowledge, exploring themes of sustainability and the techno-utopian idea of extraterrestrial ascent.

The chasm in Butler's eco-catastrophic world that divides the employed from the unemployed, homeowners from the homeless and the educated from the illiterate is also explored in a science-fictional work with a very different tone – Kim Stanley Robinson's *New York 2140* (2017). With a more playful touch, Robinson's distinctly hopeful novel foregrounds the economic impact of severe flooding. When global sea level rise reaches fifty feet, Manhattan is swallowed up and midtown becomes an intertidal zone. Despite the collapsing tower blocks and the return of cholera, New Yorkers discover new water-based pleasures, adjusting to flood life and even marvelling at 'the whitmanwonder [beauty] of it'.

Robinson's earlier *Science in the Capital* trilogy (2004–7) focuses on the interrelationship between government and climate scientists working at the National Science Foundation to implement climate change mitigation policies through research into the melting of Arctic ice sheets, changes in the Gulf Stream, the potential of carbon sinks for storing emissions and the biotechnological mitigation of diseases exacerbated by climate change. His novel *The Ministry for the Future* (2020) returns to these earlier themes, as climate scientists are tasked with running the eponymous Ministry. Here, however, the bureaucracy of scientific research has calcified into a more violent, activist sense of urgency. Alongside geoengineering, debt strikes and good old-fashioned socialist agitation (staples of Robinson's fiction), protagonists also entertain the necessity of bioterrorism, political assassination and industrial sabotage to advance their ecological cause.

As we enter the sixth mass extinction event, the first time in sixty-five million years when species are becoming extinct much faster than they can be replaced by evolution, arguably all literature that considers itself to be realist should now include the issue of climate emergency within its narrative world. Science fiction has become a booming genre – an important imaginative and critical tool in the ongoing struggle to connect climate change's unfathomably

15. Cover artwork by
    Stephan Martinière
    for Kim Stanley
    Robinson's *New York
    2140* (2017).

vast geological scales and timeframes with our own human sense of time and history. Thus, while non-genre works have moved closer into science fictional territory (with a proliferation of post-apocalyptic and dystopian stories, zombie viral apocalypses, flood fictions and portrayals of increasingly torrid temperatures by writers such as T. C. Boyle, Maggie Gee, Jeanette Winterson, Ian McEwan, Claire Vaye Watkins, David Mitchell, Jenny Offill and Will Self, to name but a few), many recent works of science fiction have delved into the murky realms of horror, the Gothic and the weird. These non-human worlds are characterized by their inscrutable and frequently spine-chilling rupture of species boundaries.

Jeff VanderMeer's *Southern Reach* trilogy (2014) is an important example of the ambiguity that these works pose. In the flourishing ecosphere of the alien Area X, which has landed along Florida's moss-drenched north-western coast and is rapidly spreading across the region, interloping human researchers meet a variety of grizzly ends – at least, as their recognizably human selves. In Aliya Whiteley's *The Beauty* (also published in 2014), a small clan of men eking out a desperate post-apocalyptic existence are either brutally massacred by a sentient mycological network of mushroom women, or forced into an accreting web of fungal power. The alien biodome that crashes into a dusty backwater Nigerian town in Tade Thompson's *Wormwood* trilogy (2016–19) offers readers a similarly weird tale of fungal colonization. A superior interstellar alien race has undertaken a programme of slow settlement on Earth at the cellular level, through the 'xenosphere', which absorbs people into a biological information system that is harvesting human cognitive activity and, ultimately, 'sooth[ing] them into extinction'. N. K. Jemisin's science fantasy *Broken Earth* series (2015–17) imagines a similar transformation of the human body, this time by an ancient race of sentient rocks that drag Jemisin's protagonist deep into the bowels of the Earth.

Not all contemporary science fictions that use the tradition of literary weird to deal with climate disaster are so gruesome. Nnedi Okorafor's *Lagoon* (2014) rewrites the Wellsian tradition of the alien invasion, relocating the devastation to Lagos, Nigeria. The alien Ayodele offers a much more compassionate extraterrestrial ambassador than Wells's terrifying Martians in their glittering metallic tripods,

and her mission on Earth is the restoration of the planet's exhausted biosphere. Cleaning up oil spills, restoring marine diversity and introducing alien green technology to replace Nigeria's dependence on oil, *Lagoon*'s use of an extraterrestrial ecological redeemer positions this novel as a post-oil ecotopia unlike any other.

Video games have similarly addressed the catastrophic impact of fossil fuel-based capitalism. Based on Sid Meier's original 1991 strategy game, *Civilization VI* (2016) encourages players to reflect on the ecological cost of development and industrialization. Where earlier versions of the franchise saw players starting out in the Stone Age and competing to industrialize with no detrimental effects on the climate, in *Civilization VI* players are concerned with urgent climate mitigation, protecting coastal cities from rising sea levels, developing carbon capture and storage technologies or decelerating agricultural development to protect forests and pristine landscapes. The Polish survival videogame *Frostpunk* (2018) takes energy-conscious gameplay a step further, by setting its alternate history world in the late nineteenth century during a volcanic winter. Players lead a small band of survivors, eking out a grim existence in an arctic climate, in which every decision revolves around generating enough energy to heat and insulate buildings, automate labour in sub-zero temperatures and scour the surrounding frozen wastelands for resources.

With its Studio Ghibli-inspired visual graphics, Nintendo's popular fantasy video game *The Legend of Zelda: Breath of the Wild* (1986) is set across a diverse landscape of tropical forests, volcanoes, mountain summits and temperate grassy plains in a game world that packs ecological diversity into an area the size of Kyoto. The game's cover art playfully references Caspar David Friedrich's *Wanderer above the Sea of Fog* (c. 1818), an iconic artwork of German Romanticism that depicts the sublime beauty and terror of nature, as viewed from a rocky summit inspired by the Elbe Sandstone Mountains. *Breath of the Wild* has a similarly vertiginous sense of landscape. Its open-world environment allows players to explore the planet's climactic extremes, to rescue indigenous people and defeat monstrous creatures in a sometimes uncomfortably settler-colonialist exchange between European male adventurer and 'uncivilized' tribes and monsters.

Like other forms of digital media, the participatory form of the video game fosters civic engagement, demonstrating the educational power of game design and technological simulation. Perhaps the best example of 'green gaming' to date is the award-winning open-world game *Walden*, developed by Tracy Fullerton and the USC Game Innovation Lab and released in 2017 – an adaptation of *Walden; or, Life in the Woods* (1854), Henry David Thoreau's account of his experience of living off-grid in a cabin. Players can explore Thoreau's utopian desire to retreat from humdrum existence and live an antisocial, self-reliant life surrounded by nature. Experiencing the character Henry's first-person perspective as he builds his cabin or gathers food, the game raises awareness of the importance of access to green spaces.

As the capitalist end-times of environmental devastation loom ever closer, the American anthropologist Anna Lowenhaupt Tsing outlines an oddly upbeat account of survival amid ruined landscapes. Her influential book *The Mushroom at the End of the World* (2015), which traces the commodity chain of the matsutake mushroom from its Japanese origins to the Oregon Pacific coast, argues that we cannot live, or think, outside of 'economic and ecological ruination', and giving up is not an option. We must search to find collaborative strategies for survival – and this requires a radical rethinking of the category of the human and its embeddedness within non-human networks of matter, energy and agency.

Tsing's hopeful analysis of what might emerge from the ruins of capitalism's exhaustion of finite natural resources resonates particularly in light of the COVID-19 pandemic. Epidemiologists warn that zoonotic (wildlife-to-human) diseases will recur given more frequent opportunities for bacteria and viruses to cross from one species to another, triggered by people and livestock coming into close contact with wildlife. As COVID-19 forcefully reminds us, humanity cannot simply continue its current rate of deforestation and the destruction of natural habitats without disastrous consequences. Moreover, we cannot imagine ourselves as humans to be separate from the complex microbial worlds that in fact make our life possible – as research into the human microbiome reveals, more than half of the cells in our body are not human. These so-called 'microscopic colonists', composed of bacteria, viruses, fungi and other organisms,

play an essential role in digestion, regulating the immune system and protecting us against disease.

In her prescient video installation *Cosmic Call* (2019), the Hong Kong-based artist Angela Su explores our relationship with viruses and bacteria, re-thinking medicalized attitudes towards the non-human microbial world. Commissioned by the Wellcome Trust for its 'Contagious Cities' programme, which asked artists, medical professionals, and urban planners to respond to the theme of epidemic preparedness, *Cosmic Call* considers the possible extraterrestrial origins of the infective bacterium Staphylococcus aureus, conveyed to Earth in comets. Su's installation combines virology with astronomy in a science-fictional blend, developing an idea put forward by the astronomer Chandra Wickramasinghe, who suggested that the SARS virus – closely related to COVID-19 – was transported to Earth on a comet.

Many of these contemporary science-fictional works that rethink the relationship between humans, mushrooms, microbes and viruses sketch out a surprisingly hopeful image of collaborative survival within environmentally ravaged landscapes. As the climate inevitably shifts into a more unpredictable phase over the coming decades, perhaps we, too, can learn to adapt and evolve in concert with the animals, plants, insects and microbes around us.

16. Tardigrades, or 'water bears', are microscopic animals capable of surviving in even the most extreme environments, including outer space and irradiated zones. They precede dinosaurs by about 400 million years, and research suggests that they would survive the majority of mass-extinction events modelled.

→ These views of Earth from space are a fusion of science and art, drawing on data from multiple satellite missions and the talents of NASA scientists and graphic artists.

INTERVIEW
KIM STANLEY ROBINSON

GLYN MORGAN

Your fiction is often highlighted for its rigorous and grounded approach to science fiction storytelling, making your near-futures in particular feel very real. Which of your books do you personally feel most engages with real scientific research?

KIM STANLEY ROBINSON

I'd say they almost all engage with real science to some degree, but in odd ways sometimes. For instance, in *Galileo's Dream* (2009) I tried to show very closely how modern science began, in Galileo's career and others; but it's also a time travel novel, which is the least scientifically credible of all the ideas in my novels.

The *Mars* trilogy (1992–96) tried to hew to the science of its time. *Aurora* (2015) used science to try to kill the idea that we are going to go to the stars. Climate change science at its most current was featured in *Green Earth* (2015), *New York 2140* (2017) and *The Ministry for the Future* (2020), while *Antarctica* (1997) is about scientists doing fieldwork and also about how a scientific controversy plays out. *2312* (2021) looks at the long-term results of all the sciences combined. So it keeps coming back in different ways.

GM What drew you to science fiction as a genre, not only as a fan but also as a writer and scholar?

KSR For me, science fiction is any story that is set in the future. That means that not just the fiction published as 'SF', but also stock forecasts, demographer predictions and anything so-called futurists say are all science fiction, since we can't predict what will really come to pass, but we like to talk about it anyway. It goes back to the ancient act of prophecy, and it also works as a way of talking about what concerns us most in the present. It's a kind of modelling exercise, a thought experiment, a speculation about what's to come by judging the trajectories of things happening now. It is a form of historical thinking, projected forward into the future.

For the usual fictional forms that one thinks of as science fiction, you can see by my definition above that it has a really broad reach – it can be day-after-tomorrow near futures, a kind of exaggerated or proleptic realism; or it can be a million years from now or more, right to the end of time, and stories set that far away in time are kind of like fantasy fiction – lots of things that are 'probably possible' can be explained away by being far-future inventions, for example.

In between the near future and the far future is a middle zone that I sometimes call 'future history', which involves trying to imagine human activities about a century or two from now. This is a less occupied story zone and one I have a particular interest in. Much of my work takes place in that time zone, and in the solar system – in other words, no interstellar stories from me, except for in *Aurora*, which says it can't happen. I have an interest in humans in the solar system, often just right on Earth, in the next century or so.

GM You wrote your PhD thesis on the novels of Philip K. Dick, under the cultural critic Fredric Jameson. I have to wonder what that was like and what influence he had on your writing.

KSR I first ran into science fiction when I left for college. When I was younger I read mostly mysteries and historical fiction, but reading during my undergraduate career shifted into science fiction because I became convinced it was a better description of my youth in southern California than anything else I had read. It caught the feeling of my youth best. I majored in history and literature, but on the side I was giving myself a full education in the history and literature of science fiction. Right when I discovered science fiction (say, 1970), the New Wave was exploding the genre and its possibilities, and it was a really exciting time to get into the field. It was so full of great new work by great new writers. It was a high point that has not yet been equalled.

At that time I started writing stories, and had a little success with them. And my first adviser for my thesis (he left before I was done), Fredric Jameson, was well-versed in science fiction and very encouraging. It was a lucky thing for me. He directed me to start with Philip K. Dick, and since then we've stayed in touch and I've read all his books. His work is a really excellent introduction to literary and social theories of all kinds, always from a Marxist perspective. So I feel well educated in that regard.

GM One of the things about science fiction that I'm interested in is the idea that it is more than a collection of books or films, it's actually a way of thinking about our relationship with the future. The longer I've studied it the more I've become convinced that science fiction as a thought process is the really exciting idea, and I've started reading more and more non-science fiction as science fiction, like Richard Powers's *The Overstory* (2018), for example.

KSR Yes to the idea of Richard Powers as science fiction. That's what he does, from his own particular angle, as a realist novelist interested in scientists and in scientific ideas. Not every book fits that pattern with him, but enough that it caused him problems earlier in his career; he was always being called cerebral, etc. But with *The Overstory* he took on material that was both scientific and ecological, and very close to his heart, as he became a forest person to research it. The result was what you read. I actually think (and have told him) that he wanted to speak from the trees' point of view, but stuck to realism instead, then when he killed off the girl who was the speaker for trees, he got frustrated with his own choices and punished all the rest of his characters too much. But that immense stress, partly a matter of formal choices, added to the power of the book in some weird way that resonated with readers. For me his best book is *The Echo Maker* (2006). But no doubt he is one of our best novelists.

GM   Your first published novel was *The Wild Shore* (1984), set in a post-nuclear-war California. Each of the books in that *Three Californias* trilogy seems to be a reflection of a different aspect of contemporary American society in the 1980s and their relationships to possible futures. How were you thinking about nuclear war at that time?

KSR   Although it's true that *The Wild Shore* described a post-nuclear situation, I have to admit, it is the book of those three Californias that means the least to me now. It was a matter of filling out a design; I wanted three futures all set in my hometown of Orange County. So one needed to be post-nuclear to fill the pattern. I never thought it was the most likely. What I ended up doing in it was thinking about what might happen if the supposed neutron bomb were used, as this was being discussed as a possible, 'limited' nuclear war. Still, for me, the other two books in the trilogy, *The Gold Coast* (1988), which was very much a vision of my youth in a dystopian register, and *Pacific Edge* (1990), my notion of a utopian future, are both more important to me now.

Far more important to the general culture were those earlier post-nuclear novels of the 1950s, especially Nevil Shute's *On the Beach* (1957) and Walter M. Miller's *A Canticle for Liebowitz* (1959), but also *Alas, Babylon* by Pat Frank (1959) and Eugene Burdick and Harvey Wheeler's *Fail-Safe* (1962) – plus all the less famous stories and novels in the genre proper. Together they painted an indelible portrait of disaster, and helped to change the culture to the idea of the test ban treaty and the anti-nuclear movement more generally. It was definitely a case of science fiction making a difference. By the 1980s, the difference had been achieved, and what I did was more a literary homage to that early generation of science fiction.

While I was behind the cultural moment in terms of the nuclear imaginary, I think I was ahead of the curve when it comes to climate change. Neither one is the best place to be when it comes to making an impact on the culture. The moment has to be right. But climate change will be with us for the rest of the century, so now I'm there in the centre of things, I think.

GM   I think your feelings on *Wild Shore* are understandable, especially given how many words you've published since then, and I think it's fair to say the DNA of the other two has most clearly been passed on into your subsequent work.

Over the years your science fiction has also been read more widely, by non-traditional science fiction audiences. I think your early and powerful commentary on climate issues plays a part in that, as you were definitely – as you say – ahead of the curve and anticipated a lot of what we are only now seeing many 'literary' writers turning to. Was there a particular event in your life, or something you read or saw, that you think particularly contributed to your own 'ecological awakening'?

KSR I think it was a process of accumulation that had to do with my reading life first, plus my time in the Sierra as a backpacker, and my 1995 visit to Antarctica. But for the most part it was a gradual thing. The influence of scientists has also been cumulative, but I can point to my many conversations with scientists of all kinds in Antarctica, and also my ongoing discussions with NASA planetologists, from the early 1990s to the present, as particularly influential.

GM   People talk about how humans have evolved to recognize threat (and indeed change) when it's immediate, current and sudden, but that we're not wired in such a way that we can conceive of lengthy crises and recognize change over prolonged periods, especially cross-generational. What do you think about the idea that science fiction offers a toolkit that allows storytellers to approach the topics in new ways, allowing readers or audiences to better appreciate the issue and find new ways of understanding?

KSR   I think there is something to that. Fiction, and I think the novel in particular, is an art form that is designed to take you to other times and places, and to put you inside other people's minds. In science-fictional terms, it offers time travel and telepathy. These are fictional experiences, and yet quite moving and sometimes profound. So, science fiction is the wing of literature that sets stories in the future, and when we're thinking about the future, which we all often do when contemplating our own lives, science fiction can be a way of doing that thinking in artistic, organized and collective ways. So, if we're not wired to conceive of lengthy crises or recognize long-term changes – I'm not sure about that, but these are definitely effortful activities and not the same as perception, for sure – then engaging with a story set in the future will help us to think about various particular moments set in the future, so that we can see change more clearly. These will be fictional voyages to the future, but real thoughts in the present.

GM   Do you think science fiction can cause meaningful change in world? Or change the way scientists and engineers approach the world?

KSR   Yes, but only in the same way that all literature and art cause change, by changing perceptions, values, philosophical systems and so on. And in that they are part of a larger dialectical process in which the art has also to reflect already existing elements of a culture in order to be comprehensible. For science fiction, a couple of tangible examples will serve to illustrate: in the US, Edward Bellamy's *Looking Backward from the Year 2000* was widely read in the 1890s, with Bellamy clubs formed to read and discuss the book, which imagined a socialist future functioning very well in the year 2000. Then the progressive movement at the turn of the century brought a popularly elected Senate, food and safety laws, land protection and other socialist ideas into law. Now, the book didn't cause this, but it expressed a wave of ideas already in existence and helped people to imagine what their effect would be if enacted. Another example: at the end of the Second World War, at Bretton Woods and elsewhere, people had to reconstitute the world order, hopefully by instituting a system that would make such catastrophic wars impossible. What system was that? Well, all of them had been reading H. G. Wells's utopian novels since 1905's *A Modern Utopia* right up to the Second World War itself, and they all insisted on a scientific meritocracy guiding an integrated world according to principles of science. Again, Wells was expressing a general movement of thought, but his persistent and stubborn utopian writing helped people to see what it might be like if such ideas were enacted. This is how science fiction can cause change in the world. As for scientists and engineers, they often read science fiction in their youth and get inspired to devote their adult lives to these pursuits.

GM   Do scientists make good characters for fiction?

KSR   It's a real challenge. When I was writing *Green Mars*, I realized that I had accidentally killed off all my protagonists at the end of *Red Mars*. The story did it, not me, but there I was. And the most cliched of my scientists from *Red Mars*, a minor character, offered to me that he could be the new protagonist. So I wrote the chapter called 'The Scientist as Hero' to test out how that would work, and if it could be true. This was a revelation for me. The scientist in our culture is very well represented by *Star Trek*'s Mr Spock, I think he is the great achievement of *Star Trek*. The scientist is a bit of an alien in their 'Vulcan' rationality, living by logic, and so on. But Mr Spock has a human mother and so is half-human – though stuffed with a repressed emotionality that is very Vulcan, in that it can burst out from its repression into the world. This is a great symbol and often hilarious. Many other fictional scientists, like my Sax Russell in the *Mars* trilogy, show signs of this split nature, or our universal dichotomy between reason and emotion.
    Now, it's science itself that has shown that human rationality requires good emotional function to operate properly. This is not an either/or, but two parts of a larger whole. Understanding that means that our conception of science, and also therefore of scientists, has to become more nuanced and flexible and various. And since we live in a world utterly dependent on science for our survival, focusing on scientists is to focus on the powerful, which is something fiction is likely to do anyway.
    Another opportunity for fiction writers when trying to make scientists into characters is that very often they are in effect detectives. So, Sherlock Holmes is, like Spock, another great symbolic image of the scientist, and detective work is very well suited for fictional representation, having all the requirements of a plot – a mystery, a problem, some suspense, maybe even a clock ticking, with danger looming and clues needing interpreting, and so on. In that sense, scientists can make excellent characters.

GM   How do you approach writing a novel on the topic of climate change where the central crisis is so abstract, faceless and all-encompassing? It's not like some other topics where you can have easily visualized single villains or heroes in the more conventional sense.

KSR   It's a big problem and I guess I would say I've taken the kitchen sink approach – throw everything in and see what happens! That was true for *The Ministry for the Future*, anyway. For other novels I've taken one small group of characters, say those living in the same apartment building (*New York 2140*) or traveling together (*2312* or *Aurora*) and showed what it was like for these typical characters. Then also, the 'slow violence' of climate change occasionally erupts into 'fast violence' in storms or floods, and I've used those as illustrative moments.

GM   A number of reviewers highlight the integration of scientific non-fiction in *The Ministry for the Future*, and you are clearly integrating a lot of research into all of your writing, whether on Mars or down here on Earth. How do you see the relationship between fiction and non-fiction writing? I have heard that you may be turning to non-fiction writing next – is that because there are some things you feel fiction can't capture or articulate adequately?

KSR   Yes, but this is a bit of a coincidence – I've only turned to non-fiction briefly, to write about California's Sierra Nevada mountains and my experiences there. For that project I didn't want to be distracted by invented plots and characters; I wanted the range to be the book's protagonist, and to write about what I've seen myself up there. So it's a mix of history, geology, nature writing and memoir, but also a one-off for me. I'll go back to fiction after that, and try coming at all these issues in new ways, from new angles. Fiction is a very powerful mode, it can take on any subject, and is particularly good at portraying imagined futures. There isn't anything that fiction can't articulate, but other modes of cognition are more suited for all kinds of tasks, so I don't insist on it. It's just that I enjoy it.

← **You are here.**

In this rare image, taken on 19 July 2013, the wide-angle camera on the international *Cassini* spacecraft has captured Saturn's rings and our planet Earth in the same frame, 898 million miles (1.44 billion kilometres) away.

FURTHER READING

A wealth of books, films, comics and video games are already referred to in each section of this book. The following lists, by no means definitive, offer additional material that may be of interest to anyone looking to engage further with the topics discussed in the essays. The lists overlap in terms of subject matter, but are broadly broken up into each of the book's five parts, as well as a general list, each blending science fiction scholarship with some popular scientific writing of interest and relevance. Also included is a list of science fiction anthologies, which, in their variety of writers, themes, styles and issues, offer a snapshot of both the history and contemporary range of science fiction, to compliment the main chapters.

SELECTED FICTION COLLECTIONS

John Joseph Adams, ed., *Loosed Upon the World: The Saga Anthology of Climate Fiction* (Saga, 2015)

Djibril al-Ayad and Kathryn Allan, eds, *Accessing the Future: A Disability-Themes Speculative Fiction Anthology* (Futurefire.net, 2015)

Brian Aldiss, ed., *A Science Fiction Omnibus* (Penguin, 2007)

Hassan Blasim, ed., *Iraq +100: Stories from a Century after the Invasion* (Comma Press, 2016)

Elly Blue, ed., *Biketopia: Feminist Bicycle Science Fiction Stories in Extreme Futures* (Microcosm, 2017)

adrienne maree brown and Walidah Imarisha, eds, *Octavia's Brood: Science Fiction Stories from Social Justice Movements* (AK Press, 2015)

Grace L. Dillon, ed., *Walking the Clouds: An Anthology of Indigenous Science Fiction* (University of Arizona Press, 2012)

Gardner Dozois, ed., *The Very Best of the Best: 35 Years of The Year's Best Science Fiction* (St Martin's Griffin, 2019)

Harlan Ellison, ed., *Dangerous Visions: 33 Original Stories* (Doubleday, 1967)

Arthur B. Evans, Istvan Csicsery-Ronay, Joan Gordon, Veronica Hollinger, Rob Latham and Carol McGuirk, eds, *The Wesleyan Anthology of Science Fiction* (Wesleyan University Press, 2010)

Ed Finn and Kathryn Cramer, eds, *Hieroglyph: Stories &Visions for a Better Future* (William Morrow, 2014)

Basma Ghalayini, ed., *Palestine +100: Stories from a Century after the Nakba* (Comma Press, 2019)

Matthew David Goodwin, ed., *Latinx Rising: An Anthology of Latinx Science Fiction and Fantasy* (Wings Press, 2017)

Leigh Ronald Grossman, ed., *Sense of Wonder: A Century of Science Fiction* (Wildside, 2011)

Ivor W. Hartmann, ed., *AfroSF: Science Fiction by African Writers* (Storytime, 2012)

Nalo Hopkinson and Uppinder Mehan, eds, *So Long Been Dreaming: Postcolonial Science Fiction and Fantasy* (Arsenal Pulp, 2004)

Yvonne Howell, ed., *Red Star Tales: A Century of Russian and Soviet Science Fiction* (Russian Life Books, 2015)

Simon Ings, ed., *We, Robots: Artificial Intelligence in 100 Stories* (Head of Zeus, 2020)

Victor LaValle and John Joseph Adams, eds, *A People's Future of the United States* (Oneworld, 2019)

Ken Liu, ed. and trans., *Broken Stars: Contemporary Chinese Science Fiction in Translation* (Head of Zeus, 2019)

Ken Liu, ed., *Invisible Planets: 13 Visions of the Future from China* (Head of Zeus, 2016)

Gerson Lodi-Ribeiro, ed., *Solarpunk: Ecological and Fantastical Stories in a Sustainable World*, tr. Fabio Fernandes (World Weaver Press, 2018); originally published as *Solarpunk: Histórias ecológicas e fantásticas em um mundo sustentável* (2012)

Vonda N. McIntyre and Susan Janice Anderson, eds, *Aurora: Beyond Equality* (Fawcett Gold, 1976)

Xueting Christine Ni, ed. and trans., *Sinopticon: A Celebration of Chinese Science Fiction* (Solaris, 2021)

Sunyoung Park, ed., *Readymade Bodhisattva: The Kaya Anthology of South Korean Science Fiction* (Kaya, 2019)

Rivqa Rafael and Tansy Rayner Roberts, eds, *Mother of Invention* (Twelfth Planet Press, 2018)

Adam Roberts, ed., *Classic Science Fiction Stories* (Macmillan Collectors Library, 2022)

Franz Rottensteiner, ed., *The Black Mirror & Other Stories: An Anthology of Science Fiction from Germany & Austria* (Wesleyan University Press, 2008)

Franz Rottensteiner, ed., *View From Another Shore: European Science Fiction*, 2e (Liverpool University Press, 1999)

Wade Roush, ed., *Twelve Tomorrows: New Fiction Inspired by Today's Emerging Technologies* (MIT Press, 2018)

Tarun K. Saint, ed., *The Gollancz Book of South Asian Science Fiction* (Hachette India, 2019); reprinted as *New Horizons* (Gollancz, 2021)

Pamela Sargent, ed., *Women of Wonder, The Classic Years: Science Fiction by Women from the 1940s to the 1970s* (Harcourt Brace, 1995)

Pamela Sargent, ed., *Women of Wonder, The Contemporary Years: Science Fiction by Women from the 1970s to the 1990s* (Harcourt Brace, 1995)

Thomas Sheree, ed., *Dark Matter: A Century of Speculative Fiction from the African Diaspora* (Warner Aspect, 2000)

Robert Silverberg, ed., *The Science Fiction Hall of Fame* (Doubleday, 1970)

Sheree Renée Thomas, Oghenechovwe Donald Ekpeki and Zelda Knight, eds, *Africa Risen: A New Era of Speculative Fiction* (Tor, 2022)

Lavie Tidhar, ed., *The Best of World SF*, vol. 1 (Head of Zeus, 2021)

Gene van Troyer and Grania Davis, eds, *Speculative Japan: Outstanding Tales of Japanese Science Fiction and Fantasy* (Kurodahan Press, 2007)

Ann VanderMeer and Jeff VanderMeer, eds, *The Big Book of Science Fiction: The Ultimate Collection* (Vintage, 2012)

Ann VanderMeer and Jeff VanderMeer, eds, *Sisters of the Revolution: A Feminist Speculative Fiction Anthology* (PM Press, 2015)

Phoebe Wagner and Brontë Christopher Wieland, eds, *Sunvault: Stories of Solarpunk and Eco-Speculation* (Upper Rubber Boot, 2017)

Joshua Whitehead, ed., *Love After the End: An Anthology of Two-Spirit and Indigiqueer Speculative Fiction* (Arsenal Pulp Press, 2020)

GENERAL

Charles L. Adler, *Wizards, Aliens and Starships: Physics and Math in Science Fiction* (Princeton University Press, 2014)

Brian Aldiss and David Wingrove, *Trillion Year Spree: The History of Science Fiction* (Gollancz, 1986)

Kingsley Amis, *New Maps of Hell: A Survey of Science Fiction* (Harcourt, 1960)

Mike Ashley, *Yesterday's Tomorrows: The Story of Classic British Science Fiction in 100 Books* (British Library, 2020)

Brian Attebery and Veronica Hollinger, eds, *Parabolas of Science Fiction* (Wesleyan University Press, 2013)

Mark Bould, Andrew M. Butler, Adam Roberts and Sherryl Vint, eds, *The Routledge Companion to Science Fiction* (Routledge, 2009)

Mark Bould, Andrew M. Butler, Adam Roberts and Sherryl Vint, eds, *Fifty Key Figures in Science Fiction* (Routledge, 2009)

Mark Bould and Sherryl Vint, *The Routledge Concise History of Science Fiction* (Routledge, 2011)

Mark Brake and Neil Hook, *Different Engines: How Science Drives Fiction and Fiction Drives Science* (Macmillan, 2008)

Damien Broderick, *Reading by Starlight: Postmodern Science Fiction* (Routledge, 1995)

Dan Byrne-Smith, *Science Fiction: Documents of Contemporary Art* (Whitechapel Gallery, 2020)

Gerry Canavan and Eric Carl Link, eds, *The Cambridge History of Science Fiction* (Cambridge University Press, 2019)

Seo-Young Chu, *Do Metaphors Dream of Literal Sheep? A Science-Fictional Theory of Representation* (Harvard University Press, 2010)

Jim Clarke, *Science Fiction and Catholicism: The Rise and Fall of the Robot Papacy* (Gylphi, 2019)

John Clute and David Langford, eds, *The Science Fiction Encyclopedia*, 4e

Istvan Csicsery-Ronay Jr, *The Seven Beauties of Science Fiction* (Wesleyan University Press, 2008)

Xavier Dollo and Djibril Morissette-Phan, *The History of Science Fiction: A Graphic Novel Adventure* (Humanoids, 2021)

Rick Edwards and Michael Brooks, *Science(ish): The Peculiar Science Behind the Movies* (Atlantic, 2017)

Carl Freedman, *Critical Theory and Science Fiction* (Wesleyan University Press, 2000)

Aaron John Gulyas, *Extraterrestrials and the American Zeitgeist: Alien Contact Tales Since the 1950s* (McFarland & Co., 2013)

Roslynn D. Haynes, *From Faust to Strangelove: Representations of the Scientist in Western Literature* (John Hopkins University Press, 1994)

Nick Hubble and Aris Mousoutzanis, *The Science Fiction Handbook* (Bloomsbury, 2013)

Edward James and Farah Mendlesohn, eds, *The Cambridge Companion to Science Fiction* (Cambridge University Press, 2003)

Paul Kincaid, *What It Is We Do When We Read Science Fiction* (Beccon, 2008)

Rob Latham, ed., *Science Fiction Criticism: An Anthology of Essential Writings* (Bloomsbury, 2017)

Rob Latham, ed., *The Oxford Handbook of Science Fiction* (Oxford University Press, 2014)

Isiah Lavender III, *Afrofuturism Rising: The Literary Prehistory of a Movement* (Ohio State University Press, 2019)

Isiah Lavender III and Lisa Yaszek, eds, *Literary Afrofuturism in the Twenty-First Century* (Ohio State University Press, 2020)

Sarah Lefanu, *In the Chinks of the World Machine: Feminism and Science Fiction* (Women's Press, 1988)

Ursula K. Le Guin, *Dreams Must Explain Themselves: The Selected Non-Fiction of Ursula K. Le Guin* (Gollancz, 2018)

Stanisław Lem, *Microworlds: Writings on Science Fiction and Fantasy* (Harcourt, 1984)

Alexis Lothian, *Old Futures: Speculative Fiction and Queer Possibility* (New York University Press, 2018)

Roger Luckhurst, ed., *Science Fiction: A Literary History* (British Library, 2017)

Roger Luckhurst, *Science Fiction* (Polity Press, 2005)

David Mead and Paweł Frelik, eds, *Playing the Universe: Games and Gaming in Science Fiction* (Maria Curie-Skłodowska University, 2007)

Gavin Miller, *Science Fiction and Psychology* (Liverpool University Press, 2020)

Wendy Gay Pearson, Veronica Hollinger and Joan Gordon, *Queer Universes: Sexualities in Science Fiction* (Liverpool University Press, 2008)

Amanda Rees and Iwan Rhys Morus, *Presenting Futures Past: Science Fiction and the History of Science* (University of Chicago Press, 2019)

Martin Rees, *On the Future: Prospects for Humanity* (Princeton University Press, 2018)

John Rieder, *Science Fiction and the Mass Cultural Genre System* (Wesleyan University Press, 2017)

Adam Roberts, *The History of Science Fiction*, 2e (Palgrave Macmillan, 2016)

Joy Sanchez-Taylor, *Diverse Futures: Science Fiction and Authors of Color* (Ohio State Press, 2021)

David Seed, ed., *Anticipations: Essays on Early Science Fiction and its Precursors* (Liverpool University Press, 1995)

Tom Shippey, *Hard Reading: Learning from Science Fiction* (Liverpool University Press, 2016)

Darko Suvin, *Metamorphoses of Science Fiction*, 2e (Peter Lang, 2016)

Sherryl Vint, *Science Fiction: A Guide for the Perplexed* (Bloomsbury, 2014)

Sherryl Vint, *Science Fiction* (MIT Press, 2021)

Gary Westfahl, *The Mechanics of Wonder: The Creation of the Idea of Science Fiction* (Liverpool University Press, 1998)

Ytasha L. Womack, *Afrofuturism: The World of Black Sci-Fi and Fantasy Culture* (Chicago University Press, 2013)

Lisa Yaszek, *Galactic Suburbia: Recovering Women's Science Fiction* (Ohio State University Press, 2008)

Lisa Yaszek and Patrick B. Sharp, *Sisters of Tomorrow: The First Women of Science Fiction* (Wesleyan University Press, 2016)

1. PEOPLE AND MACHINES

Kathryn Allan, *Disability in Science Fiction: Representations of Technology as Cure* (Palgrave Macmillan, 2013)

Neda Atanasoski and Kalindi Vora, *Surrogate Humanity: Race, Robots, and the Politics of Technological Futures* (Duke University Press, 2019)

Margaret A. Boden, *AI: Its Nature and Future* (Oxford University Press, 2016)

Nick Bostrom, *Superintelligence: Paths, Dangers, Strategies* (Oxford University Press, 2014)

Rosi Braidotti, *The Posthuman* (Polity Press, 2013)

Scott Bukatman, *Terminal Identity: The Virtual Subject in Post-Modern Science Fiction* (Duke University Press, 1993)

Nessa Carey, *Hacking the Code of Life: How Gene Editing Will Rewrite Our Futures* (Icon, 2019)

Stephen Cave, Kanta Dihal and Sarah Dillon, eds, *AI Narratives: A History of Imaginative Thinking about Intelligent Machines* (Oxford University Press, 2020)

Thomas Connolly, *After Human: A Critical History of the Human in Science Fiction from Shelley to Le Guin* (Liverpool University Press, 2021)

Caroline Criado Perez, *Invisible Women: Exposing Data Bias in a World Designed for Men* (Penguin, 2019)

Carol Margaret Davison and Marie Mulvey-Roberts, eds, *Global Frankenstein* (Palgrave Macmillan, 2018)

Marcus Du Sautoy, *The Creativity Code: How AI is Learning to Write, Paint and Think* (4th Estate, 2019)

Liz W. Faber, *The Computer's Voice: From Star Trek to Siri* (University of Minnesota Press, 2020)

Terrie Favro, *Generation Robot: A Century of Science Fiction, Fact, and Speculation* (Skyhorse, 2018)

Thomas Foster, *The Souls of Cyberfolk: Posthumanism as Vernacular Theory* (University of Minnesota Press, 2005)

Hannah Fry, *Hello World: How to be Human in the Age of the Machine* (Transworld, 2018)

David H. Guston, *Frankenstein, Mary Shelley: Annotated for Scientists, Engineers, and Creators of All Kinds* (MIT Press, 2017)

Everett Hamner, *Editing the Soul: Science and Fiction in the Genome Age* (Pennsylvania State University Press, 2017)

Gregory Jerome Hampton, *Imagining Slaves and Robots in Literature, Film, and Popular Culture: Reinventing Yesterday's Slave with Tomorrow's Robot* (Lexington, 2015)

Yuval Noah Harari, *Homo Deus: A Brief History of Tomorrow* (Penguin, 2016)

Donna Haraway, *Manifestly Haraway* (University of Minnesota Press, 2016)

Katherine Hayles, *How We Became Posthuman: Virtual Bodies in Cybernetics, Literature, and Informatics* (University of Chicago Press, 1999)

Minsoo Kang, *Sublime Dreams of Living Machines: The Automaton in the European Imagination* (Harvard University Press, 2011)

Sophie Lewis, *Full Surrogacy Now: Feminism Against Family* (Verso, 2019)

Colin Milburn, *Respawn: Gamers, Hackers, and Technogenic Life* (Duke University Press, 2018)

Cathy O'Neil, *Weapons of Math Destruction: How Big Data Increases Inequality and Threatens Democracy* (Penguin, 2016)

Harry Parker, *Hybrid Humans: Dispatches from the Frontiers of Man and Machine* (Profile, 2022)

Fiona Sampson, *In Search of Mary Shelley: The Girl Who Wrote Frankenstein* (Profile, 2018)

Lars Schmeink, *Biopunk Dystopias: Genetic Engineering, Society and Science Fiction* (Liverpool University Press, 2016)

Max Tegmark, *Life 3.0: Being Human in the Age of Artificial Intelligence* (Penguin, 2017)

Sherryl Vint and Sümeyra Buran, eds, *Technologies of Feminist Speculative Fiction: Gender, Artificial Life, and the Politics of Reproduction* (Palgrave Macmillan, 2022)

2. TRAVELLING THE COSMOS

Michael Benson, *Space Odyssey: Stanley Kubrick, Arthur C. Clarke, and the Making of a Masterpiece* (Simon & Schuster, 2018)

André Bormanis, *Star Trek: Science Logs* (Pocket Books, 1998)

Simone Caroti, *The Generation Starship in Science Fiction: A Critical History, 1934–2001* (McFarland & Co., 2011)

Stuart Clark, *The Search for Earth's Twin* (Quercus, 2016)

Robert Crossley, *Imagining Mars: A Literary History* (Wesleyan University Press, 2011)

Anthony Downey, ed., *Heirloom: Larissa Sansour, Research/Practice* (Sternberg, 2019)

Alexander C. T. Geppert, ed., *Imagining Outer Space: European Astroculture in the Twentieth Century* (Palgrave Macmillan, 2012)

Kate Greene, *Once Upon a Time I Lived On Mars: Space, Exploration and Life on Earth* (Macmillan, 2020)

Paul C. Gutjahr, ed., *'Voyage to the Moon' and Other Imaginary Lunar Flights of Fancy in Antebellum America* (Anthem, 2018)

Peter Krämer, *2001: A Space Odyssey* (BFI Classics, 2010)

Lawrence Krauss, *The Physics of Star Trek* (Flamingo, 1996)

Roger Lancelyn Green, *Into Other Worlds: Space Flight in Fiction from Lucian to Lewis* (Abelard-Schuman, 1958)

Sarah J. Montross, ed., *Past Futures: Science Fiction, Space Travel, and Postwar Art of the Americas* (MIT Press, 2015)

Timothy Morton, *Spacecraft* (Bloomsbury, 2021)

Chris Pak, *Terraforming: Ecopolitical Transformations and Environmentalism in Science Fiction* (Liverpool University Press, 2016)

Carl Sagan, *Pale Blue Dot: A Vision of the Human Future in Space* (Penguin, 1994)

Carl Sagan, *Cosmos* (Abacus, 1980)

Fred Scharmen, *Space Forces: A Critical History of Life in Outer Space* (Verso, 2021)

Vivian Sobchack, *Screening Space: The American Science Fiction Film* (Ungar, 1987)

John C. H. Spence, *Lightspeed: The Ghostly Aether and the Race to Measure the Speed of Light* (Oxford University Press, 2019)

Michael Summers and James Trefil, *Exoplanets: Diamond Worlds, Super Earths, Pulsar Planets, and the New Search for Life Beyond Our Solar System* (Smithsonian, 2018)

Kip S. Thorne, *The Science of Interstellar* (W. W. Norton & Co., 2014)

Kip S. Thorne, *Black Holes and Time Warps: Einstein's Outrageous Legacy* (W. W. Norton & Co., 1994)

Gary Westfahl, *Islands in the Sky: The Space Station Theme in Science Fiction Literature*, 2e (Borgo/Wildside, 2009)

3. COMMUNICATION AND LANGUAGE

Dave Addley, *Typeset in the Future: Typography and Design in Science Fiction Movies* (Abrams, 2019)

Anindita Banerjee, ed., *Russian Science Fiction Literature and Cinema: A Critical Reader* (Academic Studies Press, 2018)

David Bellos, *Is That a Fish in your Ear? Translation and the Meaning of Everything* (Penguin, 2011)

Daniel Leonard Bernardi, *Star Trek and History: Race-ing Toward a White Future* (Rutgers University Press, 1998)

Ian Campbell, ed., *Science Fiction in Translation: Perspectives on the Global Theory and Practice of Translation* (Palgrave Macmillan, 2021)

Ian Campbell, *Arabic Science Fiction* (Palgrave Macmillan, 2018)

Ingo Cornils, *Beyond Tomorrow: German Science Fiction and Utopian Thought in the 20th and 21st Centuries* (Camden House, 2020)

Samuel R. Delany, *The Jewel-Hinged Jaw: Notes on the Language of Science Fiction* (Wesleyan University Press, 2009)

Samuel R. Delany, *Starboard Wine: More Notes on the Language of Science Fiction* (Dragon, 1984)

Jörg Matthias Determann, *Islam, Science Fiction and Extraterrestrial Life: The Culture of Astrobiology in the Muslim World* (Bloomsbury, 2020)

Jennifer L. Feeley and Sarah Ann Wells, eds, *Simultaneous Worlds: Global Science Fiction Cinema* (University of Minnesota Press, 2015)

Johannes Hossfeld, *Kiluanji Kia Henda: Travelling to the Sun through the Night* (Steidl, 2018)

Jing Jiang, *Found in Translation: 'New People' in Twentieth-Century Chinese Science Fiction* (Columbia University Press, 2020)

Brigitte Koyama-Richard, *One Thousand Years of Manga* (Thames & Hudson, 2022)

Jessica Langer, *Postcolonialism and Science Fiction* (Palgrave Macmillan, 2011)

Tanya Lapointe, *The Art and Science of Arrival* (Titan, 2022)

Walter E. Meyers, *Aliens and Linguists: Language Study and Science Fiction* (University of Georgia Press, 1980)

Nick Nicholas and Andrew Strader, *The Klingon Hamlet* (Pocket Books, 2000)

Nichelle Nichols, *Beyond Uhura: Star Trek and Other Memories* (Boxtree, 1996)

Steven Pinker, *The Language Instinct: How the Mind Creates Language* (William Morrow, 1994)

Jeff Prucher, ed., *Brave New Words: The Oxford Dictionary of Science Fiction* (Oxford University Press, 2007)

John Rieder, *Colonialism and the Emergence of Science Fiction* (Wesleyan University Press, 2008)

Andy Sawyer and David Seed, eds, *Speaking Science Fiction: Dialogues and Interpretations* (Liverpool University Press, 2000)

Sarah Scoles, *Making Contact: Jill Tarter and the Search for Extraterrestrial Intelligence* (Pegasus, 2017)

Seth Shostak, *Confessions of an Alien Hunter: A Scientist's Search for Extraterrestrial Intelligence* (National Geographic, 2009)

Eric D. Smith, *Globalization, Utopia and Postcolonial Science Fiction: New Maps of Hope* (Palgrave Macmillan, 2012)

H. Paul Shuch, ed., *Searching for Extraterrestrial Intelligence: SETI Past, Present, and Future* (Springer–Praxis, 2011)

Stephen Webb, *If the Universe is Teeming With Aliens… Where Is Everybody? Seventy-Five Solutions to the Fermi Paradox and the Problem of Extraterrestrial Life* (Springer, 2017)

4. ALIENS AND ALIENATION

Jim Al-Khalili, ed., *Aliens: Science Asks: Is There Anyone Out There?* (Profile, 2016)

Bryan Appleyard, *Aliens: Why They Are Here* (Scribner, 2005)

Neil Badmington, *Alien Chic: Posthumanism and the Other Within* (Routledge, 2004)

Debbora Battaglia, ed., *E.T. Culture: Anthropology in Outerspaces* (Duke University Press, 2005)

Walter Benjamin, *Illuminations* (Fontana, 1992)

Anne Billson, *The Thing* (BFI Classics, 2021)

Mark Bould, *Solaris* (BFI Classics 2014)

Gerry Canavan, *Octavia E. Butler* (University of Illinois Press, 2016)

Sean Carroll, *Something Deeply Hidden: Quantum Worlds and the Emergence of Spacetime* (Dutton, 2019)

Peter Godfrey-Smith, *Other Minds: The Octopus, the Sea, and the Deep Origins of Consciousness* (Harper Collins, 2017)

Elaine L. Graham, *Representations of the Post/Human: Monsters, Aliens and Others in Popular Culture* (Rutgers University Press, 2002)

Roger Luckhurst, *Alien* (BFI Classics, 2014)

Robert Markley, *Dying Planet: Mars in Science and the Imagination* (Duke University Press, 2005)

Michael Michaud, *Contact With Alien Civilizations: Our Hopes and Fears about Encountering Extraterrestrials* (Springer, 2006)

Patricia Monk, *Alien Theory: The Alien as Archetype in the Science Fiction Short Story* (Scarecrow, 2006)

Kevin Reese, *Celestial Hellscapes: Cosmology as the Key to the Strugatskiis' Science Fictions* (Academic Studies, 2019)

Wade Roush, *Extraterrestrials* (MIT Press, 2020)

Nicholas Royle, *The Uncanny* (Manchester University Press, 2003)

Ziauddin Sardar and Sean Cubitt, eds, *Aliens R Us: The Other in Science Fiction Cinema* (Pluto Press, 2002)

Nisi Shawl, *Writing the Other: A Practical Approach* (Aqueduct Press, 2005)

Merlin Sheldrake, *Entangled Life: How Fungi Make Our Worlds, Change Our Minds and Shape Our Futures* (Random House, 2020)

Peter Swirski, *Stanisław Lem: Philosopher of the Future* (Liverpool University Press, 2015)

Katie Whitaker, *Mad Madge: Margaret Cavendish, Duchess of Newcastle, Royalist, Writer and Romantic* (Basic, 2002)

Jenny Wolmark, *Aliens and Others: Science Fiction, Feminism, and Postmodernism* (Harvester, 1994

Ed Yong, *I Contain Multitudes: The Microbes Within Us and a Grander View of Life* (Bodley Head, 2016)

5. ANXIETIES AND HOPES

Jason Barr, *The Kaiju Film: A Critical Study of Cinema's Biggest Monsters* (McFarland & Co., 2016)

Mike Bogue, *Apocalypse Then: American and Japanese Atomic Cinema, 1951–1967* (McFarland & Co., 2017)

Mark Bould, *The Anthropocene Unconscious: Climate, Catastrophe, Culture* (Verso, 2021)

Paul Brians, *Nuclear Holocausts: Atomic War in Fiction, 1895–1984* (Kent State University Press, 1987)

Gerry Canavan and Kim Stanley Robinson, eds, *Green Planets: Ecology and Science Fiction* (Wesleyan University Press, 2014)

Rachel Carson, *Silent Spring* (Houghton Mifflin, 1962)

Dani Cavallaro, *The Animé Art of Hayao Miyazaki* (McFarland & Co., 2006)

Daniel Cordle, *Late Cold War Literature and Culture: The Nuclear 1980s* (Palgrave Macmillan, 2017)

Caroline Edwards, *Utopia and the Contemporary British Novel* (Cambridge University Press, 2019)

Matthew Edwards, ed., *The Atomic Bomb in Japanese Cinema: Critical Essays* (McFarland & Co., 2015)

Christiana Figueres and Tom Rivett-Carnac, *The Future We Choose: Surviving the Climate Crisis* (Knopf, 2020)

Lisa Garforth, *Green Utopias: Environmental Hope Before and After Nature* (Polity Press, 2018)

Amitav Ghosh, *The Great Derangement: Climate Change and the Unthinkable* (University of Chicago Press, 2017)

Donna Haraway, *Staying with the Trouble: Making Kin in the Chthulucene* (Duke University Press, 2016)

Frederic Jameson, *Archaeologies of the Future: The Desire Called Utopia and Other Science Fictions* (Verso 2005)

Mark Kermode, *Silent Running* (BFI Classics, 2014)

Ailton Krenak, *Ideas to Postpone the End of the World* (House of Anansi Press, 2020)

James Lovelock, *Gaia: A New Look at Life on Earth* (Oxford University Press, 2000)

Robert Markley, *Kim Stanley Robinson* (University of Illinois Press, 2019)

Bill McKibben, *The End of Nature: Humanity, Climate Change and the Natural World* (Penguin, 1989)

Andrew Milner and J. R. Burgmann, *Science Fiction and Climate Change: A Sociological Approach* (Liverpool University Press, 2020)

Timothy Morton, *Dark Ecology: For a Logic of Future Coexistence* (Columbia University Press, 2016)

Tom Moylan, *Scraps of the Untainted Sky: Science Fiction, Utopia, Dystopia* (Westview Press, 2000)

Tom Moylan and Raffaella Baccolini, eds, *Utopia Method Vision: The Use Value of Social Dreaming* (Peter Lang, 2007)

Hans Ulrich Obrist and Kostas Stasinopoulos, eds, *140 Artists' Ideas for Planet Earth* (Penguin, 2021)

Naomi Oreskes and Erik M. Conway, *The Collapse of Western Civilization: A View from the Future* (Columbia University Press, 2014)

Eric C. Otto, *Green Speculations: Science Fiction and Transformative Environmentalism* (Ohio State University Press, 2012)

J. Jesse Ramírez, *Un-American Dreams: Apocalyptic Science Fiction, Disimagined Community, and Bad Hope in the American Century* (Liverpool University Press, 2022)

Sean Rhoads and Brooke McCorkle, *Japan's Green Monsters: Environmental Commentary in Kaiju Cinema* (McFarland & Co., 2018)

Richard Rhodes, *The Making of the Atomic Bomb* (Simon & Schuster, 1986)

Adam Roberts, *It's the End of the World: But What Are We Really Afraid Of?* (Elliott & Thompson, 2020)

David Seed, *Future Wars: The Anticipations and the Fears* (Liverpool University Press, 2012)

Jerome F. Shapiro, *Atomic Bomb Cinema: The Apocalyptic Imagination on Film* (Routledge, 2002)

Patrick B. Sharp, *Savage Perils: Racial Frontiers and Nuclear Apocalypse in American Culture* (University of Oklahoma Press, 2007)

John L. Steadman, *Aliens, Robots and Virtual Reality Idols in the Science Fiction of H.P. Lovecraft, Isaac Asimov and William Gibson* (Zero, 2020)

Shelley Streeby, *Imagining the Future of Climate Change: World-Making through Science Fiction and Activism* (University of California Press, 2018)

Douglas A. Vakoch, ed., *Ecofeminist Science Fiction: International Perspectives on Gender, Ecology, and Literature* (Routledge, 2021)

David Wallace-Wells, *The Uninhabitable Earth: A Story of the Future* (Penguin, 2019)

Paul Williams, *Race, Ethnicity and Nuclear War: Representations of Nuclear Weapons and Post-Apocalyptic Worlds* (Liverpool University Press, 2011)

Keith Makoto Woodhouse, *The Ecocentrists: A History of Radical Environmentalism* (Columbia University Press, 2018)

Liam Young, ed., *Planet City* (Uro Publications, 2021)

Taras Young, *Apocalypse Ready: The Manual of Manuals, A Century of Panic Prevention* (Thames & Hudson, 2022)

CONTRIBUTORS

ABOUT THE EDITOR

Glyn Morgan is a curator of exhibitions at the Science Museum, London, and an Honorary Research Fellow at the University of Liverpool. He is a founding co-organiser of the Current Research in Speculative Fiction conference series, former editor of *Vector: The Critical Journal of the British Science Fiction Association*, and frequent contributor to academic journals and resources. His recent book *Imagining the Unimaginable: Speculative Fiction and the Holocaust* (2020) examines popular fiction's treatment of the Holocaust in the dystopian and alternate history genres of speculative fiction.

ABOUT THE CONTRIBUTORS

Charlie Jane Anders is an American writer and commentator. She is the author of *Victories Greater Than Death* (2021), the first book in a new young-adult trilogy, with the sequel, *Dreams Bigger Than Heartbreak*, published in 2022. She also co-hosts the podcast 'Our Opinions Are Correct' with Annalee Newitz.

Sir Ian Blatchford was appointed Director & Chief Executive of the Science Museum Group from November 2010 and combined this with the role of Director of the Science Museum from December 2010. He was previously Deputy Director of the Victoria & Albert Museum. Sir Ian was Chairman of the National Museum Director's Council (2017–21). He was Chairman of the Governors of De Montfort University (2011–18). He was awarded a Knighthood in the 2019 New Year's Honours for services to Cultural Education.

Chen Qiufan (aka Stanley Chan) is an award-winning Chinese speculative fiction author, translator, creative producer and curator. His works include *Waste Tide*, a novel imagining a near-future e-waste crisis in China, which was selected by *The Guardian* for its best science fiction books of 2019.

Rachel S. Cordasco is a writer, editor, translator and founder of the website SFinTranslation.com. She is co-translator of Italian science fiction writer Clelia Ferris's short story collection *Creative Surgery*.

Daniel Cordle is Associate Professor in English and American Literature at Nottingham Trent University. He is an expert in nuclear and Cold War literature and culture. He is the author of *Late Cold War Literature and Culture: The Nuclear 1980s* (2017).

Richard Dunn is Keeper of Technologies and Engineering at the Science Museum, London. Having previously worked as Curator of the History of Navigation at the National Maritime Museum, Greenwich, he has published widely on subjects including astrology, navigation, scientific instruments and museums.

Caroline Edwards is Senior Lecturer in Modern and Contemporary Literature at Birkbeck, University of London. Her research focuses on the utopian imagination in contemporary literature, science fiction, apocalyptic narratives, and Western Marxism. She is author of *Utopia and the Contemporary British Novel* (2019).

Nalo Hopkinson is a critically acclaimed author and Professor of Creative Writing. Nalo's first book, *Brown Girl in the Ring* (1998), won the Locus Award for Best First Novel. Her novel *Skin Folk* (2001) won the World Fantasy Award and the Sunburst Award for 'Canadian Literature of the Fantastic' while *The Salt Roads* (2003) received the Gaylactic Spectrum Award. In recent years, Nalo has focused on post-colonialism and resistant narratives. In 2021 she was recipient of the 37th Damon Knight Memorial Grand Master Award from the Science Fiction & Fantasy Writers of America (SFWA).

Rachael Livermore is an astrophysicist, science communicator and science fiction convention organiser. Her research is concerned with the formation and evolution of galaxies in the first half of the Universe's history.

Roger Luckhurst is Professor in Modern and Contemporary Literature in the Department of English, Theatre, and Creative Writing at Birkbeck, University of London. His numerous publications include *The Mummy's Curse: The true history of a dark fantasy* (2014) and *Gothic: An Illustrated History* (2021).

Colin Milburn is Gary Snyder Chair in Science and the Humanities and Professor of English, Science and Technology Studies, as well as Cinema and Digital Media at the University of California, Davis. His research focuses on the relations of literature, science, and technology.

Amanda Rees is a Reader in the Department of Sociology at the University of York. She has published widely on the history of the field sciences, on the history and sociology of the relationship between humans and other animals, and on the history of prehistory. Most recently, she has turned her attention to the history of the future.

Kim Stanley Robinson is an American novelist, widely recognized as one of the foremost living writers of science fiction. Best known for his multi-award-winning *Mars* trilogy (1992–6), his other works include *The Years of Rice and Salt* (2002), *New York 2140* (2017) and *The Ministry for the Future* (2020).

Vandana Singh is an author of speculative fiction, in addition to being a physicist and an interdisciplinary researcher on the climate crisis. She is an Associate Professor and Chair of the Department of Physics and Earth Science at Framingham State University in Massachusetts and serves on the Advisory Council of METI (Messaging Extraterrestrial Intelligence).

Tade Thompson is the author of numerous novels, including the critically acclaimed sci-fi novel *Rosewater* (for which he won the 2019 Arthur C. Clarke Award), the first in his award-winning *Wormwood* trilogy, *Making Wolf* (2015), and most recently *Far From the Light of Heaven* (2021). He is also a practising psychiatrist.

Sherryl Vint is Professor of Media and Cultural Studies and of English at the University of California, Riverside. research focuses on speculative fiction, especially relationships with science and technology. Her publications include *Science Fiction* (2022) for the MIT Press Essential Knowledge series, *Science Fiction: A Guide for the Perplexed* (2014), and with Mark Bould, *The Routledge Concise History of Science Fiction* (2011).

A large project such as the exhibition from which this book sprouted always requires a village to bring it to reality. This project in particular involved so many twists and turns, not least a global pandemic. Thank you to all the contributors to this volume and to everyone who has supported the work we have undertaken. Huge thanks to Charlotte Grievson, Jenny Lawson and Wendy Burford for their guidance, editorial work, and keeping the project on track through everything. Thank you to all the team at Thames & Hudson, including Kate Edwards, Niall Sweeney, Julie Bosser, Fredrika Lökholm, Anjali Bulley and Ruth Ellis. Special thanks to Anna Garnett and also to Samira Ahmed, Mark Bould, Amy Butt, Matt d'Ancona, Roger Highfield, Sing Yun Lee, Ken Liu, Anwesha Maity, Sinéad Murphy, Joanna Page, Katie Stone and Alfredo Suppia for continued support and advice. I also owe a debt to Matthew Howles and Holly Palmer, who transcribed one of the author interviews when I was too ill to sit at the computer.

Thank you for picking up this book. Whether you're new to science fiction or an old hand, I hope you found plenty that is new and delightful in it.

PICTURE CREDITS

a = above, b = below, m = middle, l = left, r = right

2–3 © 1973 Les Films Armorial – Argos Films
4–5 © Rainee Colacurcio
6 Remedy Entertainment Plc
8–9 vovan/Shutterstock
11 Photo by Rolfe Horn, Courtesy of The Long Now Foundation
12 ©The Trustees of the British Museum. All rights reserved
16 Alex Wells
17 Records / Alamy Stock Photo
18 NASA
19 Pamela Zoline
20 Ronald Grant Archive/TopFoto
22 Courtesy of SpaceWorks Enterprises, Inc.
23 © Larry Achiampong. All rights reserved, DACS/Artimage 2022. Courtesy of the Artist and Copperfield, London
24–25 Moviestore Collection Ltd/Alamy Stock Photo
26–27 Pictorial Press Ltd/Alamy Stock Photo
28, 35, 38, 53, 55b, 57, 64, 67, 94, 115, 116, 180, 199, 229, 230 © Science Museum Group
29 © Sam Chivers
30 Robbie Jack/Contributor
31a Album/Alamy Stock Photo
31b Retro AdArchives/Alamy Stock Photo
32 © Monsengo Shula. Courtesy MAGNIN-A Gallery, Paris
33 John Jennings
34 Collections of The Bakken Museum, Minneapolis
36a AF archive/Alamy Stock Photo
36b Courtesy Open Bionics
37 Andrew Lloyd/Alamy Stock Photo
39 Fabrizio Terranova
40 Courtesy of the artist and Marian Goodman Gallery. Photo credit: by Andrea D'altoè Neonlauro
42–43 Meletios Verras/Shutterstock.com
44–45 NASA Photo/Alamy Stock Photo
47 © Women Make Movies/Courtesy Everett Collection Inc/Alamy Stock Photo
48–49 Self Reflected, 22K gold microetching under white light, 96"x130", 2014–2016, Greg Dunn and Brian Edwards
52 Retro AdArchives/Alamy Stock Photo
54 gary warnimont/Alamy Stock Photo
55a Babington, Thomas A, active 1860s. [Babington, Thomas A] :[Sterndale, Totara Valley, South Canterbury. 1860s]. Ref: A-253-030. Alexander Turnbull Library, Wellington, New Zealand/records/22886736
56 david pearson/Alamy Stock Photo
58 Artwork: Helen Baribeau/Photo: Collection of The University of Arizona Museum of Art, Tucson; Museum Purchase with Funds Provided by the Edward J. Gallagher, Jr. Memorial Fund.
59 MOEBIUS PRODUCTION
60 Everett Collection Inc/Alamy Stock Photo
62 The Protected Art Archive/Alamy Stock Photo
63 Mass Effect and screenshots of it are licensed property of Electronic Arts, Inc.
65 Everett Collection Inc/Alamy Stock Photo
66 Everett Collection Inc/Alamy Stock Photo
68–69 AA Film Archive/Alamy Stock Photo
70 Courtesy Chen Qiufan
74–75 ESO/M. Kornmesser
77 NASA

78 © Archive RAS (F.555. Op.l. D.84. L.11)
79 Pictorial Press Ltd/Alamy Stock Photo
80–81 Reklamafilm, www.reklamafilm.com
83 TCD/Prod.DB /Alamy Stock Photo
84 Impress/Alamy Stock Photo
85 © Universal History Archive/UIG/Science Museum Group
86–87 Photo by Jean-Philippe CHARBONNIER/Gamma-Rapho via Getty Images
88 Everett Collection Inc/Alamy Stock Photo, Courtesy Everett Collection. Photo Ron Harvey. © Amazon Prime
89a AF archive/Alamy Stock Photo/20th Century Fox
89b NASA/Bill Ingalls
90–91 Xinhua/Alamy Stock Photo (CNSA/Handout via Xinhua)
92 © G!Film Studio. Design by Zhao Li, 2019
93 Lou Linwei/Alamy Stock Photo
95 'A Space Exodus, film still, 5', Larissa Sansour, 2009
96–97 Space Frontiers/Getty Images
98–99 Entertainment Pictures/Alamy Stock Photo
100–1 NASA/JPL-Caltech/STScI
102a Pictorial Press Ltd/Alamy Stock Photo
102b Courtesy of the Estate of Paul Lehr/Penguin Random House
103 © Universal History Archive/UIG/Science Museum Group
104–5 Moviestore Collection Ltd/Alamy Stock Photo
106 © 2022 Kurt Vonnegut LLC. All Rights Reserved. Used with Permission. Artwork by Albert Monteys.
107 Illustration by David Lupton for the Folio Society
108 Shutterstock/edobric
110 © SUNRISE
111a AA Film Archive/Alamy Stock Photo
111b MIKKEL JUUL JENSEN / SCIENCE PHOTO LIBRARY
112–113 © ESA/ATG medialab
114 © Microsoft. All rights reserved
117 NASA/JPL-Caltech
118–19 BABAK TAFRESHI/SCIENCE PHOTO LIBRARY
120 Courtesy Charlie Jane Anders/Sarah Deragon, Portraits to the People
124–25 Art Collection 2/Alamy Stock Photo
126 The Art and Science of Arrival, by Tanya Lapointe, published by Titan Books
127 NASA
128 Collection Christophel © Paramount Television/Alamy Stock Photo
129 Rod Lord (www.rodlord.com)
130 Pictorial Press Ltd/Alamy Stock Photo
131 SCIENCE PHOTO LIBRARY
132 Moviestore Collection Ltd/Alamy Stock Photo
133 DR SETH SHOSTAK/SCIENCE PHOTO LIBRARY
134–35 Courtesy the Artist and Goodman Gallery Johannesburg, Cape Town and London
136–37 Photo 12/Alamy Stock Photo
138 By Tom Gauld for the Guardian
139 MARK WILLIAMSON/SCIENCE PHOTO LIBRARY
140 © Rocket Publishing/Science Museum Group
141 NASA/rawpixel.com
142 Leo and Diane Dillon, courtesy R. Michelson Galleries
143 Gavin Fox & Liam Devereux – Framestore
145 Faberge Fractal by Tom Beddard
146–47 Xinhua/Alamy Stock Photo (Xinhua/Ou Dongqu)
149, 153b © Gianni Benvenuti (detto Gianni), with permission from Elfie Harris-Benvenuti
150 Archive PL/Alamy Stock Photo
151 "Planet of the Apes" 1968 20th Century Fox Poster File Reference # 31386 594THA PictureLux/The Hollywood Archive/Alamy Stock Photo

152 BFA/Alamy Stock Photo
153a Courtesy Penguin Random House and the Artist
154a Artwork and copyright by Victo Ngai, produced by Black Dragon Press in collaboration with Mosfilm in Moscow.
154b © Jacket illustration by Jack Gaughan and © Jacket design by Lena Fong Hor. Photo credit Type Punch Matrix, typepunchmatrix.com
155 Album/Alamy Stock Photo
156 BFA/Alamy Stock Photo
157 Novel © 2008 Liu CiXin; Cover art © 2008 Li Tao; Sichuan Science Fiction World Magazine Co., Ltd
158 © Hao Jingfang, 2016
159a AF archive/Alamy Stock Photo/Optimum Releasing
159b Courtesy Penguin Random House
161l Illustration by Maciej Garbacz for the cover of the book *Cat's Whirld*, by Rodolfo Martínez, published by Sportula en 2015
161ar Illustration by Franco Brambilla, courtesy of Delos Digital
161br Copyright © 2016 Kurodahan Press/Mike Dubisch
162–63 Courtesy of the artist and Pierogi Gallery
164 Courtesy Vandana Singh
168–69 Alex Andreev, alexandreev.com
171 Moviestore Collection Ltd/Alamy Stock Photo
173 BFA/Alamy Stock Photo
175 © Encyclopaedia Britannica/UIG/Science Museum Group
176–177 Allstar Picture Library Ltd/Alamy Stock Photo / Columbia Pictures
178a *A Case of Conscience* by James Blish, Cover art by Peter Curl, Faber and Faber Ltd
178b RTRO/Alamy Stock Photo
179 Ron Tom/CBS Photo Archive via Getty Images
182–83 Keystone Press/Alamy Stock Photo
184 PETER MENZEL/SCIENCE PHOTO LIBRARY
186–87 NASA/JPL-Caltech
188 Studio Canal
191 Allstar Picture Library Ltd/Alamy Stock Photo
192–93 CHRISTOPHER SWANN/SCIENCE PHOTO LIBRARY
194–195 PAUL D STEWART/SCIENCE PHOTO LIBRARY
196 Engraving of a flea in *Micrographia*, 1665, by Robert Hooke. Wellcome Collection. Attribution 4.0 International (CC BY 4.0)
197 Science History Institute, Public domain, via Wikimedia Commons
200 AF archive/Alamy Stock Photo/Universal International Pictures
201 Dipper Historic/Alamy Stock Photo
202–3 EUROPEAN SOUTHERN OBSERVATORY/SCIENCE PHOTO LIBRARY
204–5 AA Film Archive/Alamy Stock Photo
206 Alexander Chinneck
207 © 1973 Les Films Armorial – Argos Films
208 © Israel Museum, Jerusalem / Gift of Fania and Gershom Scholem, Jerusalem; John Herring, Marlene and Paul Herring, Jo Carole and Ronald Lauder, New York / Bridgeman Images
209 US NATIONAL ARCHIVES AND RECORDS ADMINISTRATION/ SCIENCE PHOTO LIBRARY
211 Artist: Jason Coulthard of the Adnyamathanha people in South Australia. Artwork *Urtli Yuratu* (*Star Woman*). Pen and Ink, 2020. Website: www.wakarla.com; Instagram: wakarlart
212–13 Remedy Entertainment Plc
215 Carla Roadnight
220–21 Teikoku Shounen
222–23 David Pollack/Corbis via Getty Images
225 Uncredited/AP/Shutterstock
226 *Protest and Survive*. Photomontage: Peter Kennard 1981. Collection: Tate
227 © Universal History Archive/UIG/Science Museum Group
232 Courtesy Penguin Random House. Photograph courtesy Michele Leong

233 Allstar Picture Library Ltd/Alamy Stock Photo
234 Pictorial Press Ltd/Alamy Stock Photo
236a Matteo Omied/Alamy Stock Photo Toho Company Ltd (東宝株式会社, Tōhō Kabushiki-kaisha) © 1954
236b Matthew Corrigan/Alamy Stock Photo
237 Everett Collection Inc/Alamy Stock Photo
238 Granger Historical Picture Archive/Alamy Stock Photo
239 Moviestore Collection Ltd/Alamy Stock Photo
241 Brian Cowden/photograph David Anderson
242–43 Tyne & Wear Archives & Museums/Bridgeman Images
244–45 Halldor Kolbeins/AFP via Getty Images
246 Wellcome Collection
247 © Yao Lu, 2006
248 INSPIRED MINORITY PICTURES/Album
249 © James Lovelock/Science Museum Group
250–251 Still of the Vertical Farm Stacks of 'Planet City,' 2021. Director: Liam Young. VFX Supervisor: Alexey Marfin
252 Photo is used BY PERMISSION OF RACHEL CARSON COUNCIL, INC., Credit: Brooks Studio
253 AF archive/Alamy Stock Photo /MGM
254 'Rising Tide' reproduced with permission courtesy of the Radical Ocean Futures Project, Stockholm Resilience Centre, Stockholm University. Image Copyright: Simon Stålenhag
255 Danita Delimont/Alamy Stock Photo
257 Luis Acosta/AFP via Getty Images
258 BFA/Alamy Stock Photo
259 Chris Putnam/Alamy Stock Photo
260–61 Abeer Seikaly
262 Stephan Martiniere
265 3Dstock/Shutterstock.com
266–67 NASA images by Reto Stöckli, based on data from NASA and NOAA
268 Nisbet Wylie/SFX Magazine/Future Publishing
274–275 NASA/JPL-Caltech/SSI

INDEX

Illustrations are in **bold**. Unless otherwise indicated, all titles of works are books or stories

First published in the United Kingdom in 2022 by
Thames & Hudson Ltd, 181A High Holborn, London WC1V 7QX

First published in the United States of America in 2022 by
Thames & Hudson Inc., 500 Fifth Avenue, New York, New York 10110

Science Fiction: Voyage to the Edge of Imagination
© 2022 Science Museum, London/Thames & Hudson Ltd, London

Text and Science Museum images © 2022 Science Museum, London

Design © 2022 Thames & Hudson Ltd, London

Interview with Chen Qiufan © 2022 Chen Qiufan and SCMG Enterprises Ltd
Interview with Charlie Jane Anders © 2022 Charlie Jane Anders and SCMG Enterprises Ltd
Interview with Vandana Singh © 2022 Vandana Singh and SCMG Enterprises Ltd
Interview with Tade Thompson © 2022 Tade Thompson and SCMG Enterprises Ltd
Interview with Kim Stanley Robinson © 2022 Kim Stanley Robinson and SCMG Enterprises Ltd

Designed by Pony Ltd

All Rights Reserved. No part of this publication may be reproduced
or transmitted in any form or by any means, electronic or mechanical,
including photocopy, recording or any other information storage and
retrieval system, without prior permission in writing from the publisher.

British Library Cataloguing-in-Publication Data
A catalogue record for this book is available from the British Library

Library of Congress Control Number 2022931536

ISBN   978-0-500-25239-0

Printed in Bosnia and Herzegovina by GPS Group

FSC
www.fsc.org
MIX
Paper | Supporting
responsible forestry
FSC® C118234

Front cover:
View of space from the Moon (detail).
Elements of this image furnished by NASA. vovan/Shutterstock

2–4: *Fantastic Planet* (*La Planète sauvage/Divoká planeta*),
directed by René Laloux, 1973.

4–5: Rainee Colacurcio, The International Space Station crosses
a spotless sun, 2019

6: *Control*, 2019.

Back cover:
left: still from *Pumzi* (detail), directed by Wanuri Kahiu, 2009.
INSPIRED MINORITY PICTURES/Album
right: *Difference Engine No. 2* (detail), designed by Charles Babbage,
1847–49; this engine completed in June 1991.
© Science Museum Group

Be the first to know about our new releases,
exclusive content and author events by visiting
thamesandhudson.com
thamesandhudsonusa.com
thamesandhudson.com.au